THE JOURNAL OF THE
VIRGINIA WRITERS CLUB
GOLDEN & TEEN NIBS
VOLUME 2, NUMBER 3, 2021

Dear Terri
Best wishes
for a healthy
2022. Thought
I'd plague you
with a bit more
of my
scribble.
(p141,)

2021
GOLDEN
NIB

D1716603

ISBN: 9798486796203

Editors: John Nicolay, Sofia Starnes, Marco Faust and James Reynolds

Contact: VWCJournal@gmail.com

The Virginia Writers Club is a non-profit membership organization. It is based out of Richmond, Virginia, but is open to all. Its mission is to support and encourage authors, whether established or just beginning their journey.

Cover: Sandstone Falls across the New River. This is the longest fall on the New River, spanning 1500 feet across. Dave Bieri photo from the National Park Service. Public domain.

The Virginia Writers Club: https://www.virginiawritersclub.org/

CHAPTERS

TABLE OF CONTENTS

Poetry Continued

NONFICTION   GOLDEN NIB

TEEN NIB WINNERS
POETRY

First Place Poetry Michelle Balderrama
Second Place Poetry Ross Bazzichi
Third Place Poetry Antonio James Higgins

GOLDEN NIB 2021 WINNERS
POETRY

First Place Katherine Gotthardt
Second Place Ray Griffin
Third Place James W. Reynolds

NONFICTION

First Place Nonfiction (Golden) Abbey Pachter
Second Place Nonfiction (Golden) Sharon Hostler
Third Place Nonfiction (Golden)

FICTION

June Forte First Place Sandra Roslan
Second Place Damean Mathews
Third Place Ronald Munro

These authors opted out of having their work included:

Carol Cutler, Appalachian Authors Guild, 1st Place Nonfiction; 3rd Place Fiction
Ann Dugan, Chesapeake Bay Writers, 3rd Place Nonfiction
Ann Eichenmuller, Chesapeake Bay Writers, 2nd Place Fiction

NOTE FROM THE EDITORS

The Golden Nib finds itself rooted in our traditions as an organization.

What is a writing contest without writers? Hard to say beyond the obvious, but we know that the quality of the journal and the contests that nurture it, engage chapters and the Virginia Writers Club to strive for more participation, and a fair review of the work received.

The time between the end of contests and submission to the production of this journal is short. Winners are announced at the November Annual Meeting. We strive to have the journal available shortly afterwards. October is a busy month.

This year we had 52 authors, representing 20% of our membership, submit 62 pieces. Can we do better? You speak for yourselves. We know for certain writing sits high on your list of values. Not all writers take part in contests. Not all writers feel their work fits.

A word on fitness. We are told, "I write long form. It does not fit the criteria." To this, one of our editors discussed the impressionist, Edgar Degas. The artist produced dozens of studies for a work he finally exhibited. He produced character sketches. He worked with alternative settings. He added and subtracted.

Do writers hand over a draft without revision? Without exploring? Unlikely. Then sketches, discards, and edits comprise the unseen. A novel is replete with characters whose backstories and adventures never come to life between the covers of the finished work. Each serves a purpose, if only to sharpen the denouement. When Golden Nib rolls around next year, keep this in mind. When we call for submissions to the Spring and Fall journals, send in a tease to the greater book. You never know.

The next edition of the journal arrives in April 2022. We hope you will consider taking part. Deadline March 1, 2022.

John Nicolay, Sofia Starnes, Jim Reynolds, & Marco Faust

NOTE FROM THE PRESIDENT

Dear Reader,

Last year, as the Golden Nib and Teen Nib collection shipped, we were adjusting to the grim realities of a pandemic. Like other organizations, The Virginia Writers Club had to adapt to continue to deliver resources and support to its members. To that end, we've held two virtual symposiums. The VWC board and chapters have used web conferencing to hold their meetings. But while the world seemed upside down, one thing didn't change—the ability of the written word to communicate, heal, inform, entertain, and help us stay connected. It's my hope that the 2021 Golden Nib and Teen Nib collection will entertain and inspire you.

This year we had 62 Golden and Teen Nib submissions in poetry, nonfiction, and fiction from 52 writers. These works represent the depth and diversity of members of The Virginia Writers Club.

I want to thank Michelle McBeth for all her work in organizing all aspects of Golden Nib, as well as to her and Devin Reese's efforts to rejuvenate the Teen Nib program. Thanks, as well, to the VWC journal editors John Nicolay, Sofia Starnes, Jim Reynolds, and Marco Faust, who edited and produced the collection you're viewing now. Last, but definitely not least, thank you to all the Virginia Writers Club chapters and their members for participating.

Sadly, the Virginia Writers Club lost long-time member Norma Redfern on October 23. She was an active member of Riverside Writers. She will be missed by all who knew her, and those touched by her immense talent.

Leslie Truex

POETRY

Stony Man

THE LANGUAGE BARRIER

by Michelle Balderrama
First Place Teen Nib

today i learned that what my mother speaks
is referred to as
broken english

i think it is sad to call
her efforts at interaction
broken

because i know very well
when she sits at her computer each day
repeating phrases and mumbling translations
scribbling conjugations onto worn out pages

she wants nothing more
than for her words
her sentences
her thoughts
to be whole.

for an immigrant, there are thousands of walls
to overcome
there is no need for a physical manifestation of it
on a southern border
the language barrier

INTERSTELLAR EGO

by Ross Bazzichi
Second Place Teen Nib

I am the chief narcissist.
All that ever was and will be rest under my control.
I am the captain of my ship.
I am the wielder of my fate.
Yet I find myself utterly alone,
Adrift in the cosmos.
Ranting ceaselessly, my words fall upon deaf ears.
As though I am a sole prince,
Fallen among the stars.

THE MADMAN

by Antonio James Higgins
Third Place Teen Nib

The madman speaks, his words are long,
His interests obscure.
He is not charismatic,
He has no bright allure.

This madman's logic may be sound,
Yet it is doomed to fall!
He will be mocked, for all his peers
Find *him* unusual.

"But we are like him, in some ways,"
You say, "We're madmen just the same!"
Yet you continue in your jeers,
And shame an honest name.

For you deride this *honest* man
And every honest word,
Because you think his thoughts are odd,
Yet you have never heard.

You call him mad and crazy
For saying what is true!
You lie about his character,
Is truth disturbing you?

O, madman, take up courage
Through all hostilities!
Though blind men call you blind,
You are the one who sees.

KAYAK

by Katherine Gotthardt, Write by the Rails, 1st Place
First Place Golden Nib

Something about water brings me back.
Back to the beach home,
the way we'd gather before clouds could,
fishhooks and minnows at hand,
those little sacrifices nature makes for us
so we might understand life's circle.
And yes, early blackness, August air
wrapped around our bare shoulders
like a damp comforter, warming
but warning us all at once,
that deep encouragement to get moving
before extreme weather took the day.
And yes, the fish we caught we ate, Dad first
peeling off years measured in gills and scales,
Mom frying filets in the same stainless pan
she'd used since we were children.

And then, sometimes, the ocean had a voice,
waterfront a silk sheet, yellow kayak by the dock,
sky hinting at orange, paddles already in the boat.
How could we not venture into its insistence,
explore the hush of days gone by too fast,
remembrances of last night's laughter,
children making a mess of the den?
And somehow in the morning, the call of carp,
plopping in and out of ripples they themselves created,
the first croak of blue heron celebrating itself
like the final, surviving dinosaur.
We pull the kayak into shallow water,
step in, find our balance like a miracle, push off.

It is the moistness that seems to do it,
bring tears as we navigate low tide,
salt pouring into our pores,
the sweat of the nudging wind.
It breaks the barriers between Earth and skin,
while everything – yes everything – whispers,
"This is what you were made for!"
Slowly we dip our oars into the world,
remembering to favor neither right nor left,
part the bay's water in the center.
We move away from enduring shore,
reminding ourselves it will always be there.
We launch again into introspective dawn.
Paddling toward sunrise.

SOJOURNERS

by Ray Griffin, Blue Ridge Writers, 1st Place
Second Place Golden Nib

So many lives were shattered by war's callous spears
of wrath unleashed by mankind's banal infamy.
The world was set afire with bitter hatred,
bombs and bullets and gross inhumanity.

Five years in, the war achieved its apogee
with all its mix of death and pain and endless
suffering. Our group was trapped between the highlands
and the desert from which there was no egress.

We drew near for warmth and love despite the night's distress,
and such it was at Hell's Gate when we sought the thrill
of love's release so we could face another day.
You, a nurse, to heal and I, a soldier, trained to kill.

We prayed for peace, our greatest wish to be fulfilled,
and planned for life among the vineyards near your family's home.
But life's not fair with odds against the likes
of us, sojourners, trapped in war's dark catacombs.

But when the war was won, and Europe prone
in dire distress as lives and countries were redrawn,
it was quite clear that now we had to win the peace,
But you remained, and I moved on.

It has been far too long since I have walked along
this sand and gravel path, still lined with austere
cedars, sentinels, that leads the way to where
your marble stone has lain for sixty years.

CROWS

by James W. Reynolds, Valley Writers, 1st Place
Third Place Golden Nib

I like how you describe that poem
more than the poem itself.
You see things I don't,
and the things you see have deep meanings –
deeper perhaps than the poet intended.

You see birds symbolizing change.
The young leave the old
and neither knows the impact of the parting.
Shockingly this lack of comprehension is of no consequence
because there is love in the leaving.

Even after reading the poem several times,
I see crows.

I am not sure you are right,
but I know you are not wrong.

You amaze me.

I would like to see that poem as you see it.
But whenever I see you and me in a mirror,
I am reminded:
you have poor eyesight and a temperament that is too tender.
They are your most egregious shortcomings,
and I have benefitted from both.

HOME

by Dan Swanson, Appalachian Authors Guild, 1ˢᵗ Place

During good times and bad, we often retreat
To that very special place in our turbulent lives,
A place occupied by a lifetime of memories
Of events that involve both harmony and strife.

The smell of Mom's hearty breakfasts lingers there
As the aroma of frying bacon fills the morning air
With sausage gravy and scratch-made biscuits in the oven
Served in a delicious feast to which none can compare.

Like me, a lifetime of strong values was born there,
A lasting product of childhood deprivation and toil
As we worked the hillside apple orchards and fields
And eked out a meager living from the Virginia soil.

Memories of tragedy and triumph lurk in the shadows
Of loss of family members and burying our favorite pet,
Of times of an attitude adjustment with a belt or switch
Learning education's value where life's direction was set.

A young life filled with baseball, BB guns, and cowboys
Or doll houses, Barbie dolls, and afternoon parties with tea
While our siblings and cousins slowly grew and matured
And set life's goals to be all that they could be.

Adulthood arrives with little advance warning or flourish.
We shift all our attention to managing our adult lives
And turn our backs on those magical childhood years
While focusing on our grownup roles as husbands and wives.

We return for holidays and special family events
To celebrate life's many milestones and times of joy
Or to introduce new members of our growing family
As our marital union results in the birth of a girl or a boy.

We go back there in times of turmoil and galloping fear
When the planes hit the towers, and our neighbors died,
Or our sacred vows with our spouses are tested or tattered
Or while seeking refuge from a pandemic, and we ask why.

During life's long journey, we face almost constant change:
We change addresses, jobs, and spouses, but still we find
The things that never change are the places where we were born
And the sheer joy of returning home—if only in our mind.

SUCCESS IS…
by Adda Leah Davis, Appalachian Authors Guild, 2nd Place

Success is a fickle lover casting
lures far and wide,
painting dreams of distant pinnacles and
lofty peaks to flaunt one's pride.

Success is a devious lover
whose spangled lures often enchant
with sprinkled gold along the pathway
and bewitched travelers
have no complaint.

Success is a treacherous lover extolling
precipices yet unseen
and enthusing on the glorious pleasures of
fame and fortune there to glean.

Success can be a fatal lover to
all those faint of heart
who become ensnared in success's tendrils
and find their lives are torn apart.

MATTHEW'S TOUCH

by Linda Hudson Hoagland, Appalachian Authors Guild, 3rd Place

Ella entered the TriBar with her two small sons securely
attached to her hands. Normally she wouldn't have taken
her sons to a bar but she knew the patrons
at that time of day would be the die-hard regulars who
were really nice people except they liked to tip a glass a lot.

All she wanted to do was pick up her Avon order that
had been left with the owner for safe keeping until Ella
and her sons returned from a short visit with
Ella's mother and father out of town.

Sitting about center of the U-shaped bar was a beautiful
black woman who called herself Black Beauty.
She was a working lady of the street with a smile
that could light up a room. Ella knew how Beauty lived
but she always liked her.

Matthew, a blonde haired, brown eyed boy of three years,
marched directly towards Black Beauty.
Ella's sons had spent a great deal of time with their grandfather,
who was very prejudiced, extremely vocal with his opinions.

Ella was afraid of what words might come out of the mouths
of either of her sons when seeing a real person of color.
Are they yours?" Black Beauty asked Ella.
Ella nodded her head as she tried to guide Michael,
her eldest son, to a place next to her while she waited for
Mike, the bartender to fetch her Avon order.

Black Beauty smiled at Matthew, helped him crawl upon
the stool to sit next to her.
Ella squirmed, ready to apologize
for anything ugly that might be hurled
from either Matthew's or Michael's young mouths.

Ella watched as Matthew extended his tiny hand towards
Black Beauty's face gently touching Beauty's cheek
where he softly rubbed it with his small fingertips
then pulled his hand back to look at it.
Black Beauty laughed and winked at Ella.
                          "It doesn't rub off, my pretty baby."

THE ELEGANT QUINCKE [1]

by Sharon Hostler, Blue Ridge Writers, 2nd Place

Strike out the tension:
your elegance pitted against my fine motor skills.
We signal the dance,
facing the rounded back of a wriggling six-month-old.
You, Quincke!
Sharp, sheathed, fine, graceful, and aloof in your sterility,
then I,
with latex pointers poking between the stacked vertebrae,
seek the safe space
between lumbar 4 and lumbar 5.
Now, the overture fades,
my elegant Quincke.
Your long fragile needle quivers,
ready for the treasured cerebrospinal fluid.
I press stylet to pierce silky skin between L4 and L5,
to guide your bevel,
seeking the palpable pop of baby meninges.
You stubbornly balk, deny our entrance
into epidural space.

---

[1] *Dr. Heinrich Quincke (1842-1922) was a German internist who introduced the lumbar puncture for diagnostic and therapeutic purposes (Wikipedia). The needle currently in use is called a Quincke.*

Your bevel permits my bare degree change.
Did we pierce an arteriole?
I lead with subtle pressure.
You inch gracefully through arachnoid and pia mater
into the space of cerebrospinal fluid
floating from baby's brain.
I withdraw your stylet.
Bloody contaminant?
You are discarded, useless.
Cloudy fluid? Pus cloaking meninges.
Now, a crescendo as I remove stylet,
position our test tube and pause.
Oh, my most elegant Quincke.
Crystal clear drops form and flow,
one by one, each one more glorious.
Reverence?
For your balletic pliés and jetés?
Our brava pas de deux?
Reverence! Clear spinal fluid.
No meningitis.

This Long Winding Thread of Wavering Memory

by Joy Merritt Krystosek, Blue Ridge Writers, 3rd Place

A precarious line guides me
Follows me . . .
This long winding
Thread
Of wavering memory
Fits neatly
Somewhere
Between
My heart my throat—
A tender scar exists
Where *the hurting*
Used to be . . .
Like all scars
It has no intention
Of leaving
It's only sore
If
I
Run
My
Hand
Across
It

WHAT DO I KNOW?

by L. Andrew Ball, Chesapeake Bay Writers, 1st Place

I think I know what poetry is for;
those images so delicate that if you
touch them with the rough finger
of prose, they burst like newborn bubbles.
Soft images, so sensitive and shy
that when you look at them directly,
they run away in tears and hide.
But if you glance at them obliquely
you can catch them unawares,
and that's what poetry is for.

I sometimes think I know what music's for.
When pulsing rhythms echo
through the canyons of my soul,
with harmonies I've always known
yet never heard before,
they paint immortal pictures
from beyond the ends of time,
and stir the sleeping creatures
in the corners of my mind.
Yes, maybe that's what music's for.

I used to think I knew what love was for.
What other crucible could hold
the scorching plasma of our fusion?
Yet cooling of our Universe
let gentler forces of creation
thrive and flourish. Let's stroll together
through this garden of complexity,
and find in every corner
a deeper, calmer, ecstasy.
There's so much more to love than love is for.

I wish I knew what consciousness was for.
We briefly catch this glimpse of Eden
through knot-holes in the Garden fence,
but all too soon get whisked away
to give the next in line a chance.
For centuries, we've spent our lives
distilling meaning out of chaos,
never pausing to inquire
just how progress will repay us.
Does consciousness itself know what it's for?

Will someone tell me please what life is for?
I wonder how I got invited
to wander through this masquerade,
never knowing when I will be
asked to kindly leave the stage.
Then, beckoned by oblivion,
no wiser than the day I came,
a ripple in the sands of time,
I'll leave the party much the same.
Does anybody know what life is for?

GYPSUM DUNES

by Christian Vincent Pascale, Chesapeake Bay Writers, 2nd Place

The Martian walks on gypsum dunes
He is the last one of his kind.
Once wet and warm, now left in ruins
Mars so resembles earth's cold moon.

Three billion years, or more, ago
The airboats flew cross crystal seas,
And through the wetland's rivers flowed.
The loss of atmosphere the key

To disappearance of the seas.
Hesperian age came to an end.
The solar winds caused air to flee
Then to earth's womb her life would send.

On rocket wings the cargo flew.
Archean Age when life began.
From death of one the other grew,
Five million years the rise of man.

The Martian walks on gypsum sand
Remembers breeze on summer seas
In dreams returns to former land's
Forgotten images of trees.

MY FAMILY

by Peggy Newcomb, Chesapeake Bay Writers, 3rd Place

"Of all the people in the world I had to pick you!"
exclaimed my new daughter, age six. Too late!

A few years later, new daughter number two, age seven,
stomped her foot while exclaiming: "My name
not Heidi!" I had slipped and called her
by the new dog's name.

New daughter number three, age eleven, sat in court
and watched as her birth mom stood up and told
the judge: "I don't want her. The Fosters
can have her." How horribly hard it must be
to hear your mother say that. Her mother didn't
even know the Fosters.

In time each child, not knowing that the others
had done the same thing, curled
up in my lap in the fetal position and said: "I wish
I had been in your tummy." To which I replied,
"I wish you had been there too." While thinking:
I could have spared you all the abuse and trauma
you lived through in the past.

So...this is my family (now grown) and
I wouldn't trade them for all the tea in China!

DREAMS OF THE EDGE

by Pamela Brothers Denyes, Hampton Roads, 1st Place

Spring, with her moody beauty,
with her quicksilver stormy weather,
dreamed of hot dry days, puffy clouds,
dancing nights as light as a feather.

Summer, arid without a drop, first
could not sleep for incessant heat,
then in exhaustion, dreamed of autumn,
himself prostrate at her chilly feet.

Autumn flowed with gentler winds
and rain enough for harvest's best,
but in her secret dreams one night
was shown she needed winter's rest.

Winter rose with a roaring chill,
blasting away warm harvest days.
One long harsh night he secretly dreamed
of warming green, of sweet spring's ways.

And so we dreamers will view this life,
each edge a welcoming season's change,
through storms, arid heat, bounty and rest.
That, no elegant wisdom can rearrange.

TURBULENT WINDS

by Joanne Liggan, Hanover Writers, 1st Place

Turbulent winds pass through our lives
Drastically changing,
            destroying,
                    sculpting,
or leaving a subtle glow.

Calm seas become angry demons,
A quiet existence
            now frightening,
                    complicated,
full of turmoil.

A beautiful city leveled to total ruins,
Complete happiness
            turns to despair,
                    heartbreak,
or total devastation.

Swirling snow forms soft, billowing drifts,
Shifting events
            giving texture,
                    adding interest,
The beauty of life!

Gusty breezes freshen the air,
Sudden surprises
            invigorate,
                    give peace,
Make smiles.

So, blow turbulent winds,
Forever changing,
            destroying,
                    sculpting,
And cleansing our lives.

EXISTENTIAL MORNING
by Sandra Roslan, Hanover Writers, 2nd Place

As the morning light begins to wake
and stretch with a yawn against the horizon,
wispy pastels paint the sky
and erase the night in bits and pieces,
leaving pockets of starlight still shimmering
against what's left of the fading blackness.

It's the end of something;
each night as it gives way to the expanding brightness,
but it's the beginning of something too.
And although we categorize it
by words like night and day
and yesterday and tomorrow,
time itself is endless,
looping infinitely in familiar patterns,
leaving us with a million
nows that must be appreciated
for what they are.

TEACHABLE MOMENT

by Paulette Whitehurst, Hanover Writers, 3rd Place

The infant bat,
a ball of brown fur,
found refuge in the shade
on the ledge where we could see him
through our classroom window.

After math, we observed him
while he slept.
Susan wrote about him hunching
there against the glass
in her writer's notebook and
Kellie sketched him.
Earl started an acrostic poem,
B – A - T.

After our history lesson
Sean wondered if the bat was anxious
to see what we were all about.
Zak read about bats and
announced that they eat insects
and they adopt orphan babies.
Allen asked us if we thought this guy
was an orphan. He thought that
would make a good story.
Maria proposed that we name him
after lunch.

On the way back from lunch,
we passed our principal in the hall,
and he informed us that he had
ordered the janitor to
kill that ugly thing
outside our window.
"No need to worry," he said.
"He's dead now."

Courtney wept.

WILDNESS

by Dreama Wyant Frisk, Northern Virginia Writers Club, 1st Place

There is a wildness in me,
As in the trees and birds that sing their song,
No matter how sweet the song,
Uncharted, ungraphed, unplanned
Wildness.
As in the creek that swelled and hurled its way
Down the hill,
While the laurel bloomed in a storm by the mill,
I will not be shaped.
I will not be still.
I give vent to this wildness in me,
   To baying and to howling,
   To singing and to loving.
It was at my source, my heredity,
This wildness in me.

SPINNING ILLUSIONS

by Jim Gaines, Riverside Writers, 1ˢᵗ Place

To a first grader's fresh eye
Maple helicopters
Once were signs of joy
Showers of new life
Portending the end of classes
The unburdening freedom of June
Whirlybirds that implanted and grew
Never exploding in rage
When even metal rotors saved the beleaguered
But as those giddy spinners turned to air scythes
Slicers of life
Loaded with fire spitting weapons
Gladiatorial blades shredding skies
My knowing became nauseous
And the silent descent of magic seeds
More resembled tears
For wonders that could have been

SHARDS 33

by David Anthony Sam, Riverside Writers, 2nd Place

The sunlight frees me
from the shards of myself.
What do I care if a star
becomes the nothing of its burning
into soulless dust.

> My hand moves before
> I will it.
> Does it know me?
> before I am?

I ask the winter
to forgive my understanding.
Seasons
have no knowing
and I impose my fictive self
on snow and blue ice.

The numerology of weather
fogs me in tonight.
I tend the solitary garden
that grows between
me and the world.
The loam of leaving it
will be my estate.

> I breathe from a time
> when I will have no time.

> Listen, the rain is falling.

DEATH REPLIES (For Cathy)

by Dan Walker, Riverside Writers, 3rd Place

I'm not so proud. I never claimed to be.
You call me cruel: the cold and slate-hard sea
all beaches wash upon, the fatal snow
that covers April's blossom with its own
white bloom, its water turned to stone,
a sheet that only vaguely shapes what's there
as if for movers, a carpet-covered stair
to other rooms.... I've earned all these, I know.

But I confess some pride, when ground I cloak
will hold a life that fed so many lives—
a rosebud here, those daffodils, that oak,
those students—and you say no child survives?
I'm glad to do my level best for each,
But proudest when I know: this one could teach.

FALL IN NAPLES, NY

by Peggy Crowley Clutz, Valley Writers, 2nd Place

Crisp air and apples
Bright blue skies with puffy white clouds
Geese flying in their V-honkle,
Hunters in orange clothing
Sunlight shorter and softer
Earthy smells and dewy mornings
Prickly straw on hayrides
Crunchy leaves underfoot
Grape pies from Monica's
Early morning fog on
Canandaigua Lake
Fall in Naples
Woolly bears crossing the road
Trucks with gun racks
Orange and white pumpkins
Shots ring out in the woods
Trees ablaze with colors
Squirrels scurry to bury their food
Cider and fresh donuts
Farm stands in villages
The sweet smell of concord grapes
Corn stalks decorate posts
The Naples Grape Festival
Evening comes quickly
A feeling of nesting

RAISING BEN

by Betsy Ashton, Valley Writers, 3rd Place

hold my hand
don't let go
I'll help you walk

time to eat
it's your favorite
I'll feed you

give me a sign
a smile something
show me you know I'm here

speak
one word any word
let me hear your voice

Mama

No, not Mama
just me Kathy
your daughter

HOME

by John L. Dutton II, Write by the Rails, 2nd Place

As I lie exhausted on the couch,
I dwell in slovenly comfort
During the final hours
Of another satisfyingly
Frustrating day.
I know not every task was completed,
Yet something was checked off
The never-ending
"To-Do" list of life.
I find comfort around me
And think,
"Home is where the heart is."
Clothes strewn on the floor.
Books piled in every nook.
Dog curled on my lap.
TV murmurs in the background.
Kids stomping the stairs.
Dishes stacked precariously.
Mismatched socks seeking lonely shoes.
Toys in every corner.
Wife reading in her favorite chair.
My coffee cup in hand.
I exhale and let the day fall from my shoulders.
I have found comfort in the clutter.

NONFICTION

White Oak Canyon

THE LAST CATERPILLAR

by Abbey Pachter, Hampton Roads, 1st Place
Golden Nib First Place

I
Winter approaches

The morning of December 16, 2020 broke cold and sleeting. A green, white and yellow striped, nearly frozen caterpillar clung to one matching green stem among a stand of milkweed in my grandma's garden. The plant waved wildly in the strong breeze that blew in the change from fall to winter weather. She had counted five others eating leaves during the past week when it was warmer and sunny; now many had deteriorated in the chilly wetness and developed inedible brown fungus spots. The caterpillars tried munching on the green outer layer of several unopened seed pods before giving up and disappearing one by one, into the mulch, to pupate. While the remaining leaves shivered through this stormy day, the very last caterpillar held tightly curled to its chosen stalk, conserving its tiny quota of heat and energy. It may or may not have been aware of being watched.

Petite, white-haired, and in her pajamas, Grandma checked her milkweed patch every day with her Cavalier Spaniel dog. His fur had grown out thickly, anticipating a cold winter in Virginia. Grandma loved her garden and had already pruned back most of the other plants in the small planting area of her front yard. The lawn crew had blown away most of the fall leaves, but some had escaped to add natural mulch to her garden.

Grandma emailed me photos of these caterpillars. I had enjoyed watching them as they munched and grew, and had spotted Swallowtails, Sulfurs and Monarch butterflies during a late summer visit, when my family temporarily left our crowded, Covid-plagued New Jersey neighborhood to stay with her. She had taught me to identify the Monarch caterpillars and described how they were protected from predators by their bitter taste and poisonous effect. "The bad taste comes from chemicals in the milkweed, leaves the caterpillars eat, called cardenolides. Birds who try to eat them get sick," she said. The toxin didn't bother spiders, and neither did Grandma. If a Monarch got stuck in a web, it was lunch. This was Nature's way, Grandma taught me: the "Circle of Life," like the song we gleefully sang from *The Lion King* show.

Our month-long stay was wonderfully longer than usual, but by early October we were back at our own home because, as Oz's Dorothy (and our mother) said, "There's no place like home. Even Grandma's!" Then, every few days, mom called Grandma on FaceTime and I asked her to show me the caterpillar, which she did. As the last days of fall passed, the warm sunshine departed, and the days grew shorter and colder.

Soon there were only three caterpillars remaining. Grandma hoped that the other two had heeded nature's call and crawled off to pupate. She figured those remaining would soon follow. Grandma thought about bringing them indoors, but decided it was best to let nature take its course.

Grandma was proud that hers was the least manicured garden in the neighborhood. Many plants were still flowering, even in the short December days. Fuchsia-colored annuals persisted, whose name she had to look up to remember: vinca. Milkweed was flowering last, the persistent optimist holding out for those late caterpillars.

Before retiring seven years previously, Grandma had thought about what she might like to spend more time doing once she'd cross that threshold. When she heard about the Master Naturalists, she instantly knew that was it. When asked if "naturalists" meant "nudists," she laughingly said it did not, though I would not have been completely surprised, knowing Grandma, if it had. Among many other subjects, she learned about the basic life cycle of butterflies, all of which shared developmental characteristics. She didn't know then how much butterflies would come to mean to her.

Soon she successfully nurtured Black Swallowtail caterpillars by bringing home their host plant, tall-stalked fennel that grew wild nearby. A few weeks later, there were black butterflies fluttering above the garden. The next year she created a protected habitat by hooking bed-netting onto her gutter. Tiny caterpillars, which had invisibly come along with new fennel cuttings, dutifully showed themselves as they grew through several instars. After a week of eating the fennel fronds, a few chrysalides hung at the top. She made an entry in her nature journal of their expected delivery date, or EDD, as she had done for countless of her midwifery clients in years long passed. The Black Swallowtail butterflies eclosed, or emerged as expected, in about 14 days and without complications, like most women she helped to deliver, but much more quickly than most.

Grandma described watching newly eclosed butterflies hanging upside down, their vulnerable wings gradually unfolding as the veins filled with the plasma-like serum pumped from their bodies. Soon their wings were velvety black with blue and orange, jewel-like spots edging them, dried, hardened, and strong. After each had taken its first tentative flights, she set them free. It was a thrill for her to watch them float higher and higher, then disappear.

Later, Monarch butterflies were in the news. Known for their bright orange color and mass migrations, Grandma learned their populations were rapidly declining because so many of their natural habitats were gone. Roadside wildflowers had been eliminated to make room for widening roads for more gasoline-propelled, air-polluting cars. Wild fields had been plowed for farms, super-sized and sprayed with chemicals designed to kill all plants except the intended crops. Those areas had previously provided food and nectar for butterflies and bees, including the milkweed that is essential for Monarch butterflies. It is the only plant on which they lay their eggs; their caterpillars only eat milkweed leaves. Grandma wanted to become a small part of a national effort to increase their habitat, so bought her first milkweed plant at an annual fall sale at the Norfolk Botanical Garden. It is nationally recognized for its unique full life-cycle butterfly house and is surrounded by a variety of nectaring flowers and the host plants specific for each type of local butterfly. She put hers in the sunniest corner of her garden and was rewarded when it survived its first winter, which was unusually cold and snowy. In summer, the Monarchs arrived. Their eggs were yellow, tiny and difficult to spot, but the proof came as caterpillars grew. They became just plentiful enough to enjoy the leaves without demolishing the growing stand. She knew that after their fifth instar, the cycle of growth and shedding that changed their characteristics every several days, they would walk away, pick a secret hiding place, then expose the shell that would protect their metamorphosis. Sure enough, monarchs emerged and began their life cycle again throughout the summer and fall. In this way, she became invested in their well-being.

II

Rescue

Later, on that blustery December 16 morning, Grandma decided it wasn't a completely bad thing to interrupt Mother Nature. She cut most of the remaining milkweed stalks, including the one containing the last chilly caterpillar, brought the bunch indoors, put them in a tall vase on her kitchen counter and added warm water. Within the hour, the little green, yellow and white striped caterpillar, which she felt she had rescued from freezing to death, had warmed up enough to resume crawling in search of juicy leaves to eat. It found enough of them to keep busy for the next couple of days.

Being a good sleeper, Grandma told me she "couldn't verify the caterpillar's nocturnal behavior." But the very first thing she did when she awoke was to check. It was not moving. She worried it might have died. But when she checked again after her shower, it was back to munching. She wondered whether it was stirred by the light or the warmth of the sun. It had grown overnight. It ate. It rested. It grew. "Just like you," she told me. It ate all day, tasting green seed pods only enough to reject them in favor of the leaves, which had also perked up from the warmer indoor temperature.

Later in the day, Grandma saw that the caterpillar had stopped eating. It was rippling along quickly (for a caterpillar), climbing over and between stalks, bypassing edible leaves. It seemed anxious, as if in search of something. Up and down the stalks it rippled up and down and over to another. Up and down. Grandma thought for a moment, then ran outdoors. She admired her huge Bradford Pear tree. Although not a favored species, it provided wonderful shade during hot summer afternoons. She had snapped off several dead branches the week before and left them on the ground for habitat as one of her final fall gardening activities. She selected one, broke off a thick brown twig and put it into the vase with the milkweed stalks. Within an hour the anxious caterpillar found it and quickly climbed all over it until it selected just the right spot to begin the next phase of its life. Having interpreted the caterpillar's behavior accurately, Grandma felt more at one with nature than ever before.

Before going to bed that night, Grandma saw something like spit between the caterpillar and its branch. While holding the twig with its whole body, the caterpillar appeared to be ejecting tiny bits of frothy white stuff onto the twig, rhythmically contracting and expanding its body, segment by segment, then discharging another bit on top of the last. Grandma read it was not spit, but a kind of silken mass coming from its spinneret, a gland below its mouth. The caterpillar concentrated on adding to this pad for many hours.

The caterpillar was still squeezing out more froth the next day. By late afternoon, it stopped. The pad looked like a small stalk, about the size of the lead of a mechanical pencil let out to write. It had turned around and hooked its cremaster to the strong pad, the rest of his body hanging free. Its head-end curled up to form a 'j' shape, sometimes wiggling and shivering when Grandma approached, sometimes curling up.

Curious about what would happen next, Grandma settled into a comfortable chair near her fireplace and took some time to read more about Monarch butterflies. She wondered, was there a way to confirm its gender? She learned that caterpillars, the juvenile stage before becoming butterflies, like human children, have immature organs inside that mature under hormonal influence, like during human puberty. She learned it was possible to tell by inspecting the end where the caterpillar had attached to the twig. A dark line would be visible just below the attachment, ending in two dots. If it were a female, the line would extend, but not if it were a male.

She looked closely, then looked back at her photographs from the previous day, then back at the caterpillar. She spied a tiny dark line just below the silk pad! She followed it down, seeing nothing more. She tried again, more slowly. There it was! Just beyond the short line were two small dots, one on each side. She could not see any line beyond it. To make sure, she magnified her view using her phone's camera. Still, she saw no extension of the line. It was a male, a boy. What an exciting discovery! During the next twenty-four hours, it hung this way, and it seemed like nothing was happening. Grandma had plenty of time to reflect on nature's wonders. She felt fortunate to be observing and taking part in one of life's small dramas. Her thoughts wandered to other experiences she'd known that led her to appreciate butterflies.

III
Wings over the Smokies

Over a decade earlier, as a younger and more agile woman, Grandma was hiking along the trails near the Blue Ridge Parkway in western Virginia. It was a warm, late summer day. There were few clouds in the pale blue afternoon sky. The air smelled sweet from the dark rose-colored sumac and the beginning mustiness of fallen leaves. Grandma had been enjoying a spectacular overlook towards the low, gently rolling and gradually receding pale blue mountains from which the Smoky Mountains got their name. The rocky path crossed a gap between two large boulders.

Just beyond the boulders, Grandma heard a sound she could not identify. Being hearing impaired, even noticing this was unusual. She stopped and turned around to determine its source but saw nothing. Then she turned her gaze upwards and there it was: a cloud of fluttering orange wings was making the soft noise. As she looked, she turned gently, slowly, again, to find herself surrounded. She froze motionless in wonder as time stopped. The butterflies continued to mingle, perhaps in a mating frenzy, making the sound of a hundred small wings.

IV
Human Nature

Many years later and still, several years ago, Grandma's knowledge of the life cycle of butterflies proved emotionally helpful as analogous to the process she witnessed during her father's last weeks of life. Upon hearing that he could barely eat any longer and had even lost his determination to maintain some caloric intake by enjoying his most favorite chocolate ice cream, she knew it was time to be there with her mother and sister. It reminded her of the beginning of metamorphosis when caterpillars stop eating leaves to prepare for what would follow.

Although her dad easily recognized her when she arrived, his waking hours were few. Grandma hoped her background as a nurse-midwife would help her play a similar role in (as she liked to say) sweeping the path ahead to avoid unnecessary difficulty for him. She hoped to ease his transition as she had for laboring women.

As the days passed, Grandma could ease her father's discomfort with medications left by hospice nurses for that purpose. When he asked, she wet his lips, and he expressed deep pleasure from tiny sips. Although he slept for increasing intervals, when awake, he would get up from the couch with a little assistance, determined to use the toilet. With so little intake, it surprised Grandma how often this occurred. Then she thought again about caterpillars. Approaching the end of their last instar, they stopped eating too, then took walks that must have seemed as long for them as to her father. These walks were to eliminate all internal waste from their bodies. Her dad, like a caterpillar, became physically and perhaps metaphorically lighter. Then, on one such walk after using the bathroom, he said he couldn't take one more step. As she helped him, this time to bed, he became like a caterpillar, making its attachment to a desirable resting place.

V
Transitions

While pondering life's mysteries, Grandma monitored her caterpillar, checking it nearly every hour. Stuck to the twig, his movements became less frequent. He seemed to get darker as the day progressed, matching the brief daytime hours. She hoped to witness the end of his last instar when he would shed his skin for the last time, then become a chrysalis. Her frequent checks were interrupted by distracting phone calls. When she looked again, she thought, "Drat! I guess some things are private!" In a magical moment, he had become a beautiful chrysalis, emerald-green with a gold-studded collar and several specks of gold scattered below. It was now only a matter of time before he would transition into a butterfly. She read it should take eight to twelve days and marked her calendar.

Along with friends on Zoom ™ for Shabbat services, Grandma lit the last night of Chanukah candles. In their midwinter glow and upon saying the Kaddish prayer, her thoughts turned back to her father. She remembered their last conversation. She had reassured him that everything was ok as he rested. She had given him a gentle hug and kiss goodnight. He was comfortable. She held off the narcotics he had been needing every several hours. It was late and a good night's sleep would help everyone. Soon he was asleep facing her mother in the bed they had shared for almost sixty-five years. The night turned out to be a blessing as peace and love filled their home.

The following morning, he was no longer conscious. His arms were tightly flexed, but his joints and muscles relaxed once she gave him a gentle massage, which had always been a favorite thing. Perhaps he knew that his transition was happening. What was going on inside of him was a mystery. Grandma spoke quietly but clearly, very near her father's head, saying she loved him and would stay close by, that she and her sister would always care for their mom, each other and the rest of their family, and that she had learned from his good example. Perhaps the message with the massage helped him relax further. A few hours later, his breathing changed. They gathered around and held him. Quietly, it stopped.

VI

Metamorphosis

As was their tradition, Grandma stayed with her father until further arrangements were finalized. She sat quietly across from him, thinking of many good times they had together. Although her mind wandered, her gaze was on him. Then she saw something she'd never seen before and cleared her eyes to make sure it was there. As if it were a double image, her father's body hovered just above him. The image stayed for some time. She told him, perhaps vocally but perhaps through her thoughts, that he had crossed over, that he was finished with his earthly body, that everything was fine, that she loved him and would always remember him, and knew he would watch over her, and that it was ok for him to leave. In the next moment, his spirit image dissolved, and his energy left the room. Some part of him had clearly left the husk of his physical remains behind, the skin of his chrysalis, perhaps emerging elsewhere, out of sight. All was quiet, and there was peace and grace.

Although the transition experienced with her father seemed to take only a short time, Grandma thought perhaps that was only the most obvious part of it. Clearly, he was gone. She wondered if he had just completed his own metamorphosis to a different existence, one she could touch not only in her memories but also in an inexplicable sense of presence. Then and afterwards, she said it felt like he was so close as to still be a part of her; she could feel him within her chest. "Yes," she seemed to hear him, "You're right, yes" about whatever she was thinking.

This is what Grandma told me about how watching a caterpillar become a chrysalis reminded her of her father's death. It had provided her an opportunity to ponder life's mysteries and the processes of transformation and death, or at least of the meaning humans attribute to it. I never met; I was born the year after he died. Grandma said he would have been so delighted to meet me. I have learned to love him through photographs and Grandma's stories. What would happen to the last caterpillar's chrysalis remained to be seen.

RUNNING OUT OF TIME

by Sharon Hostler, Blue Ridge Writers, 1ˢᵗ Place
Golden Nib Second Place

Jerry was on my schedule for three o'clock. I wasn't sure why. I assumed it was about dying. We had an hour.

Jerry was eighteen, mentally and emotionally competent to make his own decisions. But physically, he totally depended on his parents. He couldn't even brush his own teeth. I was trained in pediatric hematology, just learning about chronic illness and disability. My only contribution, it seemed, was to document Jerry's day-by-day decline from muscular dystrophy.

Jerry's disease was not like cancer. When kids died of cancer, it was quick. Infection or hemorrhage. I'd stood at the bedside with parents watching their little ones die of leukemia when we had no effective drugs. Now, I was a young widow with preschool kids, sidelined from acute care. I knew about death and dying.

Jerry jockeyed his chair through the door. He had enough muscle strength to operate the joystick, but not enough to shake my hand.

When I'd examined Jerry in the clinic without his braces, he was a bag of bones. Utterly helpless to sit up or even to roll over. But today, Jerry sat upright, long leg braces poking angles at the knees of his baggy trousers. His feet, too deformed for shoes, were swathed in heavy wool socks. Jerry looked dapper in a blue-striped shirt and tie.

I squeezed his shoulder in greeting and slid into my chair. "Fancy seeing you here." The space, my office, it was tight. Too close. I could smell his toothpaste.

"This isn't easy to talk about," he said.

"It never is." But I knew we had to do it. The other doctors didn't understand. They were eager to release a tight muscle or fuse a back, to *do something.* No one wanted to perform the real work of helping a patient prepare to die.

"I'm getting worse." He paused to breathe.

"Do you want to talk about it? You know, the dying?"

"To hell with the dying crap! Got it covered." Angry, he took a long, slow inhale. Then he grinned. "I've even picked out the font for my tombstone!"

"Oh, my." He was out ahead of me now.

"Pay attention, doc."

"Okay, Jerry."

He sweat, turned his head, and looked out the window. Of course, he was angry with me, angry with all of us, for not being able to cure him. I expected this.

"Living's damned limited these days." He was struggling to breathe, but it was clear he had something important to say. "I don't want to... die."

"Of course not.

He took another breath, still looking out the window. "A virgin."

I startled. "What?"

Now he looked at me and whispered, all in one breath: "I don't want to die a virgin."

This was not what I had expected him to say. But why not? He was eighteen. I remembered what it felt like to be that young.

Well, why couldn't Jerry be full of longing? Hormones were hormones! I sat up tall in my chair, crossed my legs, and resumed my clinical persona. "I have a few questions."

"Go ahead."

"Are you masturbating?" I asked. Surely, someone had asked him that before. Had I? I wasn't sure.

"Yeah, yeah, but it's not getting any easier. Use your imagination. Look at these hands."

I nodded.

"Hell, it's getting harder and harder." Jerry appreciated his joke. "When I'm in the right position, you know, upright with my hands free to jack off. Well, even then, I have a hell of a time." He stopped for several minutes to catch his breath.

"Afterwards, I'm stuck with my hands in my freaking crotch. I can't move for shit, and I get terrible cramps in my shoulders."

"And?" I asked.

"It's a mess. I ring the bell. But I'm never sure who's going to come, Mom or Dad."

"Do you and your dad talk about it?" It was difficult to imagine he did.

"No way. He cleans me up. Repositions me so I can sleep." I noticed noises out in the lobby. Wheelchairs. Clatter. No one could hear us.

"Doc, this is not what I came to talk about."

"But you said~"

"I said I don't want to die a virgin!"

I hadn't once considered this an issue? Not once, not even a fleeting thought. His parents were already stressed. The staff was focused on his breathing. None of us were paying any real attention to Jerry.

"I'm thinking."

He jostled the joystick, jerked his chair around, and slammed straight into my shins. "My days are numbered. Doc. Numbered!"

"I know." I could smell Jerry's body odor. There simply wasn't enough air in here for the two of us.

"You were the one talking about the 'developmental tasks' at the conference. I was on the panel. Remember?"

"I remember."

"Well doc, I'm on to the 'losing my virginity' task."

That was when someone knocked on the door. I think we were both relieved that our time was up.

The next morning, I was still thinking about Jerry as I drove into work. I reviewed his request objectively from each perspective - ethically, developmentally, practically, morally, professionally. I didn't trust my medical colleagues. And I couldn't involve Jerry's clinical team. Definitely not the uptight case worker.

I stared out my office window at the willow trees. It was early spring. Their buds were ready to burst into brilliant chartreuse. Clinic started in fifteen minutes. I had to think fast.

I dialed Johns Hopkins and asked to speak with Professor John Money. I'd heard him deliver a keynote about sexuality and disability. I owed it to Jerry.

"Money here."

I presented Jerry's dilemma. "You mentioned medical prostitutes in your keynote."

His voice boomed back, "Just for the transgender clinic!"

It was worth a try.

Dr. Money continued, "Any connections with the prostitute community there?"

"I'm a pediatrician, sir. No way."

"Send the kid up here."

"Not an option, sir!"

"For God's sake and with all due respect to pediatrics, use your imagination. Get the phone book."

I pulled out the local directory. "What exactly?"

"Flip through the Yellow Pages. I'll hang on." I was damned sure there were no listings for prostitutes, but I looked anyway.

"You're in a college town. You must have sexual resources. Erotic dancers or massage parlors?"

"Exotic massage?"

"BINGO. Close enough. APPROXIMATE, doctor. Make do. And good luck on a happy ending!"

Later that day, I considered the logistics, and I identified two agents. Unfortunately, it would involve use of the recreational therapy van as transport. A necessary breach, I concluded.

Two years later, on Christmas Day, Jerry's time ran out. Just before noon, after the presents were almost all opened. The sparkly white lights on the Christmas tree blinked on and off as family and a few friends crowded around Jerry's bed. There were some quiet tears as we waited for the undertaker to come. We whispered our goodbyes.

Someone handed out tissues. Snatches of carols floated in. Jerry's mother passed a tray of macaroons and brownies. A neighbor took the phone off the hook. Stories of Jerry slowly filled the room. People chuckled. His father poured brandy. The stories continued. The laughter got louder and louder.

Not all of Jerry's stories were shared.

One, at least, remained secret.

Sacred.

CROSSING HALSTED STREET

by June Forte, Write by the Rails, 1ˢᵗ Place
Golden Nib Third Place

The School Sisters of Notre Dame, a Bavarian Order, established the Academy of Our Lady in the southwest corner of Chicago in 1875. By 1892, the westward expansion of the Rock Island Railroad had slashed a day's journey into the city to less time than it took to read the morning newspaper. Affectionately called Longwood, the coed Academy evolved into an exclusive girls' boarding school in 1892, catering to the influx of upper-crust families with grand manors that overlooked the ancient glacial ridge that ran the length of Longwood Drive.

The Wall Street Crash in 1929, followed by the Great Depression, shattered the opulence of the community, reversing many of the once-wealthy families into house-poor squatters, unable to send their children to private schools. The good Sisters adapted with the times. They converted school dormitories into classrooms, added business classes, and reinvented Longwood as a girl's high school in 1935.

The school kept its Academy designation as a Music Conservatory, and the outlandishness of continuing in the vein of a finishing school. The high-minded attitude of the nuns rubbed off on their students. As a result, the local Catholic Boy's high school students dubbed Longwood "Snob Hill."

Regardless of the new diversity of economic backgrounds, the nuns prepared Longwood's graduates to marry well, except for the students who took typing and stenography. The liberal arts students and the commercial students were discouraged from associating with each other. The feelings of not being good enough had many business-oriented students fleeing to a Commercial High School after a year. College was not a financial option for me. Notre Dame Men, the Irish equivalent of marrying a Bavarian Baron, wouldn't be knocking on my door anytime soon. Nor did I envision a promising future in secretarial work.

In 1958, my freshman year, the school admitted its first Black students. One girl shared my homeroom. She commandeered a desk in the room's front, her arrow-straight spine placed inches away from the back of the chair, legs crossed at the ankles, head held high. Her first name fit her demeanor perfectly: Lucrezia, after the infamous Italian Renaissance noblewoman of the Borgia family, daughter of a Pope. Her last name, Pharaoh, invoked ancient Egyptian Dynasties. Poise accented her regal bearing; her smile radiated the warmth of a Sun goddess.

In no time, Lucrezia became Dee-Dee and a strong friendship developed between us. Easy to recognize our similarities. Education was important to our parents, enough to sacrifice to ensure it. My father worked two full-time jobs and Dee-Dee's mother took a part-time job to pay tuition.

Our love of reading drew us to the school library, devouring classics or cramming for tests. We ate lunch together, shared half-sandwiches, a piece of fruit or home-baked cookies. The campus became our domain. We promenaded along the perimeters, stopped to throw bread to the Koi in the pond, sat on the benches by the stone grotto and shared secrets. We kept roller skates in our lockers, strapped them on and raced down the open-air Cloister Walk during lunch hours. We copied popular hair styles: Page Boys, flips, bubble cuts, French twists.

We signed up for the same electives, rolled our eyes and joked our way through home economics, learning how to deal with servants and entertain 50 guests for black-tie dinners. Dee-Dee and I were more apt to end up as the laundress or the cook than the hostess.

White-cotton blouses with Peter-Pan collars surfaced under gray gabardine blazers and skirts. Strictly enforced, the uniform rules required girdles and nylons. When our threadbare nylons shredded while our money ran out, Dee-Dee and I drew dark seam lines up the backs of each other's legs with eyebrow pencils to fool the nuns.

We dreaded "no-uniform" day. Better-off students showed up in cashmere blazers and Pendleton pleated skirts, coordinated ballet flats, pearl chokers and engraved photo lockets. We couldn't compete in our Sears Roebuck outfits and everyday worn-at-the heels saddle shoes. What most students considered a festive day exposed us to direct and indirect humiliation.

Dee-Dee and I lived just blocks apart; it might as well have been miles. She lived east, and I lived west of Halsted, the unvoiced divide between Black and White. Teenagers of either color could be surrounded, robbed and beaten for stepping off the bus at the wrong place or time.

School friends, Dee-Dee and I, all those times would allow. No sleepovers or giggling on family stoops, no sharing popcorn at the movies, swimming at the pool, milkshakes at Walgreens. We parted each summer, reconnecting with our separate neighborhood friends who attended public schools.

Several of my friends lived in the projects on 95th Street, a major east-west thoroughfare. One afternoon, I took the risk and crossed Halsted. 95th had little foot traffic that day, a steady stream of cars in both directions, only me on the sidewalk. I felt confident I'd make it to the projects without a problem.

I'd walked several blocks when a posse of Black girls unexpectedly came around a corner into my path. I don't know who was more surprised. They hesitated, then challenged me.

"What you doing in our neighborhood, White Girl?"

"Visiting a friend in the projects."

They got braver and closer. "You don't belong here."

I didn't see any weapons. To my eye, a group of friends, not a gang. They weren't out looking for a confrontation when I happened by and emboldened them. I had enough sense to stand my ground and not step back. They weren't sure what to do next. I knew if it got worse, my only out would be to make a dash across four lanes of highway to the other side. A girl in the back of the group broke the standoff.

"Aren't you Dee-Dee's friend?"

"Dee-Dee Pharaoh? Yes, we're friends."

"Girl, you know you shouldn't be walking in this area." The girls seemed as relieved as I was. They let me pass.

Dee-Dee and my friendship lasted beyond graduation. We both worked downtown, where we could fashion ourselves as coworkers. I worked at an insurance company. Dee-Dee worked at the Chicago Library by Lake Michigan. We'd bring our lunch and lay claim to a bench by the water and catch up on our separate lives. In another time, in another city, Dee-Dee and I would have had a lifetime of shared memories.

We drifted apart as racial tension on the South Side increased in the 60s and made it impossible for us to maintain our friendship. It wasn't about crossing Halsted anymore.

Real-estate opportunists invaded white neighborhoods using scare tactics, convincing people to sell their houses at reduced prices <u>NOW!</u> The agents turned around and sold the same house at enormous profits to desperate house hunters, who were being squeezed out of homes and apartments by gentrification eating into historically Black neighborhoods. The only people who made a good deal: speculators and venture capitalists.

The assassination of Dr. Martin Luther King widened and deepened Halsted's no-man's-land. Armed National Guardsmen in topless jeeps roamed both neighborhoods, ensuring no one crossed into enemy territory. The divide was so wide that no mutual ground remained. Neither Dee-Dee nor I could muster the strength to jump across.

Sixty years later, I still feel the tension when I visit the South Side. Those invisible barriers of old have migrated, but still define and limit neighborhoods by race and means. Someday, I hope, they may blur the point that two friends can cross the street.

ACADEMY OF OUR LADY — 95th and THROOP STS. — LONGWOOD, CHICAGO 43, ILL.

MY DAD'S GHOST HUNT

by Adda Leah Davis, Appalachian Authors Guild, 2nd Place

My Dad married the first time in the early 1900s. He was sixteen and his bride was thirteen. I think she came from a large family who needed to get rid of one or two so the others would have enough to eat. Anyway, these two children married and set up housekeeping.

Dad had rented an old one-room log house with a lean-to attached to the side.

The house was in a hollow by itself. He and his young wife only had a bed with a feather tick, a small step stove, a small table, two pots, two plates, and I suppose two of everything else.

The stove and table were in the lean-to. Their bed was in the main room. The house had one door, one window, and a shutter over a hole in the kitchen wall.

The first night they spent in their new home was a warm night and so Dad left the door open, but a bat flew in the house and scared his wife so that he promised to shut the door after this.

The following night, true to his word, Dad shut the door and he and his wife went off to sleep in the comfort of their very own home. During the night, Dad heard a creaking, and the door came open. Dad thought the wind had blown it open and since Rosie, his wife, was blissfully sleeping, he just went back to sleep and left it open. When Rosie awoke the next morning, she thought Dad had lied to her and not shut the door. She was upset and said she would not stay if he didn't keep the door shut. Then Dad told her what had happened, which didn't help the situation. She became terrified now, since she felt the house was haunted.

Dad, who had been raised to not believe in ghosts, laughed and told her that there were no such things as ghosts. She was still unconvinced, but he assured her she could watch him shut the door that night. That night, Rosie made sure the door was closed and fastened before she would go to bed.

Sometime around midnight, the same creaking occurred and again the door came open. This time, Dad got up and went outside and looked around. The moon was full and there was no wind. Puzzled as to the cause, Dad finally went back to bed with the final thought he would investigate this thing in the morning.

His investigation revealed nothing to explain what was happening, but night after night, this phenomenon occurred. Dad put a chair against the door, hammered in a nail and turned it over the door, and finally put up two metal sleeves to hold a crossbar across the door.

With a satisfied grin, Dad said, "That door can't come open tonight". He stayed awake just to make sure. Rosie was crying and so insistent on moving that something had to be done. He was even wondering if just maybe there were ghosts.

Midnight came and went, and the door was still closed. Dad drifted off to sleep. A storm blew in with rain and strong winds between two a.m. and three a.m. and the door came open again. The storm awoke Dad. He realized the door was again open.

Getting out of bed to close the door, Dad saw the crossbar wasn't broken, it had just slipped out of the sleeves. Closing the door again and putting the crossbar back in place, Dad crawled back into bed, but was too puzzled and scared to sleep. During those long, fretful hours, he looked for another place to live. With this decision made, he finally drifted off to sleep.

Awake with the sun, Dad heard a banging and thrashing outside and ran to the door. A big rawboned mule was rubbing its back against the side of the house. Knowing the house was old and anything banging against the walls would cause something to happen, Dad laughed in relief. He ran in to wake Rosie with "Come outside and see our Ghost."

Once his reasoning was explained to Rosie, they both laughed and were much happier than they had been since their wedding.

They spent a pleasant day picking berries and gathering hazelnuts and were tired when night came. Since they now felt their problem was solved, night did not seem so terrible, and they gladly placed the crossbar over the door and tumbled into bed. The mule had been taken back to Uncle Cam Horn's, its owner, who shut him up in a barn stall.

Rosie woke Dad with a wild scream as she watched the bar slowly slip sideways, fall to the floor, and the door slowly open. Neither of them slept any more that night.

The next morning, Dad told Rosie to cook them some breakfast and then they would go over to his Pap's to see if they could stay there until they could find another house. Rosie looked in the wood box and there wasn't any wood, so Dad picked up his axe and went out to the corner of the house to chop kindling wood from the log he had pulled in the day before.

He had almost chopped enough when he gave a great swing and the axe slipped. The blade struck the post that held up the corner of the house, knocking it completely out. Dad pulled the post out, or at least part of it, because it was so rotten that it came away in two pieces. A light came on in Dad's head, but he said nothing until after breakfast. Then he said, "Rosie, if I can prove to you that there are no ghosts, will you be satisfied to stay here?" Rosie agreed, because she was so sure he couldn't prove it.

When the dishes were cleaned, they went up and over the hill to Dad's parents' house. Grandpa was out in the cornfield and Dad went out to talk to him. Soon Dad and Grandpa left and were gone a long time. Rosie helped Grandma to cook dinner and when the menfolk came back, they all had a good meal. Dad then told Rosie if she would stay one more night in the house, he could prove there were no ghosts. With encouragement from Grandpa, Rosie finally agreed.

Feeling that there would be no sleep that night, Rosie still crept into bed to lie trembling until she finally fell into an exhausted sleep. Neither of them awoke until the sun was high in the sky and shining through their one window and the door was tightly shut. Dad jumped out of bed, dancing around in his glee. He had proven there were no ghosts. He still had to take Rosie outside and show her the new post that he and Grandpa had put under the house.

"See, you little scaredy cat, there wasn't a ghost," explained Dad as he described what happened. "The post on that corner of the house was so rotten that any movement or pressure made the post give and when it did, the house was out of square and that put too much pressure on the wall, so the door came open." Rosie didn't know how he knew that, but he was older than she was, and she took his word for it. But she still wondered if a ghost had been trying to scare them away.

The Blessings from Poverty

Life Lessons from Growing Up Poor in Appalachia

by Daniel C. Swanson, Appalachian Authors Guild, 3rd Place

I stared at the screen of our Zenith TV as the NBC Evening News showed the gleaming blue and silver fuselage of Air Force One as it landed at the airport in Huntington, WV. It was May 1964, and President Lyndon B. Johnson was touring the Southern
Appalachian region as part of his 1964 Poverty Tour. He announced his plans for a War on Poverty.

During a commercial break, I turned to my dad and asked, "Are we at war? Who is the enemy?" I was a little confused.

The TV reporter showed video of the President's tour of Eastern Kentucky that featured Appalachian families in their "Sunday best" clothes smiling for the camera. It also showed video of the stereotypical Appalachian family with several stringy haired children and their father in bib overalls with their bare feet dangling over the edge of the front porch of a rundown shack on the edge of a creek in one of the many deep hollers in the region.

The War on Poverty became a critical part of a massive federal government program that became known as The Great Society. The program resulted in the passage

RODA COAL MINE, NEAR BIG STONE GAP, VA.

of over two hundred new laws that launched some of the most consequential, and expensive, social programs in the country's history. These included Medicare, Medicaid, and Food Stamps.

President Johnson declared, "the enemy is unemployment, and its ally is poverty." He promised a "cure" to poverty in the Appalachian region. I didn't realize it at the time as I watched the TV coverage from the family farm in Wise County, Virginia, but we were on the "front lines" of the battle.

Our family had dealt with a long history of tragedy and economic hardship. My grandfather on dad's side of the family was part of a massive Swedish migration in the late 1800s and early 1900s. He settled in Southwest Virginia and made his living in the expanding timber industry that ravaged the region while cutting the massive old growth timber that covered the steep ridges and deep hollers.

He eventually met and married my grandmother while working as a timber cutter in Wise County. They moved from timber camp to timber camp throughout the mountains as the logging companies logged out of one area and moved to another. By the early 1920s, they had four young children, with my dad being the second youngest. My grandfather was tragically killed in a logging accident in Bath County, Virginia, in 1924, when my dad was only three years old.

My widowed grandmother boarded a train back to Wise County with her four young children. With no husband, no money, and no job, she faced the daunting task of surviving with her children in the hard years leading up to the Great Depression. She moved into her parent's home in the Rocky Fork section of the county. Tragedy again visited the family later that same year, when her infant daughter died of whooping cough and was buried on my dad's fourth birthday.

My dad's first job came at five when he rode on the back of a mule along with his grandfather as they traveled throughout the county and sold moonshine. Most of the family scratched out a living by making moonshine, farming, and trading with their neighbors. Times were so tough that dad and his older brother resorted to hunting wild birds with a sling shot to get enough food to survive. This practice almost eliminated the wild birds in the area.

Dad attended a two-room school called Riner School until he quit school to go to work full time after completing the sixth grade. He went to work in a sawmill. He met and married my mother when he was nineteen and she was sixteen. He later went to work in non-union coal mines where he found his life's work and resulted in his premature death from black lung disease. He spent his last years selling vegetables and apples from the family farm.

My mother grew up in a remote area of Wise County near the Buck Knob. Her family eked out a meager living from farming, cutting timber, and coal mining. Her mother came from an ancestry of some tough people that included the infamous Cherokee warrior Chief Bob Benge on her father's side of the family. She would board a bus from Wise County to Eastern Kentucky with a small cage of chickens that she raised on their farm and sell them before she returned later in the day. She tragically died as the result of an operation on a goiter, an affliction caused by a lack of iodine in her diet, now commonly available in table salt, five years before I was born.

Mom only attended school at the Riner School until the third grade. She was forced to quit school to help maintain the home place and take care of the family. Even though she lacked a formal education, she was one of the smartest people that I ever knew. She was especially good with math. She often faced the challenge of only having a meager budget of twenty dollars to purchase a week's groceries for her family of five children. As she made her way up and down the store aisles and filled her cart with only the essential items, she had the uncanny ability to keep a mental tab on how much she had spent.

After the cashier rang up her purchases, the total almost always came to just under the twenty dollars in her purse! She spent most of her life as a homemaker, but she also continued her mother's tradition of entrepreneurship as she earned money by selling handmade quilts, canned goods, and produce grown on the family farm.

Life on the family farm in my early years was only slightly removed from the lifestyle that my ancestors had lived. We didn't have indoor plumbing. We did our "business" in an outhouse next to a cherry tree on the edge of the yard. Late night visits were especially challenging as we made our way from the back door to the outhouse while facing the fear of instant death from stepping on a copperhead snake!

Drinking water came from a well that provided limited water with the taste of sulfur and the smell of rotten eggs. One of my first jobs was to carry water for Mom's roller type washing machine from a creek across the holler. We carried water in a tub after scooping it up from the creek. We had to be careful to avoid scooping up minnows and crawdads with the water. Mom would then heat the water over an open fire until it was warm enough to pour into the washer. Several years later, dad installed a water line to a natural spring that flowed year-round from a coal seam up the holler.

Like our ancestors, we learned to live off the land. Some of the steep ridges around our home had been "strip mined" by running bulldozers around the mountainside to expose the coal seams. These coal seams were then "augered" to remove the coal, and it was trucked off to market. These "strip jobs" became prime areas for growing wild blackberries and copperheads. I would arise early to beat the summer sun and make my way along the ridges while filling two metal buckets with sweet, wild blackberries.

These blackberries were then canned to make Mom's prized blackberry jam for consumption during the cold winter months or made into blackberry cobbler.

Our foraging wasn't limited to wild blackberries. We also picked wild raspberries and wild blueberries, although they were less common. We even knew of remote locations in the mountains where we could pick wild grapes in the fall. We called them "possum grapes," and they made delicious grape jelly.

Much of our food came from the garden on the family farm. We grew sweet corn, half runner beans, and lots of potatoes. My brothers, sister, and I spent hours during the hot summers hoeing and weeding the crops in the fields. We itched constantly from the pollen off the cornstalks and tried to avoid painful bites from the "buck flies" that tormented us as sweat poured down our backs. The annual crop was sold to supplement the family income or canned to save for winter. Potatoes that were left over at the end of the growing season were buried underground to avoid them being frozen and retrieved for meals in the fall and winter.

We viewed all the critters in the mountains that rose from the family farm as potential food. We hunted squirrels, rabbits, and even ground hogs to provide meat for family meals. Although some of my cousins ate them, I drew the line at possums. We hunted with a single barrel twenty-gauge shotgun. Luckily, these safaris into the mountains never resulted in my brothers or me blasting off a foot. Fried squirrel was a family favorite. My sister and I often claimed that our high intelligence level later in life came from eating squirrel brains!

I got my first job when I was in the third grade. I was attending the same two-room school that my mom and dad had attended. One day Mrs. Roberts, my third-grade teacher, approached me with my first ever job opportunity. The school had no central heat or air conditioning. Heat during the cold winter months was provided by a large "pot belly" stove in the room's corner that scorched the faces of my classmates sitting near the stove while others farther removed from the stove shivered. The stove had to be constantly fed with firewood and coal that we carried in from behind the schoolhouse.

"Danny, how would you like to earn some money?" Mrs. Roberts asked me at recess. Since I seldom had any money, it didn't take me long to answer her question. "Yes, Ma'am, what would you like me to do?" I enthusiastically responded.

She replied, "I need someone to come to school early and build a fire in the pot belly stove. Then the school room will be warm when the students arrive."

I asked, "How much does it pay?"

"Ten cents a day, and I'll pay you every Friday."

I replied, "I'll take the job." I could hardly wait to start as I looked forward to the riches to come.

I didn't think of myself as poor at that time in my life. I wore hand-me-down clothes, and we didn't always get a new pair of shoes when it was time to start school in August. All of my cousins and classmates lived like we lived. We didn't know any rich people, and we had limited exposure to life outside Wise County in the days before cable TV and the internet.

The first time that I realized I was poor occurred a couple of years later, while I was in the fifth grade. I had moved over to the "big room" of the school where the fourth and fifth graders attended class. We had no cafeteria, so mom always packed our lunch in a brown paper bag. On a good day, lunch consisted of a baloney or Spam sandwich and a piece of fruit or Little Debbie's oatmeal cake. We could purchase a half pint of milk for three cents to drink with our lunch under a shade tree on the school playground. One morning, mom told me we had nothing for lunch in the house. Her only option was to give me two of her homemade fried apple pies for lunch. Now, I loved my mom's fried apple pies, but I was embarrassed for my classmates to see that this was all I had for lunch.

Lunch time came, and I quietly moved to a remote corner of the school playground so I could eat my lunch without the laughter and ridicule of my classmates. I didn't even have the three cents for milk! I finished my apple pies as quickly as possible and moved back over toward the schoolhouse to rejoin my classmates for a quick game of tag before the bell rang. I vowed to do whatever it took to escape the multi-generational clutches of poverty.

I moved on to the Elementary School in town the following year. My struggles with poverty continued. The school was just across a short bridge from the small downtown area and a local grocery store where my mom shopped. A couple of my cousins and I came up with a simple solution to our lack of adequate food for lunch. Lunch time was one of the busiest times of the day in the store. We decided we could casually roam the aisles of the store and quietly munch on a banana or bag or chips and hide the evidence in our pockets. We would then move toward the store counter and purchase a Baby Ruth candy bar for five cents so the store clerk wouldn't be too suspicious.

Our newly discovered life of crime went well for the first few days. One day, as we approached the counter, the store manager confronted us.

"I've been watching you boys." He stated in a stern voice. "Have you been stealing food from the store?"

We shook our heads to answer "No" because we were too scared to answer his question.

"Well, if I ever catch you, I'll turn you in to the town police," he threatened as we headed for the door.

That incident represented the end of my brief crime spree and provided one of the most important lessons in my young life. I concluded it was better to go hungry that to steal. I carried that lesson for the rest of my life.

The school years passed quickly, and before long I was preparing to head off to college. I decided in the eighth grade I wanted to attend Virginia Tech and become a civil engineer. There was only one problem. My family had no money available for my college expenses while still raising three children on a meager coal miner's wage.
Luckily for me, I was able to receive a full academic scholarship. I became the first person in my large extended family to receive a college degree, and it profoundly changed my life. I accepted a job offer from a large Fortune 500 company upon graduation and moved with my bride to Cincinnati, Ohio, and never returned to the family farm.

I spent the next couple of decades of my life in the corporate world, running away from the poverty in my early life and my Appalachian culture. I lost much of my southern accent and worked hard to sound like a Midwesterner. I focused on the riches and prestige that came from "climbing the corporate ladder", often at the expense of my family. By the time that the prosperous "Dot Com" years of the 1990s had arrived, I had been promoted to Vice President in a large multi-national consulting company. We lived in a palatial home in the suburbs of Cincinnati. I drove a shiny black Cadillac Sedan Deville with gold trim and a vanity license plate with my last name. We were truly living the American dream!

Late one summer, we received a call from a couple of my high school classmates. They were planning to visit family in the area and asked if it would be okay to stop by our home for a visit. We assured them we would love to see them and looked forward to their arrival. The day came, and we greeted them at the front door.

Gary and Nina had married during our senior year and lived their entire lives in our hometown. They stepped into the foyer as their eyes scanned the spiral staircase and twenty-foot-high ceilings of our home. They had strange, puzzled looks on their faces.

"Is this your house?" they stammered.

"Of course," my wife and I quickly responded although unsure of why they asked.

"We didn't know you lived like this," they replied while still having a shocked look on their faces.

We concluded a very enjoyable visit, and they left to make the drive back to our hometown. I am sure that it seemed a million miles away from the life we lived. After thinking about it for the next few days, I finally understood why they were so shocked. I hadn't seen them since high school, and they still thought of me as the "high school me" and not the "corporate me". To them, I was still that kid who wore hand-me-down clothes and never had a car, or a date, in high school.

Another key event in my "corporate life" came a few years later. I have taken a job with a startup computer technology company that was on the leading edge of the development of computerized medical records systems. I was a manager in the company, and I had made the maximum contribution to my company 401-K plan each year and used all of it to purchase company stock. I had also received several thousand shares of stock as stock options as part of my annual compensation package. I assured my wife that we would be instant millionaires when the company was acquired, as expected, by a larger company in the industry.

I was working in my home office, when one of my colleagues called with the news of the sale of the company. Unfortunately, the buyer was of a mercenary company who had used their membership on the Board of Directors to wait until the company was in dire financial straits before offering to purchase it. Instead of becoming millionaires, we barely recovered our investment, and our stock options became worthless.

My journey through life convinced me that education, both formal and learning from life's experiences, is the most important contributor to financial gain. However, incidents like these also caused me to realize that having a rich and fulfilling life had little to do with financial gain. I came to understand that the hard lessons learned while growing up poor in Appalachia had led me to appreciate the life blessings that come from having experienced poverty in my life. These blessings include self-reliance, frugality, humility, integrity, and respect for other people.

We left the corporate world to return to Virginia a short time later. Although the world to which we returned differed vastly from the one that we had left in our early adult years, we didn't miss the stress from the corporate world. We eventually moved with our son, a single parent, and his son, Noah, to a scenic town in Southwest Virginia.

On a warm spring day, I waited at the end of our long driveway to meet Noah when he got off the bus from school. He was straight-A student and one of the most popular members of his fourth-grade class.

"Hi Papa," Noah cheerfully greeted me as he stepped off the tall step from the bus. He called me "Papa" as opposed to "Grandpa" or "Papaw." This title was a hybrid title that combined the roles of Dad and Papaw that I had played as his primary caregiver when he first came to live with us as a toddler. We often used the time as we casually made our way up the driveway leading to our large, two-story brick house at the top of the hill to catch up on the events of Noah's day.

"Well, Noah, how was your day at school?" I asked as we gazed off toward the surrounding hills covered with the bright purple redbuds, white and pink wild dogwood trees, and crab apple trees.

He replied, "It was fine, Papa. I got an A on my math test."

I commented with pride, "Good job! It sounds like another chance to make the Honor Roll. It won't be long before you're in college."

Noah continued, "I have a question for you. As I was getting off the school bus today, one of my friends looked at our large brick home and asked me if we were rich. Are we rich?"

I replied, as Noah got a confused look on his face. "Well, yes, Noah, I would say that we are rich, but it has nothing to do with a large house, fancy cars, or money in the bank,"

He demanded, "What is rich, then?"

"Noah, real wealth is about your reputation, honesty, service to your community and your God, your legacy, and your family—especially your children and grandchildren."

he replied, "I don't understand."

"Someday you will, Noah, someday you will," I assured him as we approached the top of our driveway and our home.

PUBLISHING WITH JOHN GRISHAM

by Alden Bigelow, Blue Ridge Writers, 2nd Place

I was standing behind the podium at Boar's Head Inn, a premium resort and meeting destination in Charlottesville, Virginia. I did a reading from my latest book, *Killing Time in a Small Southern Town*. It is historical fiction which tells of the kidnapping and attempted murder of two African American boys by two white boys during the pre-integration struggle of the early 1960s in Charlottesville, Virginia.

I was speaking to an audience of approximately 45 and was hopeful of having a lively discussion and perhaps sell 25 to 30 books. By comparison, I had done a reading the previous week at the Batesville Market, a beautiful old hardware store circa 1920s that had recently been restored. There I had presented to a group of fifteen, eight of whom were friends of mine. They had already bought my book, so that left a sales market of seven, of which two had checked the book out from their local libraries. Of the remaining five, three left early to complete their grocery shopping, and one of the last two purchased a book. This produced a grand total of one book sold. Nevertheless, there was an enthusiastic conversation and discussion. Such is my world of marketing books, self-publishing and tilting at windmills.

I have always hoped that discussion and praise for my books, together with the occasional query letter, would not only yield more book sales but somehow lead to the world of big-time publishers. That was always my hope. And I always come back to the story of the little boy and his father walking along the beach. There was a large group of beached star fish who had been washed ashore, and the boy asked his father what would happen to them.

"Well, they'll all probably die," his father said.

The little boy picked up one of the star fish and threw it back into the water. When his father asked him what he was doing, the boy said he was saving the star fish. The father smiled and said, "well you can't save them all."

"Well, I saved that one," the boy said.

In the same way, I hoped that some big publishing company would pluck my query fish from amongst the thousands of rejected ones all around. They would nourish it and ultimately publish the intended book for its millions of readers.

These were the subliminal thoughts that raced through my head even as I fielded questions and comments from my audience at the Boar's Head Inn. They did seem to like my book. For me, that always produced a temporary "rush" soon to be followed by recurrent doubts of what had I really accomplished.

But wait! In that very moment, on that very night, I experienced a totally unexpected breakthrough. I had just acknowledged a member of the audience who had raised her hand at the end of the reading. She was an attractive blonde-haired woman who appeared to be in her 50s. She stood up and said that she loved my book, *Killing Time*, and was going to show it to her husband because she believed it deserved to be presented to a much larger audience. She identified herself as Renee Grisham, wife of John Grisham, the author. She said she was going to ask him to read it to see if he liked it as much as she did.

Wow! Maybe my time has finally come, I thought.

Three days later, John Grisham himself called to say that he too loved my book and wanted to get together to discuss it. He asked me if I would like to join him for the upcoming UVA basketball game against Duke. He had an extra seat for that game, and he knew from reading my bio that I was a UVA graduate and would probably like that.

"Yes, I would."

The following Saturday, I sat next to John Grisham on the "floor" of the John Paul Jones Arena. Grisham was a middle-aged man with piercing blue eyes and receding blonde hair. He was fit and relaxed and charmingly disarming. And his were the best seats in the House. We sat in the front row "on the floor" only a few feet away from the players. Right in front of me was phenomenon Kihei Clark, UVA's diminutive point guard. And next to him was Mamadi Diakite, the 6' 9" Grand Orange.

They were so close I could see the sweat dripping from their bodies. And three seats down from me sat the lanky silver-haired Terry Holland, perhaps UVA's most famous coach. He was talking to Ralph Sampson, who was seated to his immediate right. This is the same 7' 4" Ralph Sampson, who was perhaps the greatest UVA basketball player of all time.

Oh, what a night.

Meanwhile, Grisham and I talked and kibitzed while cheering on UVA to a thrilling 52-50 nail biting victory over the Duke Blue Devils. After the game, Coach Tony Bennett came over to shake hands with John Grisham. They apparently knew each other well.

When Grisham introduced me as a "fellow author," Tony put his hand on my shoulder and said, "It's an honor to meet any fellow author of John Grisham. I love his books and I'll be looking for yours."

After the game, we had drinks at a local restaurant, during which John said he was going to do what he could to get his agent to take on my book. "It reminds me so much of some of my books. I almost wish I had written it myself." At the end of this wonderful evening, John shook my hand warmly and reiterated that he would have his agent read *Killing Time* and get back to me in the near future.

This was all exceptional news for my writing career. My wife, Emily, seemed just as excited as I was. I could barely contain my anticipation of being published by Doubleday and Company. I could see the national book tours, the interviews on the Today Show, a one-on-one interview on the Tonight Show, and even a major book review from the New York Times.

Finally, at 73, I would be "discovered overnight." Finally, I would have the vehicle to showcase my writing talent and provide me with the publishing success I had so long sought... and so richly deserved... I thought.

Time went by, first days and then weeks ... and then a month. Had it all been a fantasy? Suddenly an email appeared on my computer. It was from John Grisham apologizing for his agent not getting back to me sooner, something about a scheduling conflict, but that he would make sure that he did so in the next day or so at the most. "The dream lives," I thought.

Grisham's parting comment was, "Go Hoos".

Again, days went by and then weeks. Nothing. I sat at my desk, gazing out the window, looking at some ducks floating on the small watery cove which touched on my backyard. At this moment, I imagined any query fish I might throw into the water today would not be rescued by Double Day Publishing. In fact, it would probably be eaten by the ducks or simply slip under the surface, never to be seen again. So much for big time publishing.

Then the phone rang. It was J. J. Snerdley, Literary Agent for John Grisham at Double Day Publishing.

"At John Grisham's firm request," he said, "I have read your book, *Killing Time in a Small Southern Town*, Mr. Bigelow. *Killing Time* is really quite a good read. It has a great plot-line, the characters are well developed, and the action is scintillating. I don't want to overuse the cliché, but it's a real page turner."

"That's terrific," I interjected.

"Well, I suppose it is." Snerdley sniffed. "However, there is one hitch. Your book reads very much like many of Mr. Grisham's books. In some ways, it's better than some of his books. That's why I can't accept your book for publication. It's simply too good. You get my meaning, right, Mr. Bigelow?"

"Well, not exactly, I began ..." Snerdley interrupted my comments and cascading emotions:

"Mr. Bigelow, it simply wouldn't be good business to put a book like yours out there, which might compete with John's books. You understand that would not be good for John. So, regretfully, I must tell you we can't take you on. But I think WTF publications might be interested. Why don't you query them? it is an excellent book, so keep on doing what you're doing. I'm sure one of those queries will work out for such a book. By the way, I understand you are an alumnus of UVA."

"Yes," I said weakly.

"Well, as John would say, GO HOOS. Bye-bye for now."

Okay, fellow writers. **Spoiler Alert**. The part about doing a reading of *Killing Time* at the Boars Head Inn for an audience of 45 is true. The rest was all a daydream conflated by my fevered imagination. It is nothing more than a cautionary tale about putting too much hope or expectation of having a major publishing company accept your book for publication. Of course, there is always that possibility, but for 99% of us, it is not to be a reality.

Of course, you should continue sending out queries and exploring all levels of publication, but you should appreciate all victories, all levels of success along the way. Embrace the process. It's fundamentally about advancing *your* writing.

Do the best you can in the writing arena every day. Respect your writing- work at it every day- whether you write a chapter of blinding brilliance or a couple of fragmentary sentences which you know you will rewrite the next day.

Do make sure you use all the publishing avenues open to you. Create interviews in the local newspapers or weeklies. Pursue interviews with the local radio and television outlets. Do as many readings as you can secure in writer's clubs, book clubs and service clubs. Enjoy them. They provide such a great arena to discuss your book ... your writing. Be hopeful. Reach for the winning query star fish. Remember, there's only one John Grisham but there's only one you... and your writing is unique to you. Help others help you. Never give up. Keep writing. You already *own* that success ... because you ... are a writer.

MY MOTHER'S LAST GIFT

by BA Morris, Blue Ridge Writers, 3rd Place

I lost Mom long before I realized she was leaving. I think this is true for all of us who live with a parent who has dementia or Alzheimer's disease. It was transparent to me only later when I found her large collection of Styrofoam containers and the bags of groceries I had bought her which she had never unpacked, and when I read the ramblings in her journals about the thieves who came and stole things from her in the dark of night.

The lung disease the doctors found, which brought her to live with me, was a blessing in disguise. It allowed me finally to see the extent of her mental instability. She had successfully hidden from me until then. Her pulmonary issues were the beginning of a four-year journey into a deep, dark place for my mother. First, there was the treatment for the lung disease with Prednisone, which caused damage to her bones, her immune system, and her mind. Second, there was the fall, which resulted in a broken hip, surgery, rehab, and then what was intended as a short stay in a nursing facility. Then there was the fall, where she broke several ribs. Following that, there were various minor illnesses and injuries, and finally a dislocated shoulder. Each blow to her body seemed to take her mind farther into a place I could not follow. When she tried to run away in her wheelchair from the facility where she was living, and then hit, bit and kicked the caregivers who brought her back, we talked about moving her to a more secure part of the facility. When she ran away again, we knew it was time to finalize that action. So she was moved to the locked part of the Sunrise Assisted Living facility.

In the last years of her life, I went every night to put her to bed. Sometimes I'd find her in the TV room, and I'd wheel her to her room and help her dress for bed. Other times I'd arrive to find the staff had her bathed and waiting for me, sitting in a chair in her room. At first, she knew who I was. Slowly it changed to sometimes she did, and more often she didn't.

I recognized early on that I had to meet her wherever she was, because her reality was the only one that was true to her. I never knew in what period of her life I would find her. Therefore, it felt as if I was time-traveling with her; going back with her to other times and other events from her past.

Often, in those times, I had not yet been born. She might be just getting home from a long day working in the factory or finishing up a day of canning quarts of tomatoes over a hot wood stove. Once she was waiting for her brother, Edward, to arrive with the new car he had written her about. She was able to tell me exactly what that shiny new car looked like, and she was excited about his upcoming visit. Another time she was supposed to meet her Aunt Ettie at the train station and was afraid she'd be so late arriving that Aunt Ettie would go away without her. I let her dictate the conversation, and I never told her she was wrong. I'd ask questions to determine where she was on her timeline, and then try to jog her brain to reveal her full memory from that time. Often, she would tell me a story from "her day" that I had never heard before. Then there were the occasional days when she was in the here-and-now and would tell me she wanted to go home with me when I left. Those were the hardest, because she knew at some point, I would leave and she would have to stay behind, all alone. Those days broke my heart, and I often sat in my car in the parking lot after I left her and cried for her loss, and mine. It was bittersweet that she knew who I was and that I loved her, but awful because I could not do the one thing that would have brought her the greatest joy.

The most amazing memory she offered me was of a time when she had been working hard all day at home: cleaning the house, washing clothes by hand, and preparing an evening meal for her new husband. My father left us when I was barely six, so I had almost no memories of my mother and father's relationship. My memories were that Daddy would come home from work at the sawmill, bathe, eat dinner, and head out to the general store to hang out with the local men for a couple of hours. By the time he came back home, I would be in bed. They were married ten years before I was born, so I never knew the sweetness of my parent's early marriage. But there Mom was, a giddy young woman, in a place nearly sixty years before, waiting for her love to come home. I could see her becoming young again before my eyes, eagerly awaiting the sound of his car. I'd never known her when she was young and in love, and it was a precious gift. I wanted to hold on to that moment as long as I could, for her and for me. But I knew her body was tired in this life and needed to get to bed. So eventually, I coaxed her to lie down and rest for a few minutes while she waited for her husband to come home. I knew as soon as I got her settled, she would fall asleep.

Mom never again went back to her early relationship with my dad. Therefore, I treasured that tiny glimpse of her as a young woman, full of love for the man she had married, with all the hope for their future still alive in her. Mom has been gone fifteen years now. Dad died ten years after her and although we formed a tentative relationship, we certainly didn't talk about his marriage to my mother. He was remarried and his second wife was the one he was concerned with. So as a balance to all the pain of that marriage which didn't survive life's storms, I hold tight to that glimpse of a time, which Mom gave me that day, when everything was good between them. It is good to know that once they were in love and happy. It is good to know that I came from that love.

THOMAS

by Terry Cox-Joseph, Chesapeake Bay Writers, 1ˢᵗ Place

His arms laden with groceries, he bypasses the front door.

"Thomas, the door is wide open. Where are you going?"

"Your grandmother likes me to use the back door," he replies, and heads around the side of the one-story, white house, on the narrow path lined with Bird of Paradise.

"But, why?" I cut through the house and scamper through the kitchen to catch him as he comes through. "That's her rule," he smiles, bowing his head, spotting something at his feet.

"It doesn't make any sense. Your arms were full."

"That is the way your grandmother likes it." He unpacks the groceries from brown paper bags, sorts through dinner items, stores the rest in the cupboards then sweeps the floor.

I grin and lean against the wall, my arms crossed. Even when he is working on the car or in the kitchen, sweating, he wears a white shirt and dark vest, as though he's going to church. I watch his chocolate wrists flick with each swish of the broom. "I like to watch you sweep," I say. "It's a nice change from having to do it myself. I like being on vacation."

He laughs. His teeth are bright against his dark skin. His head is thrown back, his flashing brown eyes cast toward the ceiling. Sunlight from the kitchen window picks up flecks of white that accent the background of his curly black hair. He thrusts the broom in my direction, pauses when he senses my alarm, then returns to sweeping. My father is watching, and I think that he and Thomas are conspiring to make me finish the kitchen. But he takes me out of the room, out of Thomas' way.

I ask my father, "Why does Thomas have to come in the back door?"

"Some things are just the way they are," my father sighs. "It's your grandmother's house."

There is an empty rectangle in the center of the driveway. Thomas has taken Grammy to the hairdresser, and the metallic blue Cadillac to the carwash. I hate the Cadillac. I hate the fins in the back. It looks like a Batman car, painted blue. Thomas loves it, I can tell. Grammy loves it, too. Their love for this car is a strange binding force. Sometimes, Thomas and Grammy are a team. Their movements, their comings and goings, are so fluid, so choreographed, they are like two sides of the same person. I think of my back-and-forth doll, soft cotton, long, blonde braids of yarn hanging past blue paisley shoulders. I think of her blue eyes, stitched in yarn, eyelashes flat against the eggshell white of her flat, round face. I spend hours lifting her dress over her head, tipping her upside down to view her other side. She has no legs, and her torsos are connected. I pluck at the black chunks of yarn attached to the top of her head in French knot cornrows. My thumb delights at the rough texture. I caress her red paisley skirt. I cannot decide which side I like the best. Back and forth I go. Except for the hair, her features are identical. It is the colors that are different.

When Thomas returns, he parks the Cadillac in the driveway. The garage door is wide open. The door between the house and the garage is open. The front door is open. The Santa Monica sun dapples the door frame, and we need neither heat nor air conditioning.

"Come in, Thomas, come in," Dad says, waving Thomas through. I smile. *Finally*, I think. But he stays at the door and studies the lock. It was jimmied the night before. Not even one of us heard it. Dad and Thomas discuss the merits of getting another lock versus repairing the old one.

Thomas walks to the kitchen to find a screwdriver. Family members wander in and out. Thomas wanders in and out. Grammy returns. She has gotten a ride home from a friend. She greets us, then studies the lock with Dad and Thomas. She remains in the living room, talking. Thomas begins to walk through the front hall. He and my father exchange glances that Grammy does not notice. Like a cat, Thomas pivots on the balls of his feet. But before he disappears around the corner of the garage, he turns again, faces me, and approaches the door in a feint. He reminds me of the football players Dad watches on Monday night TV—the ones who pretend they will catch the ball when they know a player behind them actually has it. Then, with a deliberate grin and dip of his head, he walks around the side of the house.

Days later, my little sister and I look for Thomas. "He's gone to buy a cake for the party," my grandmother tells us.

"Why can't we go? Why didn't you tell us?"

"No, no, this was just an errand for Thomas."

Once again, we take our complaints to my father. "He went to Chinatown," Dad replies. "It's a bad neighborhood. Thomas has to go by himself."

"Chinatown isn't a bad place," I argue. Visions of colorful pastel frosting flowers fill my head. I imagine the satisfying weight of the cake, the stiff, plastic container cushioned in my hands.

My father says, "You have to drive through some bad areas to get to the bakery."

"But why don't we buy the cake from another place?" I persist.

"Because the bakery in Chinatown is the best," my grandmother asserts. The subject is now closed. How can the best bakery be in a bad neighborhood? I envy Thomas and his magical powers that carry him through dangerous neighborhoods.

The guests arrive for the party one by one. Thomas greets them at the door, stores their coats, mixes their drinks at the bar, and serves canapés he made himself — without breaking a sweat. Maybe that is why he stays so thin. He never stops moving. I know he will have the dishes washed the moment the guests leave. In a week, when we leave, he will be there for Grammy. She cannot see to drive at night. She cannot carry heavy bags of groceries.

My sisters are old enough to drink. "I'd like a *White* Russian," Kathy says.

"Oh?" Thomas replies. The arch of his eyebrow is slight, the twinkle in his eye meant only for her. But I see it. She is barely 18 and pretending to be sophisticated.

"Yes," she insists, with a chuckle. "A *White* Russian." Thomas chuckles as well. He pulls a pocket guide from his tux. His eyebrows rise like waning moons.

"A *White* Russian it is." He mixes the drink. "I've never made a *White* Russian before," he tells my sister as he hands her the glass. She laughs and thanks him. Grammy's friends break out into laughter. Thomas and Kathy laugh together, privy to some joke I do not understand.

Sequins glitter under the lights. Laughter becomes louder as the evening stretches. The small band Grammy has hired is too loud for my ears. The songs are old fashioned. I am embarrassed, itchy in my polyester dress. Women in sparkling gems tell me I look *so* grown up. I know they are being polite. My chest is flat. My hair is straight. They tell my little sister, Molly, the same thing. She wears a sleeveless dress with huge polka dots and a peace symbol necklace. I like her shoes better than mine.

My grandmother's blue dress has a V in the front that reveals too many wrinkles in an embarrassing place. Several of my grandmother's friends also wear revealing evening dresses. Old people are not sexy. Their loud noises bother me. Their smoke gives me a headache. Women leave crushed butts with fuchsia lipstick imprints in ashtrays. Men douse cigars in their drinks.

I feel a pang of guilt. I love my grandmother. She has never raised her voice to me. She showers me with privileges. But I am bored. My sister and I play with the huge, red pillar candles in the front living room. We take turns dipping our fingers into the hot, melted wax to see who can stand the pain the longest. We come away with chunks of red wax on our fingers and wait for it to harden, then peel it off and drop it onto the floor. The music is louder than ever.

Suddenly, Thomas is standing over us. We know better than to continue our game. Embarrassed, we hold our hands behind our backs. Thomas reaches out, runs a forefinger through the hot wax, then blows on the mass to cool it quickly. It loosens from his finger in one piece without a single crack. The lifted wax reveals a perfect pink fingertip. For a moment, we study his pink palms so like our own. They contrast with the dark chocolate flesh on the backs. His long fingers have black knuckles and pink fingernails. His hands frighten and fascinate me. Everything he touches turns out perfectly. Perhaps his hands are magic. Or perhaps he has had years to practice his many skills. I decide that he never sleeps.

He reaches behind his back and pulls a tape recorder from beneath his tux. "I have a little game for you," he confides, squatting. He depresses the "record" button, then slides the small black tape player behind the fireplace screen. "Sh," he says with a devious smile. He covers his lips with a long forefinger. "I'll be back."

Our eyes grow round with wonder and delight. The band has stopped. The laughter is unbearably loud. Bits of conversation barge into the room and zoom into the tape recorder. Molly and I pace when guests enter, fretting that our game will be discovered. We stay on the other side of the room, so we do not draw attention to the fireplace. Later, Thomas comes and moves the tape recorder to a white carpeted bedroom.

He beckons us and shuts the door behind him. He rewinds the machine, then hits, "Play."

We are in heaven. The sounds from the tape recorder are funnier and more obnoxious than they were in real life only moments ago. Thomas stands sentry by the door. Too soon, he comes to take the tape player away. With a knowing smile, he says, "You see? It's all here." We giggle, co-conspirators, best friends.

I want to go with Thomas when he runs to the cleaners, the carwash, the bakery. I want to see where he lives. I want to meet his wife. I want to know if he has a dog.

But I run errands with Grammy. She is petite, her nails are flawless, her manners impeccable. She loves us. But she is not Thomas. Thomas lives on the other side of town, and we cannot go with him.

Thomas gets a wonderful Christmas bonus. I hear Dad talking to Grammy on the phone. It is a check for $1,000. It goes out in the mail, as it has every year. I want to hand it to Thomas at his door. He lives in a friendly neighborhood, I am told. There is an emphasis on the word "nice," and I am not sure what my parents mean when they say that. But I am happy for him. Even though I still think Grammy should let him come in the front door.

MY LIFE/MY BLOG
by Dayna Hutson, Chesapeake Bay Writers, 2nd Place

First Day

A long time ago, I was sitting on the back porch listening to a chorus of frogs. Their sounds made me think of my childhood in upstate New York and "the first day" of my life. Okay; it wasn't really the first day of my life, but it was the first day that I could remember anything. All I knew, upon awakening that day, was that I was about to be adopted by the people whose house I was in. My room was familiar, as was the woman opening my blinds. However, I was unable to recall the night before or anything before that morning.

I was told to get out of bed and get breakfast, so I headed toward the kitchen. I walked slowly across the rather dark house, while I struggled for some sort of recollection of yesterday. Upon reaching the kitchen, I remember trying to turn on the water faucet, but I was unable to reach it. How old could I have been?

Social Worker

After that day, I started retaining memories. Yet, I kept wondering what happened before? Why would I suddenly begin remembering things? What was it I did not remember? Around the same time frame, a woman came to the house regularly. She was there because of me, but other than saying "Hello," she ignored me. Often, she dressed in gray or black. Sometimes, she wore navy blue. She was older and wore ugly thick glasses that would sit on the edge of her nose. Her black stringy hair was piled on top of her head. I remember thinking she was very dumb. She fell hard for the phony show being put on just for her. There were perfectly arranged small sandwiches, and little cakes served on fine china. Tea was in a fancy pot and poured into delicate cups perched on saucers.

What interested me the most, though, was the briefcase the woman always carried with her. I so wanted to steal that bag! Surely, clues to my missing past were in there! I am not sure how long the briefcase and the woman came to visit, but after my adoption, I never saw them again. How was I going to find my lost time?

Skating Forward

The house I grew up in was in a small hamlet named Shrub Oak, about sixty miles north of Manhattan. I knew everyone within walking distance, and there were lots of other kids nearby. It seemed like we entertained each other, depending on who had the best idea of the day. One of the best distractions was ice skating on one of the many nearby lakes. That helped take my mind away from my mysterious past. By school age, I was introduced to the library. It fascinated me. I think I spent most of my time walking around, exploring the historic building, rather than reading. I wondered what it would be like to live in such a grand house. Maybe I used to live in something similar.

One rainy afternoon at the library, I found a locked door. It startled me. The library had secrets, just like I did. I felt a rush of excitement. What a perfect place to start my detective work. During my next visit, I wandered around bookshelves and discovered *Nancy Drew Mysteries*. I read every one of them in a search of ideas on how to unravel my past. Finally, I found one that gave me an idea. Why hadn't I thought of that!

Clue Searching

I felt like a detective! I began exploring the house where I lived. Somewhere, there had to be a photo album that would hold a clue, just like in *Nancy Drew*. The only problem was, I didn't know if I could ask anyone where I would find such a thing.

The much older boy in the house was mean, so I tried to avoid him. The parents were not interested in my curious mind. That left the dog, Sandy. He became my search buddy and my best friend.

I took a flashlight from under the kitchen sink, when nobody was looking. I quietly closed my bedroom door, and we began searching my closet. I knew there were more items than my clothes in there. There was no photo album to be found. Now, how was I going to get into the other closets without being seen? Maybe Sandy could distract everyone!

Hidden Photo

The next Saturday was like any other, except Sandy, and I had a plan. The father left early for work. The older boy was out somewhere. The mother worked on finances after breakfast. Sandy and I waited for her to begin her work. While she was distracted, Sandy and I headed to the parents' bedroom to look in their closet. Their room was off limits to me, but nobody said anything about the closet. Besides, I could always blame it on Sandy, right? After climbing on a chair from the old Singer sewing machine, I explored the closet shelf. There was a locked metal box. That did not make me happy. It was just like the briefcase the social worker had. It shouted out that my past was a secret, and it was being kept from me.

Sandy brought me a shoe. I whispered, "Sandy; you're right. We need to check and see if there is anything more than shoe boxes on the closet floor." He looked at me with pride and a wagging tail. Nothing could be found on the floor, so I quietly moved the chair back to the sewing machine. It was important to make sure that the chair did not look like it had been moved.

Meantime, I could hear the mother on the phone. That was a relief. She was saying something about a bill, so I knew she was still working. When I turned around, Sandy was relaxing on a thick cushion that covered the top of an odd piece of furniture. It may have been a bench of some sort. Sandy quickly jumped down. With him came the cushion. Scrambling to put the cushion back in place, I noticed a small opening on the bench's top. It looked like a half moon. Was it another secret hiding place?

Of course, I stuck my fingers inside the opening and could open the top. Inside were things I had never seen. There were handkerchiefs with someone's initials on them. A patchwork quilt was neatly folded, and an old doll with a porcelain face was grinning at me. No photo album was to be found. While closing the bench top, something caught my eye. Looking closer, I discovered it was a photograph. Why was it by itself? Who was that in the photo? Was that me? It was me, but younger! Who was that boy, and where was that house?

Now, nervousness was taking over. Sandy and I bolted back to my bedroom with the photo in hand and tried to act innocent. It was good timing, because right after, the mother came to check on me.

The Truth?

There was good news, and bad news about the photo that Sandy and I found. The good news was that the parents never noticed it missing. The bad news was that I never found out who the little boy was, how old I then, or whose house was in the photo. Perhaps it is because I had no one to ask.

As time passed, I became brave enough to ask the mother about my past. She was in her bedroom, and the door was open. I stuck my head inside the open door and asked if I could enter. She said "Yes." Her clothing was laid out neatly on the bed. There were gigantic white underpants, along with a bra that appeared to be ten or twelve inches in height. A slip had been cut in half, so she could put it over her bra. Last, and most horrible of all, was the girdle. I couldn't help but shake my head in disgust.

The mother sternly asked why I was shaking my head. I didn't want to lose my chance to talk. Stuttering at first, I said "I have a question." There was silence and the usual look of annoyance on her face that I had grown to hate.

"Why was I put up for adoption?" She stopped and looked at me, as if I had asked something outrageous. She finally responded, "Your father died of a heart attack, and your mother had a nervous breakdown. She could not take care of you." That was it. She turned away. "What nationality am I?" She glared and said "Norwegian." I went back to my room and pictured a young couple, so in love. My father was tall, dark, and handsome. My mother was blonde, like I was so beautiful. They were very excited that they were having me. Suddenly, everything changed. He died from a heart attack, maybe in her arms. She was devastated. Her crying wouldn't stop. There was no consoling her.

Then I realized I was over a year old when adopted. Something felt odd about that story. Was I really told the truth, or was that a fabricated tale?

The Fearful

As I blossomed into a young woman, my life took a sharp turn for the worse. The father became interested in me in a sensual way. Wearing shorts was uncomfortable because he stared at my legs. Perhaps the mother noticed because she became adamant about my clothing. Although I was going into my teens, she refused to let me choose my clothing. She made me wear long sleeves, turtlenecks, longer than normal skirts. All the things my peers were wearing were off limits to me. That included makeup and stockings. It was quite uncomfortable. I felt like I stood out, and not in a good way.

Every day, I was assigned a massive number of chores inside the house. My work was inspected by the mother and her white glove. Never was my work good enough. It had to be repeated. When her friends came to play cards or Yahtzee, I was ordered to wait on them, serving coffee and cake, bringing ashtrays and emptying them as needed.

A Hint

When I turned sixteen, mother was very excited about me getting my driver's license. That was the first time I had ever seen her happy about something that I wanted. It was only later that I realized her excitement was not for me. It was for her. She did not drive, and my license meant she would have a chauffeur every Saturday (while kids my age were going to football games, etc.)

After my first trip to the DMV, I asked mother if I could see my birth certificate; she held it and handed it to the employee, giving me a learner's permit. She scowled and asked "Why?" My reply was "No reason." She reluctantly handed it to me. It was one sentence and a stamp to make it official. My *adoptive birth name* was born on (*the date*) in Islip, Suffolk County, New York. I was born on Long Island! Finally, I had a clue.

Something inside me told me to write to the Capital of New York and request another birth certificate, so I did. Nobody but Sandy was told.

Clue in the Mail

After that, the mailman became my favorite person. Every day, I raced to get the mail. Finally, I received an envelope from the Albany, Capital of New York. Stuffing it in the back of my pants, I went into the house to put the rest of the mail on the kitchen table. Then I went into the bathroom and shut the door. It was the only room in which I could be sure nobody would walk in.

This certificate was different. It had boxes and more information. It still had my adoptive name, of course, but something caught my attention. Brentwood is exactly where

I was born, (a hamlet within Islip) That was a great clue. The next step was to find the hospital.

Born Where?

With the latest birth certificate in hand and the tenacity of Nancy Drew, I searched for hospitals. There were one or two in West Islip, but the only hospital in Brentwood itself was a rather odd place.

That day, as the parents were coming into the house with groceries, I blurted out, "Do you know that the only hospital in Brentwood is Pilgrim State Hospital? And, it is a psychiatric hospital!?" Father walked past me and into the kitchen without saying a word. Mother, however, walked past me, glanced back, and casually said, "I think that's where your mother was."

"I could hear myself shrieking, 'I was born there?'" The house went silent. How can babies be born in a psychiatric hospital? Where was the delivery room? Where was the nursery? Of course, there was no response. How can a baby be born in a mental hospital? Where was the delivery room? Where was the nursery with all the newborns?" What now?

A Name

The hospital information scared me to a standstill. Some years passed. I moved out on my own. Then, finally one day, I felt I could try to search again. My first move was to call the county courthouse where I grew up. A very nice woman said that the parents would have been given a copy of my adoption records. She said "Ask to see them."

That idea made me very nervous, so I practiced what I would say during my drive to their house. It did not help that the minute mother saw me, she asked, "**What** did you do to your hair?" I quickly blurted out, "A lady at the courthouse says that you have my adoption records. I would like to see them, please." She hesitated and just looked at me. Finally, she went into her bedroom. I did not follow. In her hands, coming out of the bedroom, were folded papers.

She went to the kitchen, sat down and slowly unfolded them. All the time, she was staring at them. Leaning over her shoulder, I struggled to see. Finally, I saw my birth surname. It was 'headache,' I said, "That is not a Norwegian name." Of course, there was no response, and I left without the papers. Still, I had a name.

Family

Searching for the name "Hurdich" was making me very nervous. My search began in and around where I was born. Finally, I found one such name. The phone number was in New York City. When I called, a woman answered. I identified myself with the birth name that was on the adoption papers and said, "I am trying to find my natural family." She replied calmly, "Just a moment." A man came to the phone. He said "I am your half-brother, John."

Before hanging up the phone, we made plans to get together. He and his wife and baby came to my house in lower Connecticut. He brought me a small pile of pictures. I looked exactly like my mother as a child. That was the first time I saw anyone who looked anything like me.

John did not know why my mother was at Pilgrim State. He was raised by her parents. It was his father who was Hurdich, and he was my mother's husband. So, it was he who passed away. Why was every clue bringing up more questions?

Who Are They?

Two or three pictures from John showed me with a family. In one, I was in a highchair. In another, I saw a Christmas tree, so I may have been about nine months old. "John, who are these people?" He replied he had no idea. When he was young, our grandmother would take him to their house. At that point, he did not know he had a sister.

When I met my mother's two younger brothers, they had no idea who the people in the pictures were. They knew I was born and was later put up for adoption. One uncle said my father, from what he heard, was Italian and married with children. My mother's family was from Finland. What happened to Norway?

DNA

Once DNA became available, I did a test. When the results came in, they showed Finland and Italian. I am second generation American on both sides. Somewhere along the way, I recalled that one uncle said my father's name was John Lupo. Again, that was not accurate. His last name was Lupinacci.

My biological parents were deceased, but I could see the trees of a cousin and another cousin's daughter. The family tree held two John Lupinacci's. It seemed evident that the John born eight years before my mother would be my father. Something just did not seem right, though. The connection between my first cousin and their positions in the tree did not match that idea.

I wrote to the cousin's daughter, as her tree was most detailed. She responded and gave me her phone number. When we talked, she told me that John Senior was my father. There was a rumor in the family about him having an ongoing affair with my mother. This I could not fathom.

For three nights, I tossed and turned. Finally, I called the company that processed my DNA. A very nice woman viewed the tree and explained DNA numbers to me. She said that I was most definitely the daughter of John Senior. She concluded this by how I was connected to the other members of the family.

Is it possible that my mother was put into Pilgrim State because she was pregnant by a married man, and that married man was much older than she? Even with DNA done, there more to this mystery of mine.

MEMORIES OF RICK

by Chuck Tabb, Hanover Writers, 1st Place

We are the sum of our memories. They gather in our minds like spices stored for later use, and they flavor our existence as our lives' clocks countdown to the last second. Like anyone with four siblings, many of my memories center on family. One sibling I love to remember is my older brother, Rick, who was born April 15, 1952. My parents always called him their "tax baby."

There are days I think of Rick often. He died on May 3, 2010, so it's becoming "a while" since his death. To say we fought as children would be a shocking understatement. Rick could be a bit of a bully. I was three-and-a-half years younger, so I was his easy and constant target. Yet, it's funny how growing up can change things.

We became quite close as we aged into adulthood. I even rented a room from his family on more than one occasion when I was single, since that was easier, cheaper, more fun than a roommate, and less lonely. That arrangement had the added perk of becoming a fixture in the lives of his daughters. To this day, the three of us feel extremely close because of their few childhood years I spent with them.

Some days I feel the loss of my brother considerably. It was on his birthday in 2010 that I spoke to him for the last time. There is no person on Earth I have had better times with - perhaps as good, but not better. Of course, like anyone, I recall fond moments in our lives. The memories that follow, a tribute to him, are a few of them:

In the mid-1970s, I moved back to Florida from the New Orleans area. My Chevrolet Vega did not pull a small U-Haul, even with my meager belongings, so I enlisted Rick and his 6-cylinder midsize to help.

We rented a small trailer for a "local" move because it was cheaper than a one-way move, though it may have been illegal, but the statute of limitations prevents prosecution now, so I'm safe. Leaving one night in mid-February for the drive to the west side of New Orleans, we drove overnight to our destination. I forget the exact time we left, but it was near midnight. It was also cold, in the mid-twenties.

What we didn't count on was the gas consumption when pulling the trailer. The distance from my hometown of Ft. Walton Beach, Florida, to our destination of Kenner, Louisiana, which is on the far western edge of the metro area of New Orleans, was about 260 miles. We started with a full tank and my mother's Union 76 credit card. I doubt we had forty cents between us. By the time we got to Gulfport, Mississippi, perhaps 170 miles from home, we were forced to find an open gas station. It was the middle of the night, around 3 A.M., and we were lucky finally to locate a place that was open. Keep in mind, not everyone was open 24 hours back then, and a gasoline shortage added to our problem.

Gassed up, we continued to New Orleans. After a couple of hours, we were approaching the exit off I-10 that leads into Slidell, Louisiana, just as you are getting on the six-mile-long Interstate-10 bridge that crosses the eastern side of Lake Pontchartrain. At this exit, a large Union 76 station/truck stop sat with all the gas we could need. All we had was the gas card, and it wasn't good at any other places along our route. We had almost a half tank of gas in the car - as I said, the gas mileage was abysmal - but we decided to retrieve my few belongings and stop on our way back.

Big mistake.

After loading my things in the small U-Haul, we headed back toward the Union 76 near Slidell, the only Union 76 station in the New Orleans area. Just as we topped the rise on the I-10 bridge, the car sputtered and quit. Rick put the car in neutral to allow it to roll until it stopped.

If you've ever been on this bridge, you know it is actually two separate bridges, one for westbound traffic, another for eastbound. Although we had no gas can, the card could be held for ransom, so that wouldn't be a problem. But did I mention it was cold? A lighted time-and-temperature sign in Kenner had said it was twenty-two degrees - without the wind. We flipped a coin to see who would go get the gas. Rick lost the coin-flip. Bundling himself in his thin jacket, he stepped out, glared at me as if it were all my fault, which in a way I guess it was, and started walking, sticking his thumb out for a ride.

The second car to pass stopped for him, figuring out our problem since the car was parked right beside him in the breakdown lane. I sat and waited.

Of course, it was possible to hitch a ride to the gas station at the end of the bridge, get the gas, thumb a ride to the New Orleans end of the bridge, cross over, and finally thumb a ride to the car, but that would require finding two people willing to have a young man with shaggy, long hair and a smelly gas can in their car. Not likely.

So I watched and finally saw a speck in the distance: Rick, carrying the half-full, three-gallon gas can as he walked facing traffic.

I got out of the car, bundled myself against the surprisingly strong and bitterly cold wind blasting over Lake Pontchartrain, and set off to meet him, feeling the least I could do would be to carry the gas can the rest of the way once we met somewhere on that freezing bridge. The wind chill had to be near or below zero. Rick appreciated the gesture.

We filled up at the Union 76 of course, once we got the car running, and stopped again at our previous oasis when the gas level dropped to a half-tank in Gulfport.

The adventure was not fun, but it was memorable, and remembering it is fun. Had I known what a special memory this would be, I would have tried to enjoy it more back then. But back then, we thought we'd live forever.

Another memory of Rick also involved New Orleans. He was on his way from one place to another by air, and he purposely set up a long layover so we could have some time together. I was living in Metairie, a suburb of New Orleans, and after I picked him up from the airport, we drove downtown to have some beignets and coffee from the original Cafe du Monde in the French Quarter. Our plan from there was to wander around the Quarter and see what we could see.

We ended up strolling around Jackson Square, which is right across the street from Cafe du Monde, and Rick sat for a portrait. The artist *assured* us he would be done in plenty of time for Rick to get to the airport and catch his flight. When the man was *finally* finished, it was obvious Rick would probably miss his flight, but we tried anyway.

We ran to where we parked the car as I wondered if someone might think we'd just committed a crime. I paid the attendant for parking, and Rick took my keys and pulled my car up to the lot exit to pick me up. We ran several stop lights on Canal Street, somehow avoiding getting a ticket. These lights were not "maybe red" lights; they were red - with cars waiting. Rick would pull around the cars and speed past them when it was clear enough to shoot between oncoming cars to our right and left, only to be forced to do the same at the next light. When we merged onto I-10, Rick zoomed in and out of traffic.

We finally arrived at the airport, which is about fifteen miles from the French Quarter. Rick told me to circle around and if he'd missed his flight, which was scheduled to leave about twenty minutes before we had arrived, he would be outside waiting for me. If he wasn't there, I could go home.

I circled around to find Rick standing on the sidewalk, waiting for me. Instead of jumping in, though, he told me his flight was delayed by an hour, and he had plenty of time. (Keep in mind that getting to the gate was not the hassle it is today.) Lucky break! We both could breathe again.

The next day, I went out to get in my car to go to work and found a flat tire waiting for me. All I could think was how lucky we were it hadn't happened the day before. I only wish I knew what became of that picture of Rick. It was a good one, done in chalk, and I'd love to have it, or at least be able to give it to his daughters.

Finally, anyone who knows me well is aware I am a dyed-in-black-and-gold New Orleans Saints fan and have been since the day they began playing in the NFL in 1967. Rick ended up in Tampa for his final years and became a Buccaneers fan. I forgave him. But in the last years of his life, he became quite ill and had to use an electric scooter style of wheelchair to get around. I would visit him every summer, and we would do as much as we could together. One year we went to Busch Gardens to enjoy the rides, but the best time was the year we attended The Tampa Bay Bucs training camp in Orlando.

We loaded his truck with the scooter and set off. Arriving at the sports complex where Jon Gruden led the Bucs in their training camp, we pulled up in time to see the last forty-five minutes of practice. When we got there, Rick bought an official NFL Tampa Bay Bucs football. I bought a t-shirt for my son-in-law, who is also a Bucs fan. (Don't worry; I've forgiven him too.)

When practice was over, several players stuck around to sign autographs. We had everyone there sign the football and shirt, though there weren't that many players staying out to sign.

The most gracious among the players was Ike Hilliard, who was the nephew of a former New Orleans Saint, Dalton Hilliard, a star running back for the Saints in the late 1980s and early 1990s. He went from fan to fan, talking with them, posing for pictures, etc. He was nearing the end of a good career as a wide receiver, and his willingness to spend time with his fans in the Florida heat amazed me. He remained long after all the other players had gone inside to shower and enjoy the air conditioning after a long, hard practice.

As he moved from one place to another to sign autographs and chat, Mr. Hilliard would say to Rick, "Don't go anywhere. I'll get with you before you leave." He did this at least three times.

When he finally made his way to us, he explained he wanted Rick to be his last fan so he could spend as much time with him as Rick wanted. Rick, remember, was in an electric scooter/wheelchair because of his illness, which was apparent to anyone who looked at him. (He was truly skin-and-bones.) Mr. Hilliard talked with Rick, allowed me to take as many pictures of them as I wanted, telling me not to worry as I fumbled nervously with the camera, and signed both the football and the t-shirt. I "confessed" to being a Saints fan and told Mr. Hilliard to thank his uncle for me for all the great runs when he saw him again. He was a pleasant and wonderful man to someone who obviously would not be on this earth for many more years. Rick, of course, loved every second, and we thanked Ike Hilliard for keeping us for last so the man wouldn't feel rushed to get to anyone else. A class act.

So, those are three of the fondest memories I have of Rick. He had a great life, but he died far too young. That's what happens when you live in such a way as to flame out. He enjoyed "having fun" a bit too much for his own good. But he enjoyed every second of his life that he could, too.

RIGHT-HANDED

by Elizabeth Spencer Spragins, Riverside Writers, 1ˢᵗ Place

"Let go of my hand." My younger sister swatted me away and hobbled across the knife-edged gravel in bare feet. Stung to silence, I retrieved her discarded beach towel and followed, wincing with every step. Marie had barreled down the grassy slope and cannon balled into the swimming pool before I reached the edge of the parking lot. I watched, mortified, as she drenched all the teenaged sunbathers on the concrete deck. Their shrieks converged into the shrill cry of the telephone, jolting me out of that childhood memory and back into the present. Since my cell phone had no reception here, I had increased the volume of the land line to an ear-splitting level that could be heard anywhere in the house. Stumbling over my luggage, I lunged for the receiver before the second ring.

Dr. Hassan, the specialist who was overseeing my sister's care, cleared his throat and got right to the point. "Marie is not bouncing back from the initial surgery. We drained the abscess on her spine, but the staph infection has settled in her hands. They're bright red, and the right hand is considerably worse. I've changed her antibiotics to a mix that may be more effective. However, that approach will not be enough. We need to clean out the pocket of infection beneath her lungs in case that's the primary reservoir of bacteria. Then other decisions must be made."

I swallowed hard, took a ragged breath, and tried to digest the implications. Twelve hours in airports and planes had left me too disoriented to frame questions. After outlining the schedule for tomorrow's procedure, the doctor murmured a farewell and hung up.

My eyes shifted to the kitchen window, where the last embers of the sunset were fading. Dusk brought the realization that I had not eaten all day, and neither had Marie's animals. I busied myself with the search for pet food and located a few bags of kibble in the garage. On the way back to the kitchen, I passed my sibling's art studio. An unfinished abstract of the Texas sunrise rested on an easel; a mismatched collection of glass jars stuffed with brushes waited on her worktable. The paint-splattered stool, a relic from Marie's college days, displayed her creative phases in layers. I lingered in the doorway, inhaling the scent of turpentine, until a feline yowl shattered the silence and recalled me to duty.

After feeding the dog and cat, I pulled a bag of trail mix from my purse and picked at the contents while I wandered the house. A storage closet yielded an inflatable mattress, linens, and two mismatched sofa pillows. Since the music room had minimal furniture, I hauled the bedding there. Of course, the mattress proved too large for the floor space. I surveyed the room's contents to determine what could be rearranged. The piano bench was already tucked under the keyboard. Marie's steel-string guitar was reclining on the couch; a music stand in the corner cradled a collection of Broadway tunes. Wrestling the three-seat sofa out of the room was not an option, but dragging the Victorian armchair to the hall was feasible. Within 30 minutes, I had settled into my makeshift bed and a sleepless night.

At the first hint of daylight, I extricated myself from the tangled sheets and staggered, bleary-eyed, to the shower. The animals, sensing my mood, slunk away after downing their breakfast. Most of my oatmeal ended up in the trash, but I poured hot tea into a travel mug, hoping it would calm my jittery nerves later. When I passed through the foyer, my sidelong glance landed on a full-size reproduction of Rodin's "The Cathedral." I averted my eyes from the sculpture's disembodied hands and bolted.

Six hours later, I was waiting for my sister to be returned to her colorless room in the critical care unit. The surgery had been successful, but pain control had been problematic, delaying her release from the recovery area. A commotion at the door announced her arrival, and three nurses started the well-choreographed dance of positioning her bed, connecting the monitors, and checking vital signs. I pushed myself up from the lumpy chair in the corner and stood beside a sleeping form, who faintly resembled the spirited person I knew. Her pale right hand almost matched the white sheet. I reached for it and squeezed lightly. Marie opened her eyes, squeezed back, and smiled. "You came."

I nodded and shifted to make room for a nurse. Her grip tightened. "Don't let go."

Mama, Get Better

by Carol Thomas Horton, Riverside Writers, 2nd Place

Mama was crying again. I remember hearing her in the bathroom rolling the toilet paper off the old rattling dispenser and blowing her nose into its folded creases. The baby was asleep, and my brother and I had been outside playing in the sunshine. And Mama had locked herself inside a small room for privacy and depression. No one could understand her temperament, including her own self. The mood-swings would just suddenly appear — a condition that was often my fault, or so she told me. But mostly, it was my daddy's fault, she had said. He just didn't understand how to be a good husband.

I tiptoed to the bathroom door and thought about how we couldn't afford real tissues for our noses. Maybe that's why Mama was crying this time. As a ten-year-old, my beliefs in life were mostly speculation, but I knew my mama didn't like going without things. She often talked about how she had grown up in a poor farming family and now that we lived in a decent house that was closer to town, we should be able to afford nicer things. She was sick and tired of doing without.

Standing in the dim hallway, I had considered my options. My two-wheel bicycle and the other kids were waiting outside in the freshness of early summer. We were rounding up a small group to ride down the dirt roads of nearby farmland. None of us had been exploring since late last August when school had re-opened and halted our hot-weather adventures. Now, we were all hungry for the boundless freedom given to small-town suburban kids in the 1960s—the unsupervised roaming of an endless countryside.

"Go ahead! I'll catch up!" I recall yelling as I stuck my head out the backdoor and watched my friends peddle off. As long as my mama was crying, I knew I had to stay with her.

"Mama, you okay?" I returned to the hallway and asked.

"Yes, I'm fine. Go on back outside," she had shouted.

Her answer was always the same. It meant that she didn't want to talk right now, but she knew the guilt would eat at me. I was the oldest child and the only girl. I was ordained to be responsible. Mama had anointed me to be her emotional lifeline from the time I was a preschooler. I had memories as early as age three in which she begged me to take care of her. Over the years, I had grown to resent her request. I wanted the independence that I saw in my little brothers and friends—the chance to live life without bearing the burdens of my mother. But I clung to the belief that I could help her, and that her occasional bouts of anger and sadness would disappear.

"I can go outside later," I replied, and sat down on the hardwood floor to wait, hoping Mama would come out soon, before I got too far behind my friends.

If I left without visual contact, then she would likely call me out later. Or worse, she could somehow really be hurt and I would be responsible. But her sobbing only increased, growing louder and wilder, like the high-pitched howl of a lonely forest animal calling out for a missing mate—more like wailing than crying. The echo bounced off the sterile bathroom walls and out to my ears, where it crept down my spine. I shivered a bit in fear. This episode could be a bad one.

"Mama, what's wrong?" I asked, but she avoided answering.

I had just wanted it to be over. Throughout my childhood, I had become somewhat numb to many of her outbursts in an effort to survive. The source of her tears was way beyond my ability to process and understand, so I would offer to help her more out of guilt than genuine concern. But the fear of regret sometimes threatened me and I felt I had to take action, especially when her spells escalated into mania. Then I would become too afraid to leave her alone.

Mama's bawling spell lasted for what seemed a very long time. It continued even as the clinking of glass and the running of water joined her hidden actions. I knew the medicine chest in the bathroom was full of little bottles with remedies like Mercurochrome, aspirin, and ammonia. A small dose of one or the other would cure a wide range of ailments. My mama had grown up on homemade concoctions, which didn't always bring relief, so using these drugstore medicines seemed to be a cure-all, guaranteed to be an antidote for any infirmity. And when I heard her swallowing some pills and gulping down some water, I knew she'd soon be out of the bathroom.

I listened as Mama's weeping gradually ceased and her slip-ons began shuffling around in a predictable routine on the black-and-white checkered linoleum. She flushed the toilet, turned off the facet and patted the bathroom towel. The door opened, and I rose as she exited the bathroom, watching her as she pushed back the brownness of her hair. Her eyes were puffy, and her brow remained furrowed, but she said nothing. She was slow and somber, and her breathing shivered as she moved to a living room chair where she sat down. Approaching her, I chose my words with care, not wanting to reignite an emotional fire, and yearning to be a normal kid outside in nature.

"You want some tea to calm your nerves, Mama?" I remember asking. There was always homemade sweet tea in our refrigerator. A slow sip of cold, sweet tea made folks feel better.

"I'm fine, just go on out and play," Mama had answered with the words I most wanted to hear.

Relieved that she was in recovery, I rested my hand on the arm of her chair, wanting to hug her before I left, but the frown on her face reminded me to recoil. My mother was not the touchy-feely type with me. During the summer, I was usually a sweaty kid with skinned-up knees, dressed in wrinkled shorts and smelling like grass stains. Far from sugar and spice. So I needed to cleanup before touching Mama. But I reminded myself that she was out of the bathroom now, which meant she was fine. Her problems had been solved in the same way I thought all people solved their problems. You cried for a while and then you somehow felt better.

"Okay, well, I'm going outside now." I said, feeling timid, but relieved.

"Yes, I said go on out. I'm fine," Mama repeated. And so, I left.

I walked out of the room, then quickly picked up the pace. Out the door and on my bike, I raced down our dead-in street and out toward a nearby pasture. Guilt had been temporarily lifted from my conscious. I was a kid again. A church-attending, teacher-listening, daddy's girl who was learning to balance pain with hope. I didn't use scissors on Sundays and never stepped on the sidewalk cracks. I didn't bully other kids and never had to write sentences in school, which made me a pretty decent kid, I thought. Besides, there was a lot of good to be had in the world, and I was determined to find it. Someday, I would go to college, get a great job and have a nice house. Then Mama would be so proud of me and not be sad anymore. I had been sure of it.

When I finally caught up with my kid pack, the three other girls had been petting the local quarter horse and farm dogs while the boys had likely disappeared into the woods. Silvey the mare had lifted her head and glanced toward me, only to turn back when she was sure I didn't have treats. As the only horse in the neighborhood, she was the queen who relished her royal status, which entitled her to frequent carrots and head scratches. Parking my bike, I petted the hounds that had gathered around me, then walked toward the barnyard fence, grabbing a handful of grass from the ground to feed Silvey.

"Where are the boys?" I asked, extending my hand to the chestnut mare.

I had not been surprised to find the girls near the barn without the boys. All the girls I knew loved horses. Each of us seemed to have a grandparent or relative that lived way out in the country, and we all romanticized about getting our own National Velvet steed, although owning a pair of Western riding boots was the closest any of us had ever come to horse ownership. But for now, I needed a ride-along bike-companion to help me find the boys, who I knew would be knee-deep in adventure.

"Did the boys go down to the creek?" I asked again, rewording my question.

"Probably, but who cares what they're doing?" the oldest girl, Danna, sniped. But no matter what she said, she always knew what her little brother was doing. Every big sister had that responsibility.

"Well, are y'all going down there?" I replied, feigning innocence.

I already knew the likely answer, but the shaded path to the creek was a little unnerving. Bums were rumored to sleep in the ditches along the trail, although none of us kids had ever seen a homeless person, except on black-and-white television re-runs. That's how we knew to watch out for people wearing raggedy old coats, smoking smelly cigars and carrying dirty, rolled up blankets—all trademarks of genuine bumhood.

"Not me," all three girls had refused to budge from the barnyard.

"We might find arrowheads," I lied, sort of. There were plenty of tri-shaped stones on the creek banks.

"There're no arrowheads in the woods. The Indians didn't live around here. They lived down near Jamestown. I learned it in school," Danna quipped, tossing back her perfect, golden locks. She was a grade ahead of most other neighborhood kids and always had the answers. Her crisply ironed summer blouses and white-trimmed navy Keds established her superior rank.

"The Indians lived here, too. They lived all over the place in Virginia," I challenged, then braced myself, knowing Danna would slam my words. Yet I wasn't giving up. I needed to coax someone into riding the trail with me.

"You don't know! You're too young. You don't know enough about history."

"But remember what that boy Rocky said? You know—the kid who comes over and visits his grandparents near the country market? He said, Indians used to live right here in this area."

"He knows nothing. That kid annoys me. He's just a showoff," Danna shot back, as she fluffed up the ruffles at her shoulders.

"But he said his mom was a real Indian," I insisted. I had to stand my ground. "She's not an Indian! I've seen her. She looks nothing like an Indian. She has short hair, and her clothes are just like a regular mom. And she's white as a ghost."

I backed off to consider my rebuttal. Everyone I knew had either light or dark skin, but the true color of real Native American Indian skin had always been a mystery to us kids. As Virginians, we had heard the familiar story of Pocahontas since early childhood. How her father Powhatan had captured John Smith of Jamestown, and how Pocahontas had rescued him from her father's warriors. Then she had married a white man named John Rolfe and had a white baby. It was in the kids' picture books. But we had never been taught what happened to the rest of the Virginia Indians. We had just figured they had all become white folk. It was like being around white people had made the Indians want to wear white people's clothes and have white babies. Rarely did we encounter a local person with tawny skin who still claimed to be a Virginia Indian. People like that never said much about their lives.

"When the Indians married white people, they had white babies," I finally said, recalling the local stories of Indian intermarriage. "That's why Rocky's mama is white."

"Rocky's stupid and his mama's not an Indian," Danna quipped. She could not be persuaded.

I held my tongue for a moment, silently wondering the extent of Danna's knowledge about everyone's mothers and hoping she knew nothing about my mama.

"Then next time, when Rocky comes over, I'm going to ask him about his mom," I answered. I was not about to give into Miss Fancy Pants.

"Okay then, go talk to him right now! He went down to the creek with the other boys," Danna snarled.

"He's here?" My heart had leaped, and the drama of Danna's debate faded. A visit from Rocky meant adventure was afoot, for he was not like the other boys. He was short, talkative and told a bunch of wild tales that had to be taken with a grain of salt. None of the girls ever believed him, but the boys hung on his every word like it was the King James Bible. Given that his thick hair was coal black, and his skin tanned a mellow brown in the summer, I felt there had to be some authenticity in Rocky's Indian stories.

He had sworn that long ago, the King of England had sent soldiers to kill the Indian men in Virginia, but the Indian women had become the property of the white men and had white babies. That's how Rocky's great-great-whatever grandma and the other Virginia Indians had become white.

I had hesitated, knowing that ending my conversation with the other girls meant an unaccompanied ride into the shadows. But the news of Rocky's presence called to me. I jumped on my bike, pointed it toward my destination, and peddled as fast as I could. Excitement had taken control. Speed was one of the most adrenaline-charged, carefree activities a kid could experience. It was the simple days of no bike helmets and low-top tennis shoes, and a bicycle was the easiest way for a kid to travel. I raced past the infant cornstalks—inhaling the smell of freshly turned sod—and coasted downhill to the emerald hayfields. A quarter mile ahead lay the woodlands, where I hoped to find Rocky and the other boys. Skirting alongside the grassy meadow, I quickly reached the edge of the trench-filled forest, where I froze. A tattered jacket hung on a nearby branch, and I dreaded an encounter with a crafty stranger. Mama had filled my head with images of crusty old men kidnapping little girls, and I feared the forest ditches were filled with bums. What if I was captured by a troll-like madman and forced to live under a bridge? But a familiar voice in the distant compelled me to move forward.

"Not there! Com'on over here!" Rocky's southern draw was slightly twangier than the rest of us, yet somehow still debonair—like a rustic version of Rhett Butler. It was the voice a kid could both love and hate at the same time. Charming yet firm. The magnetism of his voice drew me in, and I dashed along the woodsy pathway, feeling more secure as the conversation between Rocky and the others grew louder.

"Hey, what are you doing here? We didn't invite girls." My little brother Raymond was usually the first to speak up when I crashed the all-male gatherings. I ignored him like any other big sister.

"She ain't no regular girl. Cat is an explorer like us," Rocky had always defended me, knowing I was his ally. He was also one of my few childhood friends who called me by my nickname. To everyone else, I was just plain-ole Carol Ann.

"You wanna help us find Indian relics, Cat?" he asked.

"Yea, that's why I came down here. Did you find anything yet?" I asked, eyeing the displeasure of the surrounding boys. They knew I'd be second in charge next to Rocky.

"Nah, not yet. I think most of the stuff around here has been dug up already. Too bad 'cos I know there must have been some really neat arrowheads along these creek banks."

"How do you know?"

"The Indians always hunted beside creeks and rivers." Rocky explained, straightening his back to look taller. He was barely my height.

Feeling a little foolish, I crossed my arms to gather strength, regretting my misspoken words. Of course, the Indians hunted beside the waterways. Every school library around was stacked with books that illustrated the Indians hunting and fishing along the numerous Virginia rivers and streams—stalking the deer and turkey and filling their baskets with sturgeon and oysters. The creek bank must have once been littered with old arrowheads and spear tips. Looking down, I scanned the earth for evidence. And that is when I saw it.

Reaching up from the dark ground below me, barely noticeable as it stood upright among the dead leaves and broken branches, was a large feather. I bent down, plucked it from the ground and examined it while the others surrounded me. Together we scrutinized it, silently at first, noting its smooth edges and rounded tip. Its feather barbs were deep brown and imbedded into a long, cream-colored shaft. Perhaps just another buzzard feather or maybe from a hawk, as many of these birds scouted for mice high above the nearby hayfields. The difference was the soft-white fluff, which was wrapped around the base of the feather like the morning mist at the foot of a tall-brown tree.

"It's an old buzzard feather. Lots of dead animals around here," one boy announced. A chorus of adjacent males agreed. The verdict was in.

"No! It's an eagle feather," came Rocky's rebuttal and the looks of confusion had followed.

"I never saw an eagle. We have eagles around here?" My brother Raymond and several others knew a teachable moment had arrived.

"Oh yeah, eagles are all over here. They're looking for mice and fish. That's what they eat," Rocky answered.

I stepped back and shielded the feather against my chest, anticipating the gang's curiosity. Roaming hands often led to broken treasures, and I didn't want to risk losing my prize. I had never seen an eagle, except in photographs, but I knew they were the symbol of my country. A beacon of strength. A symbol of power. But when Rocky reached out for the coveted quill, I had to surrender.

"Yep, for sure it's an eagle's feather," Rocky announced. "See them white, fluffy feathers at the bottom? That's eagle's down. And it's really a tough feather, too." Then, with a quick motion, he grabbed the feather with both hands and bent it. My heart stopped, only to restart when the feather rebounded, unscathed.

"This is powerful Indian medicine," he had announced. His eyes remained on the plumage. "A sign of bravery. Cat, you've received a great reward. This feather is gonna protect you and give you special powers. Guard it with your life!"

I stood motionless in thought. Rocky's words were like gold to me. I had found the Holy Grail of the Indian world and it was mine to keep! My eye fixed on the prize, I could feel the respect of the others surrounding me as I moved forward and gently retrieved the feather from Rocky. Even as I grasped it, my glare remained fixed on the feather, fearing it would be stroked by too many hands. Or that I might drop it and possibly extinguish the spell of its powers. I knew I must somehow protect it. And the thought of weaving it into my hair briefly passed through my mind. But as the boys closed in around me, I tucked the long, slender shaft of the feather into my waistband.

"I need to keep it close to me," I assured the others. "If it breaks, it could bring us all bad luck."

"You're a real warrior now, Cat. A real warrior," Rocky had told me.

Clutching my waist, I mounted my bike and turned to depart. I had to carry my feather to safety. To peddle home and bury it deep within the old chest of drawers beside my single-framed bed. Hidden from the cat and the spring cleanings and the curious fingers of my little brothers. There, my feather would rest with my other secret treasures—a small mica-covered rock, a charm bracelet of the Ten Commandments, and a five-stick pack of Wrigley's spearmint gum. The feather would bring me wisdom and luck. The other kids would look up to me now—at least for a while. Ghosts would fear entering my bedroom. Happiness would embrace my family. I had taken full possession of the great power of Indian medicine. Surely, I could help Mama get better now.

SKI LESSON

by Danielle Dayney, Riverside Writers, 3rd Place

We were at a small ski resort in upstate New York with friends. They invited us on a whim, our first vacation in over a year. But I had never skied, so while my husband and our friends left me to ski the real mountain and my daughter went to pre-ski school to play with other toddlers, I got a lesson from Gunther.

I stood on the bunny hill with restricting boots, and peripheral vision-limiting goggles, suffocating base layers and fleece. I reconsidered my choice to come here. I was not adventure-seeking. I would've rather been inside enjoying hot coffee—or something stronger—by the fire. I reminded myself to not be a chicken.

"First toe, dann heal," Gunther said. I didn't even have the skis on yet. That task seemed impossible.

I removed my goggles to get a better look at him, an elderly, slender man with blue reflective sunglasses on. In them I saw myself bent into awkward right angles. Hunched, tense. I rolled and straightened my shoulders, then focused on the skis. Fat snowflakes had started to fall. White clumps landed on the skis, illuminating each scratch and dent from inexperienced skiers who wore them before me. They looked like big green boats. I hated the ocean, hated being out of my comfort zone.

The temperature crawled towards 20 degrees, but didn't quite make it, and the cold air bit all my exposed skin. My upper lip, my cheeks, my nose were all numb. Still, I was overdressed. Underneath my ski coat, fleece, and base layer, sweat had gathered at the small of my back.

I replaced my goggles over my eyes with mitten-covered hands, then pulled down the neck warmer for a dose of oxygen. I inhaled the icy air, exhaled steam, and returned the neck warmer to its position over my mouth. After that, I again focused on the skis or, more specifically, the scratches on the skis. I wondered how many beginners did Gunther coach down this hill with these exact skis on? How many actually lived to tell about it?

And why in the hell did I let my husband talk me into this?

"Toe dann heel," Gunther repeated. "Downhill ski first." His German accent was thick and strict.

Kids less than half my size zoomed around me, first to my front, then to my back. They traversed the mountain easily, back and forth, keeping their skis in a perfect pizza shape. Each of them safely stopped at the bottom, not far from me and Gunther.

Toe. Then heel. I can do this.

Balancing on my left foot, I picked up my right foot like I was told. The boot weighed at least five pounds. After several tries and misses, I got the toe of my boot lined up with the binding. I stepped down hard and heard a *click*.

"Das ist gut!" he said. "Now your left foot. Dig the edge of your right ski in. Balance. Use your poles for support, right? Toe, dann heel."

I tightened my grip on the ski poles and tried to dig them into the snow. One pole slipped on a patch of ice, and I lost my footing. I fell forward, but Gunther caught me with a firm grip on my upper arm.

"Again," he said, righting my shoulders. "Das ist easy. Don't think too much. Just do."

"Okay, just do." I found my center on my right ski and dug the edge against the mountain. I pressed my left boot in, and it clicked. "Yay!" The small victory was huge.

"Cool, right?" Gunther asked. The wrinkles on his face announced themselves as his mouth stretched into a wide grin. He appeared to be having fun with my lack of experience.

"Yes," I said. "Very cool."

"Good. Now, we ski."

"Crap," I said.

"Follow me, keep your skis in a wedge, like pizza. We go slow." He went ahead of me, making gradual "s" shapes left, then right. I kept my feet in the wedge like he said, leaning my hips left, then right. My "s" shapes weren't nearly as pretty as his, and I sailed slowly down the mountain in a zig-zag. But I *was* skiing, and I *didn't* fall.

Towards the bottom of the run, I came to a full stop. The mountain had flattened out, and I didn't have enough speed to cruise along. I had to push myself with my poles to catch up to Gunther, who was waiting for me by the lift with a giant smile.

"See!" he said. "Das ist easy!" He patted me on the shoulder a bit too hard. "Ready for the lift?"

I looked up at the rotating chairlift, ascending up the mountain, and gulped.

"It's fun. You'll see," he said, already gliding toward the lift.

I trudged along behind him, panting as I dug my poles into the packed snow to push myself. By the time I met him, I was gasping for breath. Exhausted. "Skiing is hard work," I said.

He laughed and motioned for the lift operator to slow down the chair. "Hold your poles in one hand and look over your shoulder," Gunther said. I followed his direction, and soon the chair was sweeping beneath my butt and we were gliding up the mountain, higher and higher.

"Can we put the bar down? I don't want to fall." I said, gripping the handrail tight with my free hand. My back was pressed against the chair, frozen from fear.

He lowered the armrest and said, "Look around. At the beauty. This is why we ski." He was right. All this time I had been so focused on the fear of falling that I forgot to enjoy the views. I looked around us. The snow-capped mountain lined with evergreen trees and wide-open white trails took my breath away. I tried to find Justin among the skiers, but before I could find his tan jacket, Gunther interrupted me.

"We have to raise the bar and unload," he said. I moved my hand away from the armrest so he could lift it. "Ready to ski again?" he asked.

Don't think, just do. I nodded yes.

A LETTER TO MY DAUGHTERS

by Betsy Ashton, Valley Writers, 1ˢᵗ Place

Dear Daughters,

I am a woman with no children of my own, a universal mother of children born to other mothers. As such a woman and mother, I want all my daughters to stand proud, be strong, and take on injustice.

In your lives, you will experience success and failure. I want you to learn from both.

You will find times when you aren't strong, don't want to do the right thing—because doing the right thing can be hard. It can bring condemnation down on you. It can bring haters out of the dark. It can hurt.

I hope you never have to experience what I did when I was in my twenties. If you do, I hope you will do what I did.

Before you read further, you'll ask why I didn't say anything to you earlier. I hoped times would change and you'd be safer than I was. Unfortunately, if anything, times are less safe. Black fathers have "the talk" with their sons; mothers have a different talk with their daughters. Because I can't talk to each of you, this letter serves as my version of "the talk."

When I was a twenty-three-year-old teaching assistant at a major football university, I had a student who registered but never attended my class, never turned in homework. I didn't know what he looked like. I had no idea how to reach him, but since he had not dropped out, I had to carry him on the rolls. He showed up at the end of class three weeks before the end of the term. He thrust a paper at me, saying, "Sign this. I need to be eligible for the big game."

I stared first at the paper and then at the behemoth standing in front of me. I was 5'8" and weighed maybe 125. He had me by a head, outweighed me by 150 pounds on a good day. More on game day. I assumed that he was on the football team because he needed C grades to play in the upcoming bowl game.

I asked how he planned to make up the work in order to be eligible. He laughed. He had no intention of making up the work, he said. He wanted me to sign, "or else." My brain didn't compute what "or else" might mean. I tried to explain that while he was still registered, without making up the work, I couldn't sign the form. He was officially failing my class.

I held out the paper, smiled my regrets, and turned to my desk to load my bag and leave the classroom.

In an instant, he shoved me onto my desk, lifted my mini-skirt, and ripped off my underwear. He unzipped his pants. That's when he made a huge mistake: he put his hand over my mouth, smothering my cries for help. I bit him. Hard. He raped me, pulled out, and walked away, leaving his eligibility form behind.

Every cell shook from the assault. I sat for a long time, glad no students came into the classroom in the hour after the attack. Ultimately, I dried my eyes, wiped off raccoon make-up, and went to my office. I ran into my faculty advisor, who took one look at my face and pulled me aside. I didn't want to tell him what happened. Then, anger set in. I had done nothing wrong. I was the victim, not the perpetrator. And I was mad as hell.

My advisor asked how he could help. By rights, I should have suspected all men, but he was kind and concerned. I told him every detail, gave him the student's name, showed him the eligibility form. He asked me what I wanted to do.

I was now mad enough to want revenge. He called another teaching assistant, who took one look at me and said, "We're going to the health center. And then we're going to the police."

My friend was one of those dynamos who at 5' tall took nonsense from no one. She walked me to the health center, where I was examined. I demanded and got a rape kit. My friend demanded the campus police be called.

The campus policeman was useless, because it was my word against the student's. I must have wanted it because I wore a miniskirt, the fashion at the time. He took no notes and advised me to go home.

My friend called the city police. They were a little more interested in my story, but in essence said the same thing: "No one is going to believe you."

My friend drove me home and stayed with me. Thursday night passed into Friday, a day when I had no reason to be on campus. By the end of the weekend, mad morphed into icy rage. I decided to act.

I marched into the football coach's office early Monday morning and planted myself outside his door until he arrived. I followed him inside, threw the unsigned eligibility form on his desk, and said, "This player raped me in my classroom on Thursday."

He didn't believe me.

I had proof, I said. I asked him to call the player to his office.

He didn't believe me.

I took my Wonder Woman pose, fists on hips, eyes glaring up at him.

He asked his assistant to bring the player to his office.

"What proof do you have?"

The player walked in, shot me a dirty look. He had a thick bandage on his right hand.

"I bit him when he raped me. Check under that wrap."

The coach, to his credit, told his player to unwrap the hand.

Do you have any idea how filthy the human bite is? His hand was infected, teeth marks vivid against his skin, red lines climbing his arm.

I had my revenge. I exposed a rapist. I stood up for myself. I was a survivor of something no woman, no daughter, should have to survive. No one was going to put the blame on me. I couldn't prevent him from playing in the bowl game—a different teaching assistant signed his eligibility form—but, miracle of miracles, our team lost. Big time.

The Virginia Writers Club
The Golden Nib, 2021, page 87

Years later, I wondered what happened to the player. I Googled him. He's doing thirty to life for multiple rapes, many when he was armed with a knife. With that, I wiped his name from memory.

Shaking set in again. He could have killed me. He could have killed my spirit. HE DID NEITHER.

My daughters, if you ever find yourselves in such a situation, maybe not rape, but something that you shouldn't keep hidden, tell someone the truth and only the truth. Act. Be proud of your strength. Stand tall. Embrace it. You will feel better about yourself. Don't wait as long as I did to tell your own daughter. Remember, I'm right there, proud as hell of you.

I love you all,
Mom

Two Tears

by Jerry Barnes, Valley Writers, 2nd Place

A young boy, about fifteen, herding goats near Zagania, Iraq, accidentally stepped on a buried self-detonating IED. Planted by al Qaeda and likely meant for unsuspecting US troops, the device exploded.

Cherry, a young medic on patrol, came upon the badly injured teenager only a few years younger than me. He checked his vitals, found him still breathing, and put him in the back of his vehicle. He rushed the boy to the FOB, a distance of five miles or so. Just trying to save another's life, he frantically drove without the protecting a convoy or gunship. Cherry's courageous act, though noble, had put his own life in jeopardy.

When Cherry reached the aid station, we quickly checked the lad's vitals. Sadly, we found two holes in his body, one in the middle of his chest, the other in the middle of his forehead. Both entry sites appeared round, telling us he likely stepped on a ball bearing IED. Because of the intense agony he expressed when trying to breathe and his extensive injuries, we knew he would not live long.

His family arrived moments after he passed. With his body still on the examination table, we went outside to give them the news and comfort them as best we could. We asked for time to prepare his body before they saw him.

Through sobs, they agreed.

After washing his body and plugging the holes with Kirlex (a gauze), we put a bandage over the two holes and dressed the surface wounds on the rest of his body. We wanted to make their son's body as presentable as possible.

We used a beautiful black and red wool blanket to wrap his body in before presenting it to his folks. This blanket, donated to our unit at Christmastime, seemed the perfect covering to prepare him for burial. We left the boy's left hand outside the blanket, knowing his folks would want to touch him. After placing his wrapped body in a body bag, we positioned his outstretched hand for one last caress.

While finishing with the body's preparation, something strange, yet wonderful, happened.

Although thirty minutes had elapsed since he passed, I distinctly saw two tears flowing down his cheek. For a moment, I questioned myself and thought, "Is he still alive?"

Sure enough, I checked all his vitals. He had neither pulse nor oxygen saturation. Yet thirty minutes after his passing, I stood there watching him cry. Was this a muscle reaction? His body had already relieved itself of waste, which we cleaned up.

I could think of nothing in my medical training, which would explain what I saw. I somehow felt in his tears as he said to us, "Thank you for what you've done. It will make things so much easier for my folks." For me, it brought comfort and closure to a very sad and heart-rending situation.

EYES OF TRUST

by Peggy Crowley Clutz, Valley Writers, 3rd Place

You looked like a lion when you returned from getting your first clipping, which left a mass of fur around your neck and a pompom of fur at the end of your scrawny, trimmed tail. Your black, coarse, curly fur turned soft gray later and those beautiful dark brown eyes were more prominent against long lashes. If only separated by minutes, you were always happy to see us and ready to join in the fun, except in the pool, your safe spot being the steps where you lay in inches of water to cool off. If there was even a hint of being dragged in, a low growl would escape your throat, which happened one day when Colin took you in his arms and toured you around the pool, a look of terror on your face until the steps came into view and you leaped to safety. You loved it when we would hide your huge rawhide bone, flipping sofa and chair cushions in the air with your nose as you scrambled from room to room, searching for your treasure, which you always found. Gwen loved to blow a loud raspberry because you would turn around and check yourself, like it was you who made that farting sound. Your body wore out at age 12 1/2, old for a big dog. As we headed out the door, Bryan said his goodbyes and through his tears dug your grave. I hugged the vet, who drew the short straw, and we both held you in our arms as you went to sleep, those big brown eyes staring so trustingly into ours.

Mr. Max and son, Bryan.

FICTION

Little Stony Man

DEATH AND PEANUTS

by Sandra Roslan, Hanover Writers, 1ˢᵗ Place
Golden Nib First Place

Grim straightened his desk nameplate because it was crooked again. The brown plaque announced he was Reaper 82. He told himself he wasn't offended at having been reduced to a number instead of using his actual name.

Once certified, reapers went by the identification number they were appointed after graduation. Unimaginative, in Grim's opinion, but the practice had been in place for literally forever. He added the last information on the report for his previous assignment and clicked submit.

35 lumbered by to lunch, tucking his scaled tail around him to avoid knocking over trash cans and loose objects as he walked. Grim assumed that's what happened to his nameplate.

Upon receiving his diploma from The Institute of Reaping and Afterlife Studies, Grim spent his rookie year shadowing 35. Post-graduate reapers had a year of watching and learning from more experienced colleagues before they could take their own cases. Other than being swatted by his notorious tail, Grim enjoyed 35's company.

Not all reapers looked alike, as proven by 35's squat body and posterior appendage that was twice as long as he was tall. This misconception was sown throughout history regarding Soul Collectors or The Angel of Death or La Muerte or Psychopomp or Shinigami or whatever name used for the entities chaperoning people through death, but they were every shape and color imaginable. Another common belief was only one existed; there were hundreds, people died constantly, and no way could one reaper handle that influx.

However, as with all stories, there's a ring of truth to the hyperbole. Turns out, the original reapers were the classic depiction whispered about during sleepovers and midnight campfires.

Grim's ancestors were a species that closely resembled what most lore presumed they did. He was seven-foot-five, and deceptively strong, being as he was a walking skeleton. Despite no mandated dress code for his position, he adorned himself in traditional reaper garb—long black robes, dark hood. He liked the predictability of knowing what he'd wear every day.

Long ago, he'd answered a listing looking for soul collectors. After completing his education and his year of shadow-reaping, he liked the work, so he stayed. The benefits were standard and included Grim's favorite: travel. He relished seeing different parts of the world. Reapers were immortal, but they were allowed sick and personal leave, especially following complex cases like natural disasters or plane crashes.

Humans intrigued him, and that was the main reason he pursued the job. Observing their diverse customs entertained him. The code of conduct didn't forbid interaction with the living, but except for a couple of blurry glimpses when he started out, Grim avoided being seen, because of the mortals' tendency to fear what they didn't understand.

Souls went to one of two places. Above or below. There were no layovers in Limbo or detours through Purgatory, as some believed. Grim rotated shifts, filling in where he was needed since he didn't have a preference for which celestial realm he reaped.

He respected his bosses. The Devil was more hands-on with those transported to his domain, whereas God delegated duties. Lucifer had demon hordes, but he took pride in meting out punishment to those deserving. The tales of the Devil's evil reach were exaggerations, barely resembling the initial narrative. Lucifer made the best of his status— Old Scratch himself admitted the rebellion idea was hasty—and was an expert at dispensing justice. He may not have been inherently evil, but he had a mischievous streak and was always ready to hear (or spread) a juicy rumor.

The Almighty was not so accessible or sociable. He'd wave if he passed you in the hallway, maybe give a curt nod, and most often, an all-knowing look, but he rarely stopped to chat, unlike his damned son.

Grim's phone beeped with an incoming case alert. The screen illuminated, providing an address and details: Casualties: 5; Heaven-destined: 4; Hell-bound: 1.

When numbers like these came across, they were almost always because of violence. He tapped 'Confirm' to verify his acceptance.

He was reaping for Hell tonight, and he wondered what awaited him. Reapers navigated to locations at will, so he concentrated on the address until he felt the fabric of space and time bending.

In seconds, Grim arrived on-scene to controlled chaos in a convenience store parking lot where police swarmed, taking witness statements and shooing gawking bystanders. Folks sobbed while others stared ahead in stunned silence. The Coroner and forensic investigators were clearing paths so they could begin their work as soon as possible.

On the corner, a group was already creating a spot for one of those vigils humans erected after a tragedy. Cop cars lined the street, their syncopated blue and red flashers casting everything in dramatic relief. News crews congregated behind barricades, discussing how to capture the most shocking visuals and sound bites.

Grim brought his mental cloaking shields to full strength, rendering him invisible as he entered the establishment. His thick-soled boots traversed broken glass and decimated foodstuffs without making noise or displacing them.

Grim analyzed the gore before him. A cashier was shot in the face, unidentifiable beneath the dense tangle of hair, blood, and bone fragments. Dark drops decorated the confections and impulse buys near the front counter.

The air crackled with an underlying static of anger and terrified energy. Grim tapped into the field and watched the incident unfold in his mind's eye. A single gunman entered and demanded the till money. Grim saw the worker trip a silent alarm as he cleared the register out while the robber fidgeted, brandishing a semi-automatic weapon at the clerk's head. After the cash was handed over, the assailant ignored the cashier's pleas and shoved the gun against his forehead and pulled the trigger.

Grim paced, continuing to absorb the residual current that permeated the air. Next, the gunman panicked and took the patrons, who weren't lucky enough to escape, as hostages. Police arrived and started negotiations. The murderer grew increasingly agitated, and he executed the innocent shoppers.

Finally, out of leverage and raging about having his demands denied, he fired into a snack display, leaving it looking chewed up and spit out. Grim felt a severe pull in his chest and suddenly, he *knew*. He circled around the destroyed end cap and saw a small body, prone on the floor, shirt soaked in blood. The child was only seven. He sensed her parents begged her to hide, hoping to keep her safe.

Reapers saw every manner of atrocity during their careers. Humans inflicted pain and suffering upon one another in myriad ways and, mostly, reapers were desensitized. The exception was children. Reaping children was the worst job duty. It was bitter enough when little ones were sick, but at least they would be free of the agony of their affliction once they crossed, but when they departed like this, in such a cruel method, it was intolerable. Since Grim was reaping for Hell, he wouldn't be the one taking the child to the afterlife, but his non-existent heart still twisted at the senseless loss.

The reaper working for Heaven materialized beside him. He'd met 134 at work conferences and they shared a look, wordlessly acknowledging the dismal circumstances. They stood by while the souls of the deceased started leaving their mortal bodies. One by one, tendrils, like wisps of colored smoke, appeared and hovered, confused, and directionless. Most adult souls had an amalgamation of hues based on their experiences and choices. This was the case for the adults here, pastels and light gray mingling together.

Children were made of bright, happy colors. As expected, vibrant pinks and sunny yellows mixed with sky blues and springtime greens curled above the girl, reminding Grim of sweet, giant lollipops he once saw at a fair.

While Grim and 134 waited patiently for the souls to detach from their bodies, he noticed his co-worker's appearance soften and become nonthreatening. This trick was taught the last year of school and helped calm mortals about to cross over.

Grim underwent no compunction to alter his image. The soul he was here to reap deserved no such niceties or respect. Instead, he made himself more foreboding, exuding menace, chilling the atmosphere near his individual like a freezer. The murderer's soul had yet to show itself. Occasionally, souls refused to vacate and clung to life. Grim wondered if this killer desired to live so badly, why put a bullet through his own head instead of facing the consequences of his behavior? Suicide to escape karma? Never worked. Karma always got its pound of flesh, even if that flesh was reconstituted and stripped off piece by piece in Hell.

Heaven's reaper rallied her souls with gentle gestures and reassurances while she showed them the light they would walk through, and with watery smiles they entered The Great Beyond to be greeted by loved ones who passed before them. Heaven was indeed an exquisite place, conforming to each person's vision of happiness in the afterlife.

Grim's bounty still hadn't relinquished its body, and it was time to act. The presence of a working reaper should've drawn the soul out, but this one was stubborn.

As Grim towered over the perpetrator's form, he could smell evil wafting off him. Diabolical souls were putrid, with black, oily consistencies marring any of the cloud-like beauty most souls maintained. Grim recoiled at the reek of it, and he'd been exposed to so much gruesomeness over the centuries, he rarely reacted to such things.

He used his power to extract the soul and a viscous ooze seeped from the man's pores, invisible to all but the reaper. The cobalt secretions gathered around Grim's feet. As Grim further exerted his command, the pools combined, fusing into a puddle the size of a massive rodent.

The thick liquid fought Grim and crept toward its fleshy remains. It didn't matter. Even if it reattached, the body was beyond repair. The soul realized this and instead of boring into its human vessel; it changed course and surged in the opposite direction.

Great, a runaway, Grim thought. He'd never lost one, and he didn't intend for this miscreant to be the first. His utmost concern was it attaching to a living human. Then he'd have a possession to deal with and those were exhausting. Plus, the paperwork went on for days.

Grim willed his scythe into existence. He didn't enjoy using the scythe and stored it in a pocket dimension to avoid lugging it around. In moments like this, though, it came in handy. He hefted the familiar weight, driving the point into the dark mass attempting to escape.

The soul screeched, a ghoulish sound that was only outdone by the eerie metallic scrape of Grim's supernatural blade dragging along stained linoleum. The impaled soul thrashed and jerked on the tip, wrenching the tool sideways, yanking Grim forward.

Grim's clavicle dislocated and popped back into place. He sighed. *That'll be sore tomorrow.* Even with immortality, reapers could be injured if collections went amiss. Grim set his jaw and twisted the blade, securely skewering the soul on the honed weapon. Satisfied he had the absconder, Grim shifted planes and headed for Hell.

An ornate archway greeted him. Hell-forged steel stretched in each direction until ash-laden fog swallowed it from sight. Red filigree sigils marked the surface every three feet; wards sealing the denizens inside. Grim felt the pulse of Hell in his bones as he approached the drop-off located to the right of the entrance. He rang the bell, which clanged a sonorous, out of tune cacophony, like mangled church chimes.

The receiving door opened and Belladonna, the demon taker, welcomed Grim by contorting her face to reveal jagged teeth. She gnashed them in a terrifying rictus, and Grim was glad he knew it was amicable.

Once on the grounds of Hell, the blob of soul goo reformed into the remains from topside, the hole in his head knitting together to repair the self-inflicted injury along with other damage the body sustained. Since the human reanimated while still run through on the scythe, the internal wounds continued trying, and failing, to stitch themselves.

Belladonna chuckled as the body convulsed, ravaging the reconstructing insides. When the demon grew bored, she ripped the newcomer from Grim's weapon, tearing him raggedly in half. She deftly dodged the viscera spilling from the gaping wounds. The human howled in pain, hitting decibels that would shatter a normal being's ears.

"I've got it from here," Belladonna purred, gazing at the arrival like a toy whose limits she wanted to test. Grim signed the transfer form and turned to leave, a bit of glee creeping in when he heard another scream explode from the gunman. Lucifer and his demons would give him his comeuppance.

Grim's satisfaction was short-lived as his attention flashed to the earlier devastation; mostly of the child. He felt anxious and unsettled in a way he usually didn't after rough cases. His report could wait.

Grim willed himself to his favorite bench at the scenic overlook of an extensive park. In years past, it was undeveloped land, but progress (like death) stopped for no one. Rolling idyllic hills were now a vast cityscape, bustling with inhabitants.

Grim still found peace here, it was relaxing differently than before. At night, city lights stretched below him, and he could forget for that one day he or another reaper would deliver each of the populace to the afterlife.

He slouched on the bench and let the sounds of insect nightlife soothe him.

His "me time" was interrupted by a droning diesel engine from the parking lot. He glanced over and saw a gigantic white vehicle with spinning bristles gliding along the property's perimeter. Grim recognized the contraption as a street sweeper, designated to retrieve trash left by untidy citizens. The humming ceased as the operator cut the motor.

The driver's door opened, and a man hopped down, landing lightly on the concrete. Tufts of brown hair poked from under his cap and he wore a uniform with a logo matching the one on the truck. Grim activated his cloaking guards and observed the worker as he strolled toward a fast-food cup that had migrated from the lot to a grass patch near Grim's bench.

As he approached, the guy spoke. "Hey, man. Nice out here tonight, isn't it?"

Grim was startled. The living shouldn't be aware of him when his shields were up. Maybe something was malfunctioning. He assessed himself and detected no gaps or problems. Grim tensed, sure that as soon as the male realized Grim was otherworldly, he would lose his mind and run.

When nothing happened, Grim fluttered his arm in what he hoped was a polite, although dismissive gesture, taking care his white finger bones stayed covered. He'd already had a tough night, and now apparently his powers were glitchy. He didn't need a human freaking out.

As the other man bent to snag the cup, a wind gust blew it from his grasp. It bounced once against Grim's boot and settled there. On instinct, Grim reached to grab the debris. As he did, his sleeve rose along his forearm, revealing his long slender digits and gleaming wrist bones. They sparkled in the moonlight, like a beacon, a warning of danger. Grim meant no harm to the human, though, and he withdrew and shook his robe down, covering his slip-up.

There was no way the guy hadn't noticed. He'd gone for the trash, too. His tan fingers nearly brushed Grim's bleached ones.

The night went silent in Grim's ears, the quiet all-encompassing as he contemplated. Should he disappear and let the man think he was seeing things? What was one more story of a paranormal sighting?

His thoughts scattered when the bench creaked, and wood yielded as the man's weight settled beside him. What was happening? Why was this person not hot footing it to that monstrosity of a vehicle and tearing away as though he'd come face-to-face with death? And in this situation, not a euphemism.

Grim tried peeking out of his hood without exposing his skeletal visage. He wished he attended the seminar on glamouring human countenances, but he'd been super-busy that week. Until tonight, he never considered he'd have use for that illusion, anyway.

He gauged the figure next to him; a black patch with 'Sam' in white cursive was attached to his beige shirt. Sam didn't notice Grim's scrutiny or absence of response. "This is one of my favorite places to take a break," he said, adjusting his hat. "The view is beautiful. Reminds me how much more there is to see when you look at the big picture."

Grim felt a stab of admiration for the human, so many of them hurried through life and never appreciated the *more*. Also, seeing a reaper drove humans mad or caused them an existential meltdown. Sam wasn't suffering either as he gazed placidly at the shimmering landscape, and Grim awarded him brownie points for that too.

"By the way, I'm Sam," he said.

Grim didn't know what to do. He lacked vocal cords but could speak when he wanted. His voice was coarse and after years of disuse on Earth, it was bound to be harsher and more dissonant.

He cleared his throat, and the sound rumbled down his spine, vibrating against vertebrae and between his ribs. His robes whooshed out with the force of it. "You can call me Grim," he rasped, his words echoing around them. Was he nervous? Reapers didn't get nervous. He chalked it up to all people he'd ever interacted with were dead.

Sam tipped his hat. "Good to meet you." He dug in his cargo pants pocket. Grim watched warily. He couldn't be gravely injured, but with his shields impaired, his ability to discern danger might also be off.

Sam coaxed a bag from the depths of his pocket. As the plastic surfaced, Grim saw roasted peanuts. Sam ripped the package open and dropped several in his hand. "Want some?"

Reapers didn't require food. Their stamina was tied to the ever-present energy of the universe, but they could ingest it. For reapers built like Grim, without a digestive system, the food disappeared once passing through their jaws. They didn't taste the food so much as absorb its essence, leaving them with a suggestion of a flavor or emotion.

Grim nodded. He hadn't eaten peanuts in ages, and he remembered them as having a warm and comforting nature. He hesitated, then extended his arm, flinching as he exposed the pointy phalanges hiding under the thick cloth of his outfit. Sam didn't react. Fabric rustled as Grim's forearm slid through the cuff, catching at his knobby wrist joint. He squeezed his fingers together to form a cavity. Sam put some in Grim's hand before shaking more into his own palm.

"Thank you," Grim said, tamping the cavernous roll of his voice, hoping to lessen the ominousness.

Sam crunched peanuts between his teeth. "Sure."

Grim remained astounded. The human was calm. By now, Sam must've evidenced he was preternatural. Did Grim possibly glamour himself somehow?

Sam offered the bag again and Grim accepted more. They shared the peanuts until Sam crinkled and returned the bag to his pocket. He stood and stretched with a satisfied grunt. "Well, I have to go."

Grim nodded, and Sam ambled to his sweeper, taking with him the cup responsible for their introduction. Grim watched him, feeling a pang of remorse he'd again be alone.

Sam clamored into the truck cab. Before shutting the door, he called, "Hey, Grim! Maybe I'll see you again. I'm here most weeknights. Later, dude."

Grim waved as Sam's engine turned over and he puttered to the lot's exit.

As Grim pondered the last half hour, two birds landed on the bench, searching for stray crumbs. That was odd. Birds were fanciful creatures, spooked at any unusual thing.

He'd thought his shields were on the fritz.

As a test, Grim concentrated on lowering his cloaking powers. The birds squawked in surprise and took flight quicker than Grim could blink. If he had eyelids. They heckled him from a tree limb, irritated their foraging was disturbed.

If his shields were working and he hadn't glamoured himself, it meant Sam had seen him for who and what he was and still stayed and shared his food with him.

Happiness sparked inside his hollow core, chasing away the rest of his melancholy. He knew evil would always exist, but good would, too. He opened his remote-work app and clocked out for the night. He'd write his report tomorrow, he had relaxing to do.

THE DAY THE LIGHTS WENT OUT

by Damean Mathews, Appalachian Authors Guild, 1st Place
Golden Nib Second Place

"There are no more monsters to fear." That's what they told us. That was the last thing we heard before the world went dark, before the things that had waited for centuries crept out to take back what was theirs.

It's an experience I'll never forget, but many will never remember. Even now I can hear the things outside. I pray they don't get in here, that I can hide until the world returns to normal. I don't know what state anything is in anymore. The news broadcasts have stopped altogether. I only heard one anyway. It ended in screams. I've never been more scared. The eclipse wasn't supposed to be a big deal. My friends and I heard the stories and rumors and laughed, like most young adults would. I never imagined there might be some truth to it. I'm afraid I have little time to finish this. I have to write as much as I can. If anyone survives, they have to know. It can't happen again.

The news reports of an impending eclipse came in about two weeks ago. We'd all known for a while that one was coming, but what we didn't know was that intense solar flares would begin surging towards the planet at the same time we were getting into position. NASA warned the world that the flares could grow worse. At first, they just caused the auroras to extend beyond their normal borders. Mankind viewed this as more of a blessing than anything until cell towers began failing. At first it was mild interference; you'd have some text messages not go through, and a few more calls than usual would be dropped. A mild annoyance, but no real danger. Then entire cities, states, and even countries found their communication systems collapsing.

Specialists worked around the clock to ease the fears and quell the rumors that sprang up and spread like wildfire.

"The world is coming to an end," one headline would say.

"The sun will cook the planet before the eclipse can block the rays," read another, less reliable one.

Thousands of stories like these covered the globe, with everything from government conspiracy to the collapse of the dwarf star that gave us life being named as the cause of our sudden technological trouble. None of us dreamed the truth of what was going on, or what we would have to go through in just a few hours' time.

A press conference was scheduled for the exact minute before the eclipse was to begin, with the President speaking as the eclipse was at its apex, his voice going out to comfort the masses as the sun disappeared, leaving part of the world in a shadow wider than it had seen in centuries. The president stood on a podium, joined by the head researchers at NASA and countless other individuals who all laid down the facts as they saw them. The solar flares had been only slightly higher in power than one we had seen before, but the effects had largely been amplified by the drought North America was facing, the lack of cloud cover assisting in the potency the radiation had on our delicate electrical systems. I don't know how many besides me saw the look in the scientist's eyes as he uttered these words to those among us who could watch or listen. My computer, its indicator light flashing relentlessly as I drained the last of its battery to watch these reports in the darkness of my powerless home, a reminder of the advancement's men like him had made in the last 50 years.

He met the president's eye and grimaced, his face showing every ounce of lie he'd just vomited onto an unsuspecting and terrified people. The President came at last, the camera catching the podium and the diminishing sun in the same shot, a feat which surely took weeks to plan, the most minute calculations able to ruin the spooky effect. He strolled to the podium, giving a million-dollar smile to the audience, who seemed to lean collectively forward as if begging him to free them from their own fears and the possibility that something serious was actually happening. I felt the rumble before he spoke. The surrounding ground seemed to roll within itself, a rush of sound coming from everywhere at once as he opened his mouth.

"These events are not what rumors have told you. Humanity is not in danger. We have no more monsters to fear."

His microphone cut out before the camera did. Darkness seemed to swell all around him as the few lights that remained picked out the faces of those who saw what was coming for them. The moon swallowed the last of the light from the sun as the creature's humanity had forgotten they were afraid of emerging from the shadows to take back what was theirs.

I heard a cacophony of screams from all around me. My computer died as an impossibly beastly figure stepped into the frame of the camera, its eyes seeming to meet mine and seal the fate of everyone around it. In the split second I saw it, the face became burned into my brain. Huge fangs jutted from its gaping mouth, bloodshot eyes the size of dinner plates dwarfed only by hands that looked big enough to wrap around a full-grown man with no trouble. The thing stood every bit of nine feet tall and looked as if it hadn't seen daylight in centuries.

The screams from outside my house grew louder as I sat there in shock, terrified that the same thing I'd just seen was attacking my neighbors, soon to come searching for me. My fears seemed to be proven correct as I heard pounding noises on the walls all around my house. Some noises seemed to come from the first floor, as if fists were pounding the doors and windows, but a few resonated through the very room I was sitting in, as if something even more monstrous than what I'd just seen was searching for me, waiting to taste my flesh with teeth I could only imagine would rip me limb from limb. I leaped up from the desk and ran to my closet, grabbing the shotgun I hadn't touched in years. I loaded it as if I'd handled it only that morning, praying that the five boxes of ammo in front of me would be enough firepower to get me to safety.

A hunter at heart, with a paranoid tendency, I had a pistol by my bed and a large bowie knife under my mattress. I grabbed these and every spare bullet I could find and crammed them in a duffel bag. Running to my kitchen, I packed whatever food and water I could make fit in the pack, dragging a spare case of water bottles behind me down the basement stairs as I locked the door from the inside. The house I live in belonged to my grandfather during the '50s and fortunately had the safehold I am in now—the same strong room from which you probably recovered this book if I didn't make it. The bomb shelter had three-foot-thick steel walls and a submarine door that was supposed to be able to withstand any blast short of a direct nuclear assault, according to family legend.

I can hear them again. The growls are louder than ever. They're just outside the door now. Oh God. The noise is deafening. How could this have happened? Why did it have to happen? I don't know what to do. I hear claws on the door. How did they find me? What the hell are these things? I hope I'm not the last one. I hope someone can find this. If you do, never give up. Never believe you are safe. Hunt these things down, destroy them. You will never be safe if this can happen again. They're pounding on the door now. The entire room is shaking. Whatever is out there must be huge. I don't know if the door will hold. God have mercy on me. It's bending. The door is bending inward. My guns are fully loaded, but I don't know what good they will do. I will not give up without a fight. The hinges are giving. I can see fur, claws, blood. I can smell the stink. Darkness is creeping in this room as I write. I don't have long now. They've smelled me. I will not go without a fight. Fight. Fight. They are here. Oh God, it's hu...

TREASURE OF THE WOODED FOREST

by Ronald Munro, Chesapeake Bay Writers, 1ˢᵗ Place
Golden Nib Third Place

I was nine years old at the time, and sometimes I was left on my own in the afternoon while my mom took a nap. If I got snippy with her about it, she'd say, "I need ta 'cuperate from them never-endin' chores 'fore yer daddy gets hisself home." M'dad, ya see, did mainly road construction in the summer. There was always work on the roads for a sturdy back, and m'dad's back was wide and able, my momma said. But when he came home at the end of the day, he'd be achin' and tired and out of sorts most nights. That's why momma wanted t'nap in the afternoon, so she'd be "a ripe peach on a sad tree" for him. That's what m'dad would say sometimes, and it always made momma snicker so she'd have to say "G'won with ya, then." Mostly, she just wanted to be enough rested so she'd have no call to be imposin' on him after he'd been breakin' his back all the live-long day.

`She was a saint that way, my momma was. Everybody said so, especially our neighbor, Missus Armstrong. A while back, when Missus Armstrong fell and broke her hip, momma took care of her. "No need t'ask. 'Course I'm gonna take care o'ya," momma told her, an' she brooked no nonsense about it neither. She pitched in with all their chores, doin' the laundry 'n such and fixin' dinner for Misstuh Armstrong and their kids. They had two of them, Billy, who was m'best friend, and his older sister, Clarisa. Clarisa was always special to me because our birthdays fell on the exact same day, except she was a full-grown woman of sixteen years to my nine.

Afternoons, I generally played out back so's the house'd be quiet while momma was doin' her nappin'. The backyard was fenced-in with a six-foot wood fence "made with pressure-treated lumber," m'dad said. "Remember that," he scolded me. "Don't never skimp on what's needed, and don't never be dressin' it up to what it ain't." He lived by that, and that's why we didn't use no sissy painted pickets like some of our ritzy neighbors did closer t'town.

Beyond our fence, there was a path that ran alongside a wooded area. Somewhere deep inside the woods, people said, there was a secret hidden pond. Some called it a lost lagoon, but others said it was just an ol' swimmin' hole. A few folks took to warnin' us young'ns that it was a kissin' well, and if you kissed somebody there, you'd be soulmates forever. I never put much stock in all their tales, but I was curious about it though, 'specially since nobody would take me to see it. Momma said the woods was too dangerous for kids, so naturally, t'my mind, that meant they was hidin' somethin' for certain sure. I figured I'd just have to go see it for myself one day. Danger and adventure. I could fill a whole month'o Sundays with that.

Ever since I watched a Jungle Jim adventure on TV, I saw myself as a brave explorer. I wanted to be just like Jungle Jim, afraid of nothin' and nobody. In one of my favorite episodes, he's hacking his way through a dense jungle, face all sweaty, armpits all soaked through, and him about to fall over. Just when it seemed the most hopeless, Jungle Jim hacked one more bunch'a prickly shrubs, and there, bathin' in the glorious light shinin' straight down from heaven, was an ancient treasure, long ago lost and waitin' to be discovered by a brave explorer.

I just knew there had t'be a lost treasure in my woods too. Thing is, there wasn't nobody brave enough to go lookin' for it. Not 'til me, that is.

One day, I worked my way over to the farthest corner of our yard where a tool shed stood close by the fence. In the shed, I found a scythe used for cuttin' down weeds. It had a curved steel blade and a handle so long you could hold onto it with two hands like a baseball bat. I could just see myself hackin' through the densest jungle with it.

Outside, I dragged an empty wooden box over to the fence where I could use it like a ledge. I hoisted myself up onto it and hurled the scythe over the top. Then, quick as a squirrel, I scaled the fence, landin' on the other side without major injury. I didn't fall or nothin' on the way over, but I did scrape my trailin' leg as I pulled it over the top of the fence boards. The scratch marks runnin' down my calf looked like I'd been clawed by a savage lion I'd had t'fight off with m'bare hands. I was right proud of that scratch and bravely bore the pain of it. Us explorers, y'understand, expect wounds and scars, and we just treat them ourselves. I was in luck because the path was lined with all kinds of weeds and stuff, including one that had these ginormous green leaves about the size of elephant ears. I picked one, then I spit on my hand and rubbed it over my wound before wrapping the leaf around my leg like a bandage. I tucked the end of the leaf under itself to hold it together. I guess it wasn't real tight 'cuz it fell off five minutes later. But no matter, I pressed on, 'cuz that's what brave explorers do.

From there, I swaggered on down the path, flailing away with my scythe to cut down all the imaginary underbrush that dared to stand in my way. When I got to the point where the path turned out of sight of the houses, I swiveled and peered squarely at the trees that people said were too fearsome to be explored. My bones tingled, and I just knew, hidden in the darkest belly of this uncharted jungle was the long-lost treasure of the wooded forest. I drew my scythe up across m'chest, holdin' it with both hands, and swore in solemn oath, "Wooded forest, I salute you." Then whoopin' a blood curdlin' yell, I plunged into that fierce forbidden realm, muscles tense, scythe at the ready.

After a good fifteen minutes of walkin' and whoopin', I started to worry. The path from my house had disappeared from sight, but I hadn't yet hacked through a single jungle vine tryin' t'snatch me off my feet. Not a branch or bush stood in my way, and not a single rocky ridge did I have to climb. This was a great disappointment, and my thoughts started to wander back to home where my mom would soon be gettin' up from her nap, ready to start her afternoon bakin'. Whenever she made cakes or cookies, I usually got to lick the bowls and spoons, and I hadn't planned on missin' out on that. I thought maybe I oughtta be turnin' back. But then, I thought of Jungle Jim, and I was sore ashamed of myself. He wouldn't'a turned back for nothin'. So, by golly, neither would I. I sucked up my courage, swished my scythe through the air, and trudged on, brow all sweaty and armpits soakin' through.

It was just about then that the trees started to thin out, and straight ahead of me, lord a'mighty, the trees parted an' they was gone. Where I looked, there wasn't nothin' t'behold but empty space, just a vacant sky filled with blue. M'feet suddenly rooted where I stood, and I gasped with breath takin' excitement. *This was it!* Just like in a Jungle Jim movie, Heaven itself had swooped down and swallowed the ground clean away, and where its light beamed brightest was the very spot where the lost treasure was waitin' for a brave explorer to find it. None but the bravest would ever see it, an' that was me. One step more and it'd be mine by right of discovery.

Raising my scythe in homage to Jungle Jim, I broke into a delirious run. As I rushed past the last of the trees, the ground fell away into a steep slope. A bush lying low to the ground snaked out an' snagged the scythe right outta m'hands. It yanked me so hard the ground went clean out from under me, and I tumbled countless yards down the slope, bouncin' an' turnin' an' twistin' clear around, somersaultin' in a never-endin' whirl with trees 'n rocks flashin' past me helter-skelter 'til I came to rest on a flat rock that was wider than I was long.

I was crazy dizzy from tumblin', but m'heart was jumpin' so bad I just had t'lift m'head up quick t'see the treasure I'd so bravely discovered. Eyes flarin' wide, I was instantly stunned by what those selfsame eyes beheld. Before me lay not a treasure, but somethin' more precious than jewels. *The fabled hidden lagoon of the wooded forest!* I was right on the very lip of its magical waters, the same enchanted waters that glistened in all the fables I'd ever heard, an' I just knew, nobody but me had ever seen it for real. Awe such as I'd never known washed over me in waves of wonder like blessed eternity had opened its wondrous gates.

While I swooned in all that rapture, two earsplitting banshee shrieks, the equal of which I ain't never heard before, suddenly shattered the bejesus out of my awe and wonder.

Heart thumpin', throat raspin' an' chokin', I twisted hard t'see what bestial creature had issued such a spine-chillin' sound. What I saw stole m'breath clean away – two women sittin' on towels, sunnin' themselves beside the lake, strands of wet hair reachin' down from their heads 'til they curled atop their shoulders. Below that level, they bore not a stitch of thread to cover their naked bodies.

Dumbstruck, I gawked while they scrambled to shelter behind their towels. Until that instant, I'd never seen a naked woman. Heck, I'd never seen a naked girl.

I was gaspin' an' wheezin' an' tryin' t'breathe when a twangy voice sharp as a crack of lightning split the air. "Jake Tucker! What are you doing here?" My head snapped hard around, and there, risin' outta the lake like a nymph with angel's wings flarin' in the sunlight, stood Clarisa Armstrong. *Billy Armstrong's sister!*

Mounted on a rocky ledge, feet still in the water, hands on her bare hips, naked eyes flashin' at me like stars blazin' in a clear sky, she demanded again, *"What're you doing here? Were you spying on us?"*

Her voice was going shrill, and I feared she was about to have a temper tantrum like Suzy Wilson did in first grade when she got real mad an' heaved stones at everybody. I know I should'a been gone an' runnin' hard away, but it was Clarisa, and I couldn't move m'feet no more'n I could take m'eyes off a her.

But she could, and she did. Steppin' outta the water, she marched straight at me with a menace in her eye that would'a stopped a chargin' rhino, which I wasn't. *"Answer me, you twerp,"* she shouted. "How long have you been watching us? Who's with you?"

She was now standing right in front of me, only two steps away, arms arched on both sides like she was ready to draw down on me in a cowboy shootout. My head was shaking vigorously, denying everything. "No," I stammered. "I wasn't. Honest, I wasn't. It's just me. Honest. I wasn't lookin'."

She glanced away to scan the woods, then turned back to glare at me. "What're you doing here?" she demanded again. I told her I was lookin' for lost treasure, and criminy, I thought she was gonna go berserk. "Treasure?" she shouted at me. *"Treasure?"* The scorn on her face screamed "liar" louder'n words. She planted her hands on her hips again, and her lips started workin' like she was fixin' t'have a righteous conniption fit. That worried me some 'cuz I was scared I was gonna start cryin' right in front of her. But she thought better of it and pointed instead to a big rock. "There. Sit," she commanded, "and don't you move an inch until we decide what to do with you."

Clarisa turned away from me to look back at her friends. They were cowerin' behind their towels like I was a troglodyte come t'drag them off to my cave. "Oh, for crying out loud," she scolded while laughin' and shakin' her head at them. "He's just a kid. What're you thinking?"

They must've seen some wisdom in that 'cuz suddenly they were laughin' too and set about at once to straighten their towels, making them smooth and parallel. Clarisa knelt down with them in a huddle, and suddenly they were whisperin' and wavin' their hands. Then they stopped whisperin' an' set to scowlin' at me.

Clarisa demanded, "Who else knows you're here?"

"Nobody, I swear." I was sacred, and I think I bit my lip tryin' not to look it.

She squinted hard at me, aimin' her sharpest glare straight into m'head. If she'd'a told me she could see what m'brain was thinkin', I'd'a believed it. She didn't say so, but I thought it anyway. Presently she nodded and said, "And that's how it's going to stay. You understand?"

I did, and I shook m'head vigorously to prove it.

"Swear it. Cross your heart and hope to die."

"I swear it, I do."

And you'll never tell anyone, ever."

"No, I won't, not ever."

Clarisa looked at her friends who looked back at her. Then she was looking at me again. Me, I could only look at her. She hesitated. "You can find your way back?"

"Course I can." I said it like I was miffed that she'd even ask. That caused her to grin at me like she understood. Then she stepped over to me and placed her hands on my shoulders. She bent over and kissed my forehead. "There," she said. "That seals your promise."

She left her hands on my shoulders for another second, givin' my shoulders a reassurin' squeeze. Then abruptly she straightened up, and my eyes shot up with her. I was holdin' my breath and couldn't otherwise move. She put her hands back on her hips and tilted her head. "Well?" she asked like I was supposed to say something. Her friends were giggling at me again, but I didn't care. My eyes were riveted on Clarisa. She was so close...

"Men are so silly," Clarisa pronounced over me, tryin' t'sound vexed, but the words I heard came tender as a fond embrace. "Alright then," she commanded, pointing up the slope, "so go." Her face was stern, but not so the smile in her eyes. "Remember," she added, "it's our secret."

I didn't want to go, but I couldn't seem t'stop myself from obeyin' her command. Standing up from my rock, eyes still riveted on her, some unseen force drove my feet into churnin' and stumblin' up the slope. I didn't bother to pick up the scythe. I just scrambled 'til I rounded the crest and hit level ground; then I broke into a run, dodgin' an' weavin' through all the sinister trees and shrubs now stretchin' out from all sides t'trap me in their pernicious limbs. I didn't stop 'til I felt the worn trail beneath my feet and saw the shaggy weeds linin' the path that would carry me back home. I halted there, stoopin' over an' bracin' my hands against my knees to catch my breath.

When my heart stopped poundin' in my chest, I turned back to look deep into the forest, my forest, where danger lurked behind every tree; my jungle, where I'd thought to find a great treasure, but didn't.

And yet...I did.

Grinning, I leaped into a whoopin', stompin' dance-a-jig. It wasn't the treasure I expected, but it was a treasure nonetheless, the rightful treasure of the wooded forest, and it wasn't even hidden. My treasure was in plain sight, a treasure who was a goddess, and her name was Clarisa Armstrong. A nymph of the lost lagoon; a sprite of the wooded forest; maybe even a flesh and blood angel; and she was sealed to me with a kiss.

I didn't know it then, but this secret would become a constant of my existence, guiding me for the whole of my life, steering me through wicked times, and ushering me to wondrous places where the real treasures of life awaited a brave explorer to discover them. Years would pass with a lot of hard lessons learned before I would understand life is often like that, finding what you need more than what you want.

BROKEN DREAMS

by Daniel C. Swanson, Appalachian Authors Guild, 2nd Place

Peter Andersson shielded his eyes from the summer sun as he exited the dreaded Registry Room at Ellis Island and gazed westward toward his new life in America. His excitement was tempered by the challenges that he faced as a nineteen-year-old Swedish immigrant, barely able to speak the English language, while being thrust into a strange world with no family and far from his native land.

Cunard R.M.S. Caronia   TONNAGE 20,000

The year was 1906. He had endured the grueling two-week voyage across the stormy North Atlantic on board the RMS Caronia from Liverpool, England. The inspections by the medical personnel started as he ran a slow gauntlet from the dock up to the Main Hall with its iconic barrel-vaulted ceiling. He had been told that he needed to walk swiftly with no sign of a limp to avoid scrutiny by the inspectors.

Peter did not expect a problem in passing the physical examination. He took a deep breath and entered the Main Hall amid a sea of humanity. The air inside the Main Hall was heavy with the stench of body odor, vomit from the trans-Atlantic voyage, and fear. Peter's turn finally came, and he approached the doctor clad in a long, white laboratory coat.

The typical physical examination took approximately eight seconds. He winced in pain as the doctor used a sinister looking medical device shaped like a buttonhook to raise his eyelids, covering his sparkling blue eyes as part of the examination for eye disease.

During these few precious seconds, Peter's fate would be determined. He would either be waved on by the doctor, or a chalk mark with a capital letter signifying the infirmity (L for Lameness, E for Eyes, H for Heart) would be placed on his clothing, barring his entry into America. Peter's hands grew moist with sweat as he waited for what seemed like an eternity, as the doctor decided. His heart soared as the doctor waved for him to proceed to the next station and not toward the entrance to the Ellis Island Immigrant Hospital as the first stop on his return trip to Sweden.

Peter's English-speaking skills were extremely limited. As he waited on the wooden benches following his medical examination, he was unsure if he could interpret and successfully respond to the infamous twenty-nine questions that new immigrants were asked before being admitted to the country. His prayers were answered when he was approached by a kindly gentleman in a gray tweed jacket and red bow tie.

"Are you Peter Andersson?" he asked in Swedish, as he extended his hand with a warm greeting.

"Well, yes, that's my name," Peter nervously responded.
"I'm Johan Ericsson from the Swedish Immigrant Aid Society, and I'm here to help you communicate with the inspectors. If you're ready, let's get going so we can get you on your way."

"Thank you, Mr. Ericsson. I'm so grateful for your help," Peter replied.
They proceeded to the next open inspection station. They were greeted by a gentleman with wire-rimmed glasses. He looked over the rims of his glasses down at Peter and started with the first of what seemed like an endless list of questions. Peter's answers to these questions would be the final test before his admission to America.

"What is your name?" he demanded.

"My name is Peter Andersson, and I am from the Village of Ramdala in Sweden."

"What is your occupation?" he asked.

Peter confidently responded, "In Sweden, I worked as a timber cutter. I plan to make my living as a timber cutter in America."

"Do you have any family in America?"

"No, but I intend to meet my sweetheart from my village who came earlier."

The inspector looked down at his notes and offered one last question. "How much money do you have in your possession?"

"Twenty-five US dollars, sir," Peter replied as he checked to make sure his life savings
from working as a timber cutter in Sweden was still in his buttoned inside coat pocket.

The inspector banged down a stamp on the immigration form and told Peter that he was free to leave Ellis Island.

Peter thanked Mr. Ericsson and pushed his way through the crowd until he emerged from the Registry Building onto the street.

Peter stared in amazement at the scene in front of him. The tall buildings across the Hudson River on Manhattan Island rose into the sky in the distance. The air was filled with a symphony of languages, including German, Irish, French, and English, most of which Peter did not recognize. Many of the new arrivals were having tearful reunions with their loved ones at a wooden column just outside the Registry Room. Peter had heard that the column was commonly known as The Kissing Post, although Peter had no loved one to greet him and welcome him to America.

Peter snapped back from his daydream with the realization that he had a job to do. His long journey had included a train trip from Kalmar to Gothenburg, a ferry across the North Sea to Hull, England, another train trip from Hull to Liverpool, and finally the voyage to New York. The cost of his journey had been paid by a recruiter from an American steel mill who was seeking immigrant workers to operate the machinery of their rapidly expanding business. Peter had agreed to work for a year in a place called the National Tube Works in a city whose name he could not pronounce—McKeesport, Pennsylvania. He wasn't even sure where Pennsylvania was located.

Peter boarded the ferry that would take him from Ellis Island to the New Jersey shore and the Central Railroad of New Jersey Terminal. He was told that he would be met by a representative of the company at the base of the large clock tour. He made his way to the terminal and scanned the crowd. Much to his relief, he noticed a man waving a white sign with the names "ANDERSSON", "DABROWSKI", and "MCGINNIS" in all capital letters. He approached the man and did his best to introduce himself.

"*God morgon*," Peter offered as he extended his hand toward the stranger.

His host replied, "My name is Jones, and I am here from the National Tube Works. Just wait here while I locate the other new arrivals, and we can start our journey to Pittsburgh."

Peter took a seat on a bench in the terminal and waited. Before long, two other young men had walked up to their host and introduced themselves. One of them seemed to speak Polish, and the other was speaking Irish. Jones motioned for them to follow him to the track for the train leaving for Pittsburgh. The train announced its arrival as the engineer sounded the shrill whistle, and the steam engine belched black smoke and steam from its coal-fired boiler as it screeched to a halt in the station. They boarded the train, and before long, it rumbled as it exited the station.

Overcome with a combination of anticipation and sheer exhaustion, Peter leaned against the frame of the train car seat and tried to sleep as the train traveled west through the Allegheny Mountains toward Pittsburgh. The sun was just setting as they approached the bustling city. It hung like a fiery orb suspended in a pale gray mixture of fog and smoke from the smokestacks of the many factories that lined the banks of the rivers that defined Pittsburgh, and just like that, the sun was gone. Night had descended on the city as the engineer signaled the arrival of the train at the B&O Station near downtown.

Jones motioned to his traveling companions to gather up their belongings and exit the station. They would be met by a driver from the National Tube Works to transport them to the boarding house that was home to many of the immigrant workers at the mill. Peter peered out the window at the rows of houses of the many ethnic communities that dotted the landscape of the Monongahela River valley. He could see the stark silhouettes of the towering mills and factories, with their tall smokestacks belching smoke and soot into the night sky.

Their vehicle finally pulled over to the curb in front of a dingy three-story brick building with "ROOMS FOR RENT" sign permanently affixed to a metal pole in front of the building. Jones escorted the new employees to the lobby, and the desk clerk gave Peter a key to his room on the third floor. Peter opened the door to his room. He surveyed a single light bulb hanging from the ceiling in the center of the room, a narrow bed with a lumpy mattress, and a wooden chest in the corner for his clothes. Peter unpacked his suitcase and collapsed onto the bed without eating dinner.

Peter awoke around 5 a.m. Workers moved down to the kitchen for a quick breakfast and a cup of strong coffee before being transported to the mill.

As he arrived at the factory gate, he was told to meet the foreman of his work crew at the flagpole in front of the Mill Office to start work. Peter had been waiting for only a few minutes with other members of his group when they were approached by the foreman. He motioned for the group to follow him to their workstations.

The foreman gave them a brief description of the facilities as they walked. He exclaimed with pride in his voice, "National Tube Works is the largest mill of its type in the world, covering over sixty-six acres with fifty acres under roof."

As they entered one of the many long, grimy buildings, Peter was immediately struck by the noise, heat, and dust in the air. This was not exactly what he had imagined what his work life in America would be like. Still, he was a man of his word, and he decided he would make the best of the situation until he fulfilled his contract with the company.

Peter was soon to learn that McKeesport was home to a large population of Swedish immigrants. He met several Swedish co-workers, both at work and at the boarding house. He almost immediately began his search for his sweetheart from his village of Ramdala, Kristin Olson, who had told him she would work as a maid in the home of one of the wealthy mill owners in McKeesport upon her arrival in America.

As Peter continued his search, he slowly assimilated into the local culture of the Swedish American community. His English-speaking skills improved, and he could travel confidently around the city. He was invited to join members of the community at Olympia Park for the celebration of Midsummer's Day on June 21, the date of the summer solstice, a traditional Swedish holiday. He attended the First Swedish Baptist Church. He became a member of the local Odd Fellows Lodge.

At a meeting of the Odd Fellows Lodge, Peter met a man named George Kipling who would become one of the most important people in Peter's life. Mr. Kipling was born in New York, but he had moved to Pennsylvania where he met and married his wife, the daughter of a prominent McKeesport family. He was a timber cutter by trade, and he had made his living by cutting trees in the forests of Pennsylvania. However, he often spoke of moving to the pristine forests of old growth timber in Virginia or North Carolina to make his fortune as a timber cutting contractor for the large lumber mills in the area. He became friends with Peter, and he invited Peter to join him when the time was right.

The right time would come sooner than Peter had expected. He had been frustrated in his search for his beloved Kristin when he discovered she had left the employment as a maid for one of the mill owners in town only a couple of days earlier. The only clue that he was given to her whereabouts was that she had taken a job as a camp cook for one of the large lumber companies in Virginia.

Despite his attempt to live a pious life, McKeesport in the early 1900s featured more than a few temptations for a young single man like Peter. He avoided the infamous red- light district known as "Brick Alley." However, he joined some of his young Swedish American friends for an occasional pint of beer at one of the local pubs. On one raucous Saturday night, Peter and his friends were "blowing off a little steam" from another grueling week in the mill when William Malden, the arrogant son of the mill manager, entered the bar with a couple of his friends.

As they made their way up to the bar, pushing Peter and his friends out of the way, he loudly announced, "Will you square heads get out of our way and make room for some real Americans to get a beer?"

Responding to the insult, Peter and his friends got into a shoving match with William and his friends. The mass of bodies surged back and forth, and a few punches were thrown.
No one was hurt until William stumbled backward and slammed his head into the brass rail at the bottom of the bar.

Peter and his friends didn't wait around for the police to arrive. It would be their word against the word of Malden and his friends, and they will be blamed. Peter headed straight from the bar to Mr. Kipling's home. He saw that the light was burning in the living room. Peter walked up the steps and nervously knocked on the front door.

Kipling asked, "Peter, what brings you out at this time of night?"

"Mr. Kipling, will you be traveling down to the timber camps soon?"

Kipling replied, "Yes, Peter, I'm leaving in the morning. You're welcome to join me." Peter was torn between fulfilling the rest of his contract to the mill and the opportunity to pursue his dream when he came to America. With the risk that his life could be ruined if Malden didn't recover from his injuries, especially if he were to get the blame for the accident, Peter responded, "What time do we leave?"

"Be here bright and early at 6 a.m., and we'll depart. Bring all of your belongings. I don't know when we'll return to McKeesport."

Peter bumped into his friend Hans in the lobby of the boarding house and told him he was leaving for Virginia. He arose around 5 a.m., quietly exiting the boarding house for the several blocks walk to Kipling's home.

Kipling gave him a warm greeting and told him to put his suitcase in the back seat of the Ford Model A for the journey. They began their arduous trek south through the rugged mountains of West Virginia to the thriving timber camps in Southwest Virginia.

Peter had made the right decision. Mr. Malden had a concussion and about a week later, succumbed to his injuries. His father, Joseph Malden, the mill manager, immediately summoned the lead detective from the Pinkerton National Detective Agency, who provided mill security and "goon squads" to intimidate union organizers to his office.

"Detective, I'm sure that you heard about my son," Malden offered. "Yes, sir, and you have our condolences," the detective replied.

"Well, I need your help in tracking down the young Swedish bastards who killed him. A new immigrant, Peter Andersson, is said to be the leader of the group."

"I'll put two of my best men on the case, and I'll get back to you when we apprehend
him." The detective promised as he pivoted on his heel and left the office.

Pinkerton detectives were renowned for their ability to track down some of the country's most notorious fugitives, including Jesse James, so they didn't think that finding a young Swedish immigrant would pose much of a challenge. From interviewing Peter's friends, they learned he had departed McKeesport for the timber camps of Virginia, and the chase was on.

Peter and Kipling could land quickly their first contract to cut timber for the Currier Lumber Company in a remote region of Wise County, Virginia, on the South Fork of the Pound River. One day, Peter was surprised to see Hans, his Swedish friend from McKeesport, in the timber camp.

Peter asked, "Hans, I didn't think that I would see you again this soon. What brings you to Virginia?"

"I didn't see a future in the mill. I decided to pursue my fortune, like you, in the timber industry," Hans replied. A solemn look came over Hans' face, and he turned to Peter after checking that no one was close enough to hear their conversation.

"Peter, I have some bad news. William Malden died from his injuries at the bar. They think you're responsible, and they have hired Pinkerton detectives to hunt you down."

The blood drained from Peter's face. He thanked Hans for the warning and told him he would see him in camp.

Peter began a nomadic lifestyle as he moved from timber camp to timber camp as the logging companies finished cutting all the large, old growth timber and moved to the next location. To avoid easy detection, Peter used his father's last name, Nilsson, instead of his last name. He earned one to two dollars per day. He paid eight dollars per month in rent to live in very primitive "string houses" that were built on skids so they could be moved when the camp moved. The timber companies laid narrow-gauge railroad tracks into each area as the timber was harvested, and they tore up and moved the tracks when the camp moved.

Peter continued his relentless search for his beloved Kristin. At each camp in

Southwest Virginia and eastern North Carolina where Peter worked, he kept asking everyone that he met if they had heard of her while he kept looking over his shoulder for any sign of the Pinkerton agents. They were closer that he realized.

At the end of a hard day in the woods, Peter was sitting down for the evening meal at the camp dining hall when he was approached by the camp manager.

"Peter, there were a couple of shady looking guys in camp today asking if we knew a young Swedish immigrant named Peter Andersson, who was involved in some kind of trouble up in McKeesport. Their description sounded a lot like you. I told them I didn't know anyone with that name, and they moved on."

Peter replied, "Thanks for telling me, sir. I'm glad that they weren't looking for me." Peter's search for Kristin had become more hopeless with each passing year. He was well into his twenties and felt that it was time for his search to end and for him to start a family. While working in Wise County, he met and married a strong local woman, Nancy Bolling, who had spent her life in the mountains or Southwest Virginia. They had their first child six months after the wedding.

By then, over ten years had passed since the accident in the bar in McKeesport, and Peter returned to using his real name. Although he felt he was no longer being pursued by the Pinkerton agents, he was experiencing an increasing bias against immigrants that seemed to have peaked around World War I and culminated with passage of the American Immigration Act of 1924 that effectively ended mass migration to the United States.

Animosity toward immigrants had grown to such intensity that Peter no longer felt welcome in his new land. By the time of the 1920 US Census, Peter, Nancy, and their young children were living in a rented house with a maid because of Peter's increasing financial success in the timber industry. When the census taker visited Peter's home, his response to the census' questions was very revealing.

The census taker asked, "Where were you born?"

Peter responded "Pennsylvania."

He continued, "Where was your father born?"

"Pennsylvania."

"Where was your mother born?"

Peter sadly replied as he bowed his head, "Pennsylvania."

The story of Peter Andersson and his family and their pursuit of the American dream became a part of America's story, a story of millions of immigrants who built the country.

Peter's story became a story of a dream deferred by prejudice, personal tragedy, and the struggles of the Great Depression. Through the tenacity and indomitable spirit born from the challenges faced by Peter and his family, his descendants became doctors, engineers, college professors and entrepreneurs. His spirit lives on in each of them over a hundred years later.

Elena's Story

by Mary Ellen Jantzi, Blue Ridge Writers, 1st Place

Afternoon sunlight flooded Elena's small bedroom, stained the pine floor, and sprinkled the pale violet walls with lemon drops of light filtered through the young leaves outside the west window. She loved this room, infused with her mother's essence. Mom was like sunshine, blond and smiling, often offering a bakery treat or a trinket from a second-hand boutique; and her fragrance, lavender bubble- bath and lilac spray-cologne, wafted from the sachets tucked into Elena's chest of drawers.

Exhausted from a day of school followed by an hour of track-team practice, Elena sprawled across her bed, reading Pride and Prejudice. The wry humor amused, sparking images from the DVD she'd recently watched. Mom and Brad had teased each other during the film, and even kissed (when they thought she was too engrossed in the movie to notice); until her exaggerated eye-roll indicted them. She sighed, recalling their family-like togetherness.

She and Mom have lived here, in Brad Foster's house, for two years. Chesterfield, Virginia, wasn't congested like the DC area or boring like the boon-dock villages scattered around the Piedmont region. The junior high school had the latest computers, well-kept athletic facilities and nice- enough students. The librarian had become a friend and shared her love of literature. For the first time in her life, she fit in, both at school and at home.

Elena relinquished her reverie and returned to the novel. The bedroom door opened, hinges squeaking like timid mice. "Hey, kid."

At the unexpected voice, her head jerked up. "Hey, Brad. Where's Mom?" She closed the book and scooted to the edge of the bed, bare feet dangling inches above the floor. Her heart skipped beats in the wake of Brad's somber stare. "What's happened? Something bad happens to Mom? Blurry visions of car accidents skidded through her imagination.

Brad lifted her ladder-back chair and placed it backwards in the doorway. He straddled the cane seat. As usual, Brad was honoring Mom's number one rule: no one ever goes in Elena's room but me. The air, infused with petroleum odors from Brad's coveralls, prickled her nostrils. The scent was familiar, associated with the friendly camaraderie of the auto-repair garage.

"Your mom left this morning, Elena. Said she was going to Las Vegas."

"What?" Mom had never taken off before, let alone without telling her. "You mean on a vacation? Why didn't she tell me?" Her fingernails dug into the edge of the mattress while her eyes searched Brad's for truth.

"She was afraid you wouldn't understand."

"I can deal with her needing a vacation, Brad. I'm not a baby, I'm fifteen. How long a va-

vacation? A week or-"

"Slow down, kid." Brad frowned.

He rarely frowned. This must be serious. "Why are you staring at me like I'm from outer space? Tell me what's going on. It's not like Mom not to share this with me."

Brad glanced quickly around the room. "She met a man. Harry, something or other... wouldn't tell me his last name. She claims it was love at first sight."

"Oh, G-God—not again."

"What do you mean?" He asked, pinning her with his stare.

"Nothing. Uh... so, when is she coming home?" This was no trip. She knew that now. "Elena."

"You always use my first name when you're super-serious." She stiffly backed up, propped a pillow against the iron bar headboard, and tucked her feet beneath her. If only she could hide her stutter as easily as her feet. "Do I?"

"Yep. Otherwise, you call me 'kid'. I don't mind, I... "Marlena said she'd call when she got settled in Vegas."

"So she plans to take me there? To Vegas?" Brad's stare made her go still, slowed her breathing. "Of course, she does. She's my mom. She loves me more than anybody, more than this Harry ass ho—sorry, Brad."

"Don't apologize. You're allowed to be upset."

"Well, thank you, but I'm way past "upset. I'm closing in on angry and totally pissed off. Mom never learns. Now she's gone all Thelma and Louise over the edge and dumped me on Brad. The only truly good guy she ever hooked up with. He doesn't wear a gold chain around his neck or drive a gas-guzzling ash-stinky Cadillac or dye his hair to pretend to be younger than he is. He doesn't leer at me or talk down to me like I'm a moron. I don't need to lock my bedroom door when Mom's at work, like I did when we lived with other guys."

"She said to tell you she loves you. And that she's sorry."

"Sorry for leaving or sorry for not telling me? Sorry for what, Brad?"

He returned the chair to her desk, then leaned against the jamb, hands shoved in his pockets. His chest expanded with a huge intake of air. She listened for the exhale. They ran long-distance together at least three times a week, so she knew how he looked, how he smelled, and how he sounded. He was not in cool-down mode; rather, just taking a breather, preparing for the next mile.

"Elena, your mom's not planning to come back."

"Huh?" No way she believed that. She and Mom were tight, best friends, loyal to each other. Yet she hunched over, gripped her sides, and felt the flimsy lower ribs. Her lungs constricted. "Mom's b- been with me every day of my life. Now she's sorry and gone? D-dumping me? What k-kind of mother abandons her kid?" Dang freaking stutter. He thought he was cured, had outgrown it. He hadn't been afraid ever since they moved to Brad's.

"It's a complicated adult thing. She wanted a more exciting lifestyle, I guess. She had her dreams. Apparently, I wasn't it."

"But you're the best guy we've ever known. How c-could she do this? Why'd you let her go?"

"I had no right to stop her. You know she and I had little in common."

"Yeah, but you and I do. You're the closest thing I've had to a dad-person. Didn't she see how g-good it was for me here? How much I like my school and get good grades?"

"I promised her I'd see you graduate high school. Elena, your mom thought you staying here was best for you."

"Best for me? No. She did what she thought was best for her. That's why we've moved from place to place all my life." Sniffling, she moved back to the edge of the bed, focusing on her glittery purple toenails. Mom had painted them yesterday, on her birthday. "I need to talk to her, Brad. Can't we go find her? Leave now and catch up with them?"

"No, sweetheart, we can't. She left no address or number to call. Ditched her cellphone."

"Sweetheart. He never called me that before. What about the police? Can't they track her down?"

Brad shook his head."

She was overwhelmed with fear, confusion, and frustration. Her chest convulsed, and she struggled to draw breath.

Brad strode to the bed, pulled her to her feet, and wrapped her in a fierce hug. Her quivering arms clutched him like someone tossed overboard clutches a lifebuoy. Mom's rule number two no longer applies: hug me, Brad, and never let me go.

Sunlight drained from her bedroom and shadows moved in. Half an hour had passed. "I have to pay Ricky and Curt. It's Friday. Close the garage," Brad said, pulling a clean bandanna from his back pocket and wiping her face. "I'll get dinner for us when I come back in. Will you be all right 'til then?"

What did that even mean? No, she would not be all right. This situation was all wrong: moms don't abandon their kids. "Go. It's okay. Thanks for telling me." Her fake fortitude surprised her. The last thing she wanted was Brad witnessing a more embarrassing meltdown.

"This conversation isn't over, Elena."

"Can we go for a run after dinner? Maybe stop for ice cream?"

Anything .... to make this all go away. "Whatever you want, kid. I'm all yours."

The back door slammed. She peered out her bedroom window at Brad walking to the long concrete building where FOSTER GARAGE was printed in large red block letters above two high overhead doors. "I'm all yours" reverberated in her mind as she replayed Brad's comforting hug. Never had she been held so tightly, nor felt so secure. This was home.

She sat on her bed and surveyed her room—her cocoon, her Alamo. She swore to defend it. It seemed like just last week, instead of two years ago, that she and Mom and Brad had painted her room. She'd been allowed to choose the color at Home Depot. Mom and Brad, in worn out jeans and stained sweatshirts, masked the woodwork and painted the walls. Mom's platinum-blond curls bobbed playfully. Brad looked cute, too... muscly and sexy ... like a Marine with his hair trimmed short for active duty. The image of perfect parents. Mom hit the jackpot when she met Brad. Why did she have to take off for Las Vegas?

Purple balloons from yesterday's birthday party huddled in a pile in the corner by her dresser. One had deflated. That's me, she mused. Stories had always pumped her up, and in the middle of her bed, nestled on the new deep purple duvet, her book beckoned. What kind of pride and prejudice hid inside? Her own pride comprised having a pretty— no, glamorous—mother, a fun-loving guy who treated her like a dad or big brother might, a room of her own, and good grades in school. Prejudice haunted from a distance. Some people probably pitied her not having a dad. And some teachers probably assumed she was mentally deficient because of shyness and stuttering.

Both problems had almost been conquered. Was she born with the stutter? Or was it caused by being scared to death by the strange men her mother had brought into her life? Or by frequent moves and the stress of frequently being the new girl at school?

The memory of her worst episode grew vivid: she was eight, or maybe nine ... reading in her room. The door was locked because Mom was at work. Her doorknob rotated slowly, silently. She had stopped breathing and stared until it stopped. Then she'd considered climbing out her window; but it had grown dark outside and there were big dogs in the neighborhood—a scary black German Shepherd and a mean-looking pit-bull. Mom had warned her to avoid those dogs.

When Mom got home from work at the diner, and checked in on her, she couldn't speak at all. The next day she tried to tell Mom what had happened, but she stuttered so horribly she couldn't express herself. Two days later she managed to tell. Mom left the man that day. Later that week, a doctor told them that there was no cure for stuttering.

Today confirmed that stress caused her to stutter.

Merlin, a stuffed white unicorn she'd chosen at Toy-R-Us for her eighth birthday, sat on his haunches next to her desk. In the privacy of her room, she used to read to Merlin as if he were a younger brother. She never stuttered when reading aloud to him. The last books she read to him were the Harry Potter series. Even though she'd outgrown her need for Merlin, she still treasured him. Pressing him against her burning throat and stroking his velvety coat, she whispered, "It's just you and me . . . alone again."

It was six p.m. when Brad called up the stairs that dinner was ready whenever she wanted to eat. It wasn't fair to Brad to keep him waiting. It wasn't freaking fair? Nothing was fair anymore. She'd been an obedient daughter, and it wasn't fair that Mom had ditched her.

When they'd moved into Brad Foster's, when she was thirteen, things had changed. Brad insisted she stop being "a Hermit crab" in her bedroom. He invited her to run long distance with him in the evenings. And he'd taught her how to use his workout equipment in the basement. Now, in the full-length mirror on the inside of her closet door, she admired the toned muscles on her slender tomboy frame.

Mom trusted Brad, even when she was at work. A lock had never been installed on her bedroom door, like before when they lived with Mom's other men.

At the bathroom sink, she rinsed away the tears dribbling down her cheeks and toweled her face dry, brushed her silky hair into a high ponytail, and secured it with a purple scrunchie. Speaking to the girl in the mirror, she proclaimed, "I refuse to be like Mom. In fact, I promise to be totally opposite." She crossed her heart and went downstairs.

Brad rested his elbows on the kitchen table and cradled his forehead on the heels of his hands. He straightened up and smiled when Elena slid into her chair. "I'll cook the hamburgers if you're ready to eat."

She nodded yes. He'd told her about protein, muscles and all that health stuff when they worked out on his Nautilus. She knew he'd be pleased if she ate. He didn't need to know how nauseous she felt. Not real nausea from food, just nerves.

When she and Mom first came to live here, she was scrawny, a twig of a girl with a stutter and nervous blinking. She avoided looking directly at people. Now a taller twig with defined calf muscles and tiny-but-firm biceps, she looked athletic. She needed to keep her strength up to try out for the high school track team.

Brad sliced a tomato and a sweet onion and opened a bag of potato chips—kettle-cooked, her favorite. He set a cold can of Pepsi on her Boston Marathon placemat. Drops of water, like tears, rained on the runners. Condensation, sweat, tears. There was a lot of wetness in the world. No wonder she felt like she was drowning. She cupped the cold Pepsi can between her palms, letting it douse the hot sadness banked beneath her skin. Hamburgers sizzled in the skillet. Her mouth watered.

"Y-you don't owe me anything, Brad. Don't feel bad about f-finding me a p-lace to go."

"Let's eat first, kid." He handed her a plate crowned with a thick burger. "We'll figure things out soon enough."

Car tires squealed out front. Brad's house and auto shop were on a corner lot near an intersection, and she had learned to distinguish the starting-up from the slowing-down sounds of cars and trucks. Their inside joke was about to say, "Don't she purr?" when a loud sports car showed off its power. That line came from the movie Scent of a Woman, their mutually favorite movie.

"Here's what I think, Elena."

There it was again, the use of her proper name. A tremble reverberated through her body, from knees to shoulders.

"This *is* a Foster home, pardon the pun. I suspect Marlena will regret leaving you and come back soon. In the meantime, you'd have less disruption in your life if you stay here. What do you think?"

Stay here? Alone with Brad? Mom had taught her to never trust men. But Brad was a good guy, and she totally liked him. "I'm scared. W-what if Mom doesn't come back?"

Brad leaned forward and wiped her cheeks with a paper napkin. "We'll take a day at a time. I care about you, Elena, and I'll keep you safe."

She closed her eyes and relief washed over her like a waterfall on a sweltering summer eve. She had a choice. "Okay. I app-p-reciate-"

"Elena. I know."

Back in her bedroom, she couldn't pick up her novel. A love story was the last thing she wanted to read about. Mom was supposed to love her most. She loved Mom most. Where did Mom's love for her go? She burrowed between her new lavender sheets, scissoring her legs through the smooth coolness as if treading water. Treading water was all she could do until Brad had taught her swimming strokes.

He'd called her his little porpoise and his little mermaid, and she'd overcome her fear of water just to please him. Virginia Beach was their favorite vacation spot. Just a day trip, two hours from home, but still... she'd never experienced the ocean before Brad. So many parts of her life, her memories, were categorized as before Brad or after Brad.

She was wiped out, like when a breaker catches you unprepared and slams you into the sand, scraping your knees and scaring you half to death. Time to sleep. As she reached for her bedside lamp switch, she noticed the purple paisley-covered diary, a birthday gift from Brad. Was it only yesterday that the three of them had celebrated her fifteenth birthday? It seemed like weeks ago. Throwing back her sheet, she dove into her school backpack and fished out a ballpoint pen.

April 28, 2009
 Dear Diary,

Mom took off for Las Vegas with some sleazeball–without telling me goodbye! Why? I never saw it coming. Brad says I can stay here until she comes back for me. Even then, I don't want to leave. Not Brad, not my home, not my school, none of it. I love it here. Thought Mom did, too.I'm 15! Had a totally purple birthday: balloons, purple bed sheets and covers, purple flip-flops, and a sparkly purple swimsuit from Mom. Brad got me you–he knows I love to write stuff–and a Jane Austen book (we watched the movie and he thought I'd enjoy the book). He made grape-flavored popcorn (purple, of course), and we watched the movie The Color Purple.

I swear I'm not going to be anything like Mom: pregnant at 16, a high school drop-out, a waitress barely able to make ends meet, and a woman unable to settle down to a normal family life. And I totally won't ever abandon my child.

OMG! I totally forgot that Brad must hurt, too. I'll take over Mom's chores and cook our dinners. When Mom comes back, I'll try to convince her to marry him.

Elena Cristina Ford

The days ran together in a blur. Then school was out, and Elena lined up babysitting jobs and otherwise kept busy doing chores around the home and Brad's auto garage. She opened a savings account at the bank and dreamed of college. She read avidly and wrote short stories, which she tried out only on Merlin. He never complained, and that fanned the flames of her self-confidence.

Brad took her often to visit his sister and his brothers, all married, two with young children. His parents treated her like a younger Foster child. The weeks ran together, and the deep-sad sense of abandonment eased as the Foster family adopted her as one of their own. Her stutter receded and her determination to be a track star pulled her forward. Brad helped her figure out a training regimen for track. His interest in physical fitness included an interest in physical therapy, and he often studied the field when he had time. Elena asked him why he hadn't gone to college. He had attended the University of Virginia for two years; she found out but didn't think it was productive. Plus. he had a passion for fixing cars and trucks. Once he had the auto repair garage up and running, there was not much time for anything else.

Brad was happy and she could learn from that: follow your dreams, follow your heart. But be practical and smart about it.

Even as her heart ached for her mother, she considered the possibility that she was better off without her. Fortunately, she had been left with Brad Foster, a fixer of broken things.

THE FIERCE NANAS CLUB
by Elvy Howard, Blue Ridge Writers, 2nd Place

Lecia Maye Donahue Johnson Park Staunton stood in the doorway of her daughter's kitchen and stared at her daughter's shoulder blades, moving under a tight-fitting athletic shirt while she washed dishes.

Lecia's narrowing eyes were trying to decode her daughter's thinness as a sign of health or veering dangerously into something else. It was a calculation her daughter wouldn't have allowed had she'd known of it.

Everything had to be washed by hand because Vonnie wouldn't allow her mother to repair or replace the dishwasher. It hadn't worked in months, which was a source of annoyance to Lecia, who, after all, was the one who washed most of the dishes.

Balancing a shiny colander on top of plates and pans in the dish drain, Vonnie hadn't yet noticed her mother or her mother's calculating stare.

Lecia's therapist insisted if she wanted to work on her relationship with Vonnie, she must cease any criticism of her daughter and engage only in positive interactions. Sometimes this edict left Lecia with little to say. Lecia's progress on this goal was charted daily in a journal and brought to counseling sessions. *But how was anyone supposed to stop their critical thoughts?* Lecia wondered.

Remaining unnoticed wasn't possible for long. Colorful cats began circling Lecia's ankles while Tina, the Chihuahua, jumped from her basket beside the stove and clicked across the tile floor. Her clicking nails alerted the other dogs, who scrabbled up scarred wooden steps from the downstairs family room and poured into the kitchen. Lecia was swamped in fur when Vonnie turned around.

"Hey Mom, where are you going all dressed up?"

Feeding various animals tiny treats, Lecia said, "You know."

"No, I don't. I wouldn't have asked if I did."

Bent over the smaller dogs to pass out their treats while shooing away the bigger ones, Lecia buried her face in pelts. In a whiny voice, the one she hated, she said, "You know where I'm going, that meeting." Straightening, she roughly brushed off her jeans.

Vonnie stared, sighed, and turned back to her dishes. "Oh, yeah. I forgot. What your therapist told you to do."

"Right."

"The therapist you go to since you cracked up."

"C'mon, Vonnie. I didn't crack up, and you know it."

The thin woman at the sink turned again. "Well, whatever you want to call it, it must have scared the hell out of you if you're willing to go this far."

Lecia desperately searched for something positive to say, some straw she could offer the moment. The only response she could think of was despicable. "Maybe you're right about that."

Vonnie locked eyes with her mother, a curious expression on her face. "Well, you look nice."

"Thanks, but I'm not dressed up."

"You've got makeup on."

"Well, yeah." Lecia looked at the clock on the wall. It was from the house on Huckleberry Lane when she was still trying to create a family. The clock told her she had half an hour to kill before it was time to leave. "Want me to let them out?"

"Yes, please."

Lecia took diapers off a Boston bull terrier named Sally and let her and the rest of the herd, minus the cats, out the back door to a screened-in porch. Patrick, the Irish setter, was in the lead when she opened the screen door, waving his tail like a flag to encourage his platoon. Two boy Labradors penned at the back of the fenced-in yard barked their greetings as the rest of the canines followed Patrick down wooden steps and spilled onto muddy grass patched with snow.

Lecia thought about hiking across the yard to let out the Labradors, but didn't want to ruin her suede boots or have muddy Labrador feet jumping on her. Sighing, she shut the screen door and wrapped her sweater tighter. Patrick raced away, his red coat blazing against snow and patches of green grass.

Vonnie would let the Labs out later. Vonnie was an excellent caretaker of all creatures. Going back inside, the steamy warmth of the kitchen was welcome. Vonnie still washed dishes. Without turning, she said, "Hey, Mom?"

"Yeah?"

"Did you let out Frick and Frack?"

"No, sorry." It was impossible not to hear them barking.

"That's okay. I'll go out in a minute."

"The boys still asleep?"

Vonnie glanced at a monitor on the windowsill. "Yes, thank God. I'm hoping to get this pile done before they wake up."

A twinge of guilt struck Lecia because she'd thought about doing those dishes earlier when Vonnie was at Church and hadn't even though she was responsible for the mountain of dirty dishes and pots.

It had taken nearly a week to talk Vonnie into having the dinner party and getting her to invite two childhood friends and their husbands. Vonnie was much better at hanging onto people than her mother was. Along with Vonnie's husband, Charles, there'd been six for dinner.

"Last night was great, Mom. Thanks again for making me have some fun."

Lecia noticed steam from the sink, curling Vonnie's hair around her face and reminding her mother of the adorable toddler she'd been. "I'm glad it was a good time. You two deserved a night off."

Lecia had catered the affair with a Greek salad, a leg of lamb, hummus, Mediterranean green beans, rosemary-garlic crusted roasted red potatoes, and a basket of good, crunchy rolls. They had four bottles of an inexpensive yet delicious red wine to accompany the meal. Dessert was a warm apple tart with vanilla ice cream, and the pastry was the only thing leftover from the meal.

Lying in bed and listening to adult laughter coming through the walls for the first time since she'd moved in, Lecia had smiled into the dark. She'd fallen into a sleep as deep as the twins in their cribs, listening to men's deep bass, joyously loud, and screams of laughter from women. Lecia's last thought before dropping off was *making merry.*

Realizing Vonnie had no idea what time she had to leave, Lecia said, "I'd better get going," and left.

Even when taking the scenic route and avoiding all highways, Lecia arrived at an Episcopalian Church forty-five minutes early on another cold, gloomy February day. Pulling a zip-lock plastic bag from her purse, she began beading.

Upon discovering the incompatibility of caring for her grandbabies and sewing, Lecia stumbled into making beaded pocketbooks. The piece she worked on was indigo silk in a hoop. Pearls and crystals nestled against white silk ribbon embroidered in paisley shapes.

Lecia was the type of person who could lose herself in spatial problems and was soon absorbed with the question of where to put three oversized oblong pearls and how much to surround them with smaller round pearls. The clutch would be a one-of-a-kind item in a specialty shop and destined to be owned by someone wealthy.

A car door slammed, and Lecia's head jerked up, having never heard the electric car arrive. An older, tired-looking couple holding onto each other maneuvered across the buckling asphalt.

Lecia imagined telling her therapist she couldn't go inside. She'd say something like, "I got there, but I couldn't go in. I don't know why."

And then Selena would grill her until she confessed to whatever emotion it was she didn't want to know about right then. She took a deep breath and opened the damned door. Two cars pulled in and parked nearby. Neither of their female occupants looked at Lecia. Both began walking toward the same side door of the Church the older couple had entered. Lecia put her work back in its bag and wished to zip her anxiety in as easily. She got out of her car.

Wondering what emotion Selena would uncover if Lecia could not make it across the parking lot, her anxiety increasing with each step, Lecia hobbled on. *What's the worst that could happen?* She argued with no one. *So what if I'm bored for an hour? What is the big damn deal? Why in the hell am I so scared? It's insane to be freaking out over a stupid 12-step meeting.*

Lecia didn't recall "feeling like absolute shit" as an emotion on Selena's chart when discussing her life. She was sure it should have been listed somewhere between mourning and desperation.

Selena believed denial was Lecia's most significant issue and insisted she attend two Adult Children of Alcoholics and Dysfunctional Families meetings before their next appointment. Selena said ACA would help Lecia grasp the damage done in families like hers, not only the family she came from but also the ones she tried to make.

Lecia believed Selena might be her most significant issue. Voices came from down a dark hall. Lecia stood where light from a window allowed her to brush the fur of varying colors off her tan cashmere coat. Despite what she'd said to Vonnie, she worried she might be too dressed up after all. Her longish white hair was French braided to the base of her neck. A bandana wrapped the bottom of the braid, and her silver earrings were probably too big and shiny. The denim shirt might tone it down some, but her long knit vest was dramatic. None of it mattered, though. She had committed to this. Lecia lifted her chin and went to where the voices led.

Two women placed chairs in a circle. The older couple sat next to each other as the chairs went around them in a ring. A short, gray-haired lady pulled pamphlets and books from a plastic bin and placed them on a table. She laughed at something the other woman said. When she noticed Lecia in the doorway, she straightened and came near, saying, "Hi there, didn't see you. My name's Tubby. Is this your first meeting?"

"Tubby?"

"Yeah, long story. My real name's Susan, but everyone calls me Tubby."

Lecia realized Tubby was waiting for a response. "Um, yes. This is my first meeting. This is ACA, right?" Embarrassment was an emotion she could identify. She didn't deny all her feelings, and that proved it.

"You're in the right place." Tubby went back to her plastic bin. Pulling an envelope from it, she brought it to Lecia. "First 12-step meeting ever?"

"Yes."

Shocked by the fingers suddenly gripping her upper arm, Lecia froze and looked into friendly hazel eyes. Tubby said, "Good for you. The first step is always the hardest." She handed Lecia the envelope. "This is a newcomer's packet. Lots of good information in it."

Feeling like a fraud, Lecia wanted to say, *I'm only here because my therapist made me come,* but she knew how that would sound and could not think of an alternative.

Tubby grinned. "Brand new. Isn't that just wonderful?"

Certain she wasn't wonderful, Lecia only stared at the older woman dressed in casual slacks, a loose top, and a baggy oversized cardigan. She had short, gray hair and wore dangling cat earrings.

Tubby didn't appear to notice Lecia's silence. "I know you have a lot of questions. Let's speak after the meeting, okay?"

"Sure. Thanks."

"See you after the meeting, then."

Women trickled in. One of them hugged Tubby and began speaking in low tones.

Anxious, embarrassed, and fraudulent. I should write it down, so I don't forget. Lecia took a seat across from the older couple.

More women and two men filtered in, all of them chatting precisely as people did before any function Lecia ever attended. It was weird how matter-of-fact they were.

At their last session, Selena told Lecia she didn't have to speak. She only had to show up and listen.

"Hi everyone, I'm going to start the meeting now. My name is Velda, and I welcome you to the Serenity Sunday group."

The room hushed as everyone claimed seats. Lecia's attention wandered as Velda, sitting next to Tubby, read from a notebook. The group was primarily women. Lecia counted seventeen people in all. Some were sitting by themselves, some in a group like she found herself in—and no one looking blatantly weird. Stumbling through The Serenity Prayer, which everyone said in unison, called her away from checking out the group.

"Do we have any newcomers?" Velda asked, looking directly at Lecia.

Lecia, wondering about the whole anonymity thing twelve-step programs were famous for, said, "Yes, me."

"New to this meeting, or ACA?"

"To ACA."

"Welcome."   "Thank you."

Tubby nudged Velda with her elbow. "I already gave her a packet."

"Good. Let's get on with it."

Then came the introductions, something else Lecia thought odd from a group theoretically promoting anonymity. Velda began. "Hi, I'm Velda."

Tubby responded, "Hi, Velda." She turned to the woman on her other side and said, "I'm Tubby." And the introductions continued around the circle.

"Hi, Pam." The person next to Lecia said, who then turned to Lecia, saying, "I'm Bobbi."

And, even though she had watched intently as this process repeated itself, Lecia got flustered and said, "Hi Bobbi, my name is Lecia Staunton."

"We don't use last names," Bobbi hissed.

"Hi Lecia," a young pregnant woman on the other side of Lecia said before turning to her neighbor, saying. "I'm Stephanie." And the intros continued just as if Lecia hadn't made a giant ass of herself.

Velda and Tubby looked to be the same age, roughly ten years older than Lecia's fifty-seven. Velda read from her notebook. It looked as if others silently followed from the same booklet Lecia found in her seat. Peering over Bobbi's shoulder, Lecia located the page number they were reading, and just in the nick of time before again, they went round-robin, reading the twelve steps. Then read a laundry list that was unnerving in describing issues Lecia recognized.

A tired-looking, overweight, middle-aged woman was evidently in charge of the meeting's program and began by saying, "Hi, I'm Margie, a very grateful ACA. Today's reading spoke to me. In fact, it nearly knocked me off my toilet seat this morning." Everyone laughed. Lecia smiled and wasn't sure why. "It was about working the program."

She held up a small yellow book. "And I realized I was exactly as they described." She looked at Velma and grinned. "That's why I called someone in charge of today's program and asked to take her place. Thanks, Velma."

"Not a problem," Velma said.

"Anyway, I'd already decided on not coming today, which is why I'm here talking to you now."

More chuckles. Lecia thought they might as well have been speaking Urdu for all she understood.

"The reading defines what it means to work the program."

Margie read a passage and then said, "I do not go to meetings regularly, yet I believed my disappointment with the program was its fault and not mine. I do not have anyone, sponsor or fellow traveler, to partner with and get honest feedback and support from, and the biggest one, and the one I hated admitting to the most, was realizing I didn't have a real relationship with a higher power."

The woman looked around the circle. "I thought I did, but it hit me I was as superficial and distant in that relationship as I was in all areas of working the program." Tears began. "I played at being spiritual. I was never spiritual at all."

Someone brought Margie a box of tissues and silently went back to their chair. Margie grabbed a handful and wiped her face. "So, that's my topic for today. Working the program, are we worth it?"

The similarities between Margie and herself struck Lecia. Even with her Yoga classes and stabs at meditation, she'd never thought beyond getting through the next hurdle. Her entire life, she'd vacillated between wondering if there was a God to feeling like there had to be some sort of Supreme Being. It was a question she'd never really answered.

They went round-robin again, each person speaking thoughtfully about areas they could do better in

Tubby's turn arrived. She took a deep breath and exhaled before saying, "I've been in this program a long time, and it always amazes me how our eyes are opened in our own time, and not before. Last week someone close to me said something that really hurt. It was totally unexpected, and I was blindsided for a bit. I think my emotions went into lockdown or something because even though I was reeling from her comments, I made it out of this person's house without showing how upset I was." She took another deep breath. "She still doesn't know and probably never will how hurt I was." Tubby smiled. "At first, of course, I was more pissed off than hurt. I knew I was triggered, and it took me two days to get past it." She held up her hands. "But I was good to myself. I canceled all my plans and took walks, watched movies, tried not to overeat." She laughed. A few others did too.

"So yesterday, I'm finally feeling like myself again, and I call a good friend in the program to help me look at it, and I got to see again the damned abandonment stuff I grew up with. I had to see it could still define me as deserving rejection, which, trust me, feels like absolute crap." Tubby paused. "I'm seventy years old. I've been in this program forever, but there's still plenty of room for me to grow. I can recognize when I'm triggered and remind myself, I'm not the worst person in the world. With help, I can look at myself and heal instead of starting wars. It's humbling to see, and I'm so glad to have this group and the support of this program."

Lecia wondered if a fog had invaded her brain. She couldn't ever remember being deeply moved while not understanding why. She noticed a few women in the group furiously scribbling in small notebooks and wished she had one.

Whenever anyone finished speaking, others thanked them. Margie's opening was roundly received with lots of "Glad you are here's" and some applause, but Tubby's almost got a standing ovation.

A woman next to Tubby began sharing. "Hi. My name is Jennifer." Lecia focused on everything Jennnifer said, trying to sort through her comments.

"Anyway, that's when I realized what I'd thought was letting go was actually putting up walls, and that's when I learned how to truly let go with love." The woman named Jennifer smiled, and despite her efforts to understand, Lecia did not have an inkling why.

A bunch of "thanks, Jennifer" was offered, and a man was next. He cleared his throat and spoke. "Hi, I'm Nick."

"Hi, Nick," nearly all replied. Lecia noticed no wedding ring.

He rubbed his eyes. "Wow, powerful stuff. I'm just glad to be here, thanks, and I'll pass."

The woman next to him spoke. "Hi, I'm Pam."

After Pam was Bobbi, who was next to Lecia, and Lecia's palms began to sweat.

"As y'all know, I've only been coming here a little while."

Lecia listened intently, hoping for an indication of what a newbie might say.

"But today's program and sharing have helped so much. I'm so grateful to be here."

For what? Lecia's hands clenched in her lap, and she consciously relaxed them.

"I didn't want to come today, but now I see it's the exact thing I needed. And with that, I pass."

A few people said, "Thanks, Pam."

Bobbi, who Lecia had decided from her black spiked hair, black leather jacket, and black laced-up boots, was probably a lesbian biker chick near Lecia's age, spoke next. "I was wondering, listening to all of you, what a person is supposed to do when there is nothing in them that *wants* to let go." The vehemence in the woman's voice was startling.

"This morning, I was thinking I'd about had it with the crazy person in my life and came here today not wanting to hear about letting the fuck go, much less let go with love."

Dropping an "F" bomb in a church was a new experience for Lecia.

"So I'm sitting here, and it feels like a set-up, right?"

A few people nodded. Lecia could only wonder *how?*

"And then it occurs to me, all I have to do is to be *willing* to let go."

Bobbi smiled. She had a dazzling smile that nearly ruined the biker chick image. A few others smiled, too, and Lecia flat out didn't know why.

"And with that, I pass."

Bobbi's satisfied expression turned to Lecia, and she realized with an old dread, probably originating in elementary school, it was her turn.

"I guess I, um, was forced into letting go of my husband when he died. He drank too much. He did drugs, too, when my back was turned, but not that often." Lecia stared at the floor, knowing her cheeks were bright red. "I'm here because my therapist told me to come to two meetings this week. I had a meltdown." She forced her head to lift. "Not a bad one. It just had never happened before. I started crying and couldn't stop for a while. But the twins. Oh, I take care of my twin grandsons. They are only a few months old, can you imagine? But anyway, I'm here. I'm still not sure why." Feeling all of eight-years-old, and aware of how inane she'd sounded, Lecia looked back at the floor until nudged by Bobbi's elbow. "Say you pass," she whispered.

"I what?" Lecia looked at her.

"Do you pass?"

"On what?"

"Are you done speaking?"

"Yes. Oh, yes. I pass."

The rest of the meeting was a blur. A collection basket was passed around, and donations were made. Lecia put in two dollars as she'd seen others do. She was grateful when it was time to stand but startled when Bobbi grabbed her hand. The woman, *what was her name?* On the other side of Lecia, did the same.

Lecia stumbled through the Serenity Prayer a second time, and her hands were dropped. It was over. Separate groups formed. Lecia turned to get her coat and pocketbook off the back of her chair when someone tapped her shoulder.

"Did I hear you say you were a grandma?" Tubby asked.

"Yes, six-month-old twin grandsons."

"Are you're raising them?"

"No, I keep them during the day. My daughter and her husband are veterinarians. They both work long hours with a new business and all that." Lecia was exhausted. Maybe she'd go home and take a nap.

"Well, what did you think?"

"Think?"

"Of the meeting?"

"Oh. Um, wow. It's a lot to take in."

"It sure is. Hey, a bunch of us grandmas go for a late lunch after the meeting. I wonder if you'd like to come?"

"Where?" Lecia asked to stall. It was the last thing she wanted to do after her stupid outburst.

"We meet at Rosie's. It's close enough to walk."

"Sure. Thanks. I'll meet you there," Lecia said, obeying her therapist's other mandate. If anyone asked her to do something after a meeting, she had to go. No matter what. If a homeless person with no teeth asked to speak to her outside, Lecia was to accompany them. Lecia fervently wished I could still tell a lie.

Rosie's was familiar. Her second husband, Paul, had bought their first house nearby. She'd walked every one of those old, uneven sidewalks, knowing the jouncing stroller would put Vonnie to sleep. The place hadn't changed. The same vinyl red-and-white checked tablecloths, the same dusty photos and paintings of roses on the walls, and the same black and white tiled floor greeted her. The straw-wrapped Chianti bottles with layers of colored wax were gone, and the furniture more worn. Still, it was like walking into the past.

The table where they always sat with baby Vonnie, food scattered everywhere around her highchair, and Paul making it okay with a big tip, was still by the entrance. It was where they'd share a bottle of cheap wine, and Lecia would have the lovely walk home to look forward to — pushing Vonnie in her stroller with her big man at her side.

Velma, Tubby, Bobbi, *Bobbi's a grandmother? Maybe she's not a lesbian biker after all,* and another women were at a round table near the back. They gestured at Lecia, who sat in the only available chair, which was, unfortunately, next to Bobbi. A woman whose name she couldn't remember was on the other side. "Hi, thanks for asking me. I used to come here all the time, but I bet it's been over twenty years." Lecia hated the quaver in her voice.

Tubby, across from Lecia, leaned forward, a big, disarming grin on her face. "We call ourselves The Fierce Nana's Club."

"How come?"

"Because we aren't intending to go gently into that good night."

"Oh." Lecia couldn't think of another thing to say. A headache was on its way. She hoped her therapist would appreciate the lengths she went to accomplish the tasks Selena assigned.

The not-Bobbi woman sitting next to her was talking about a prickly co-worker. Velma and Tubby nodded as she spoke.

Lecia couldn't see how any of it, from saying only supportive things to Vonnie or going to ACA or having lunch with these wounded women, helped. All it did was add more stress to her life, and she wondered how long it would take to regroup from the afternoon.

A waitress mercifully appeared. Lecia scanned the menu, which also hadn't changed, and ordered an old favorite, spanakopita. She longed for a glass of Chardonnay to go with it. The group chatted about people they knew. Lecia didn't follow. She didn't have to. She only had to be there, a non-entity among other unknowns, and be ready to argue with Selena about how this could be useful. Someone spoke her name.

"Huh?" Lecia said.

"I asked what you thought of the meeting." Tubby was speaking to her.

"Oh. I, um, was really confused."

Tubby nodded in agreement. "I think we all are at first. It's a lot to take in."

Lecia's eyes involuntarily darted to the front of the restaurant, and she couldn't stop them. She forced her eyes to stare at the tabletop and her lungs to breathe. She tried to think of something to say. "My dad was an alcoholic, and two husbands were as well." Lecia never included Vaughn in those statistics, even though he was drunk when causing the accident that killed him. He'd been so young; she'd never thought it fair to label him. "My therapist believes coming to this group will help me." She looked up.

"But what do *you* think?" Tubby's warm eyes stared into hers.

"Mostly, I don't know what to think. I've been widowed twice, and I used to come here with my second husband." Lecia was horrified by the admission and by her eyes again zooming to the front of the restaurant. Filled with shame, she looked back at the table and wondered what she'd say next. She put her elbows on the table and pushed her temples with both fists. "I'm sorry, I think I'm getting a migraine." "My, gosh, Lecia. We had no idea. We could have gone somewhere else," the not-Bobbi woman said, placing a hand on her arm.

It hadn't occurred to Lecia the restaurant could be the cause of her peculiar behavior. Her head snapped up as the headache vanished.

Lecia noticed her vision was clearer, the red curtains brighter, even the plastic flowers on the table appeared more attractive. "That's okay. I'm here now. *This is the strangest afternoon I've had in a long, damn time.* I just didn't expect it to hit me so hard."

"How long has it been since he passed?" Bobbi asked.

"He died in two-thousand-eight," Lecia said.

"That must have been tough, right smack at the beginning of the recession," Tubby said.

Lecia looked at her. "You have no idea. I think cleaning up the huge financial mess he left kept me sane for a while."

"Well, no wonder you were triggered by being here."

Lecia relaxed into Tubby's motherly voice.

Bobbi asked, "Did you get a phone list?"

"A phone list? No."

"Tubby, do you have an extra in your pocketbook? All I've got on me is a debit card."

"Of course." Tubby dug in a large pocketbook and withdrew a half-sheet of paper. She handed it to Lecia.

"Do you have a pen?" Bobbi asked, and Tubby rummaged again, handing it over. Bobbi wrote *The Fierce Nanas* at the top and starred her name, Tubby's, Velma's, and Gracie N., which had to be the woman's name on Lecia's other side. "Call any of us, anytime. If we can't talk right then, don't worry, we'll get back to you."

"Okay, sure thing, thanks." Lecia tucked it in her bag.

"So tell us about your grandchildren."

"I have twin grandsons, six months old."

"I was a twin," said Gracie.

"I didn't know that? Did you?" Tubby said, turning to Velma.

"No, I didn't."

"We weren't identical, and she died when we were sixteen."

Murmurs of condolences went around the table.

"Yeah, I still miss her. Since I've been coming to meetings, I think about her more than I have in years."

The waitress interrupted, arriving with their meals.

Lecia found it pleasant to chat with a group of older women like herself in a familiar place on a gloomy Sunday afternoon. They left as a group, and she was glad for the company as they passed the table where her family used to sit—the one with the ghosts of Paul, their youth, and her only baby around it.

Beyond the Window

by Gwendolyn Poole, Blue Ridge Writers, 3rd Place

I changed the linens on Mistress Pearson's bed, polished the furniture, emptied her chamber pot, and washed the windows. I can still hear her words, "I want this room spotless upon my return this afternoon. Do you understand, Lucy?"

 Having completed the work, I took the liberty of resting my feet a spell as I sat at the writing desk and let my gaze fall on what I could see beyond the opened window.

Twenty-two years ago, I was born on the Campbell Plantation during the harvest season in Rockingham County, North Carolina. I was given the name of Lucille, but everybody called me Lucy. Although I was born to my ebony-colored mother, Drusilla, there was no denying that I was the child of Thaddeus Campbell. My light complexion, hazel eyes, and square jaw left no room for doubt. Everyone on the plantation knew the truth, even Mistress Campbell.

After Massa Campbell's death eight years ago, Mistress Campbell sold several slaves, including me and Ma, to Mr. John Pearson. That's how come we ended up here in Franklin County, Virginia. Well, Massa Pearson and Missus Adelaide are not as cruel to their slaves as the Campbells and their overseer had been. Seems like the biggest concern of Massa Campbell was that the work on his tobacco farm ran smoothly. There's big money in tobacco farming, you see.

Here on the Pearson Plantation, I work in the Big House and tend to the needs of my mistress and her young daughter, Evelyn. Every day, I have to "avail myself to the Missus…" Massa would say. Ma labors in the fields from sunup to sundown every day 'cept Sunday. Works hard too; hands stay blistered most days and back hurts her something awful I hear tell from Silas, the cook. He say that most nights after pulling tobacco all day in the hot sun, she can hardly stand upright. Makes me ashamed to complain 'bout having to clean this whole house, with Nellie's help of course, and looking after the Missus and little Evelyn. Late at night I lay in my little bed in my room just off the pantry in the Big House and think 'bout Ma sleeping on her mat on the dirt floor of the little cabin down in the slave quarters. This slavery thing is evil.

Evil. That's what I heard one day while I stood outside the mercantile, waiting for my mistress. A few men stood talking to some of the townspeople. Those men didn't talk like the men from 'round here and didn't dress like'em either. When I asked Missus Adelaide 'bout'em, she went on 'bout how they're just Northern abolitionist and for me to dismiss anything I heard them say 'cause they're only down here to start trouble for us.

Sitting here by the second-story bedroom window in the stillness of this afternoon without hearing the whine of my mistress' voice calling for me is heavenly. I see Chloe hanging clothes on the line. The fields are damp from the early morning shower, but the dozen or so field hands are working throughout the north field. I see Ma. She must be picking fat worms off the tobacco leaves. The overseer, Lucius, we call Lucifer when he's not within earshot, guides his horse in Ma's direction and stops. She places a hand on the small of her back as she straightens to look up at him. Ma nods, points, and looks down the row she has just worked. He looks in that direction, then taps his heels to get the horse to continue. I exhale. Ma's gaze follows him for a few seconds before she bends again. My heart aches for her, for all of us.

When will we be free? When will this life be…? A little bird, God's perfect creation, lands on the windowsill, so young and seemingly carefree with its soft chirping. Its freedom only reminds me of my bondage. I am not free to fly away, not free to roam and explore new places, new things.

I whisper to the little bird, "Where will you go today, Little Birdie? What plans do you have since you have all the freedom in the world?" It pushes out its rust-colored chest and chirps its answer to me. I lean forward and ask, "When you fly away, will you take me with you and Ma too?" Little Birdie flies away without me but, my thoughts and dreams fly away with it.

As I soar with Little Birdie beyond the window, I am free. In my mind's eye, I see myself leave the Pearson farm. I am not stopped by the overseer. I do not run away like so many did from the Campbell Plantation. I do not get a pass to show the patty rollers. I do not steal away in cover of darkness, afraid, cold, hungry, running, running, running. I do not watch for snakes near the water's edge or listen for the master's hounds tracking my scent. I do not check for the moss on the trees and travel only by night. And the drinking gourd is beautiful to look at in the night sky, but I do not need to follow it. My feet are like Little Birdie's wings and allow me to move in any direction I choose.

Beyond the window is a new life for me and Ma. We travel on rail cars and choose our own seats. We decide where we want to live and it is not on some massa's plantation. We live in Philadelphia or perhaps New York where people with dark skin walk the streets of freedom, dressed in their finery, walking straight and tall, no bent backs and no "yassuh or no suh." There are no auction blocks here, no humiliation of being touched, handled, and sold to the highest bidder… no more whips and chains, no more scarred backs. We see people with brown skin who are business owners. We gather to worship in churches where we don't have to sit in the balcony. We no longer have to gather in the woods and brush arbor to secretly sing our praises. We spend many days in a parlor sipping cool drinks and being delighted by great piano solos.

In Canada, we sit and dine with Queen Victoria at the same table, not in the kitchen, mind you. The meal is served on the Queen's fine china. The food is cooked to perfection. We wear elegant dresses, beautiful jewelry, and Ma's thick hair is fixed up so nice with ribbons and cowrie shells that make her look just like an African queen, our own people.

Ma stands tall now, no stooped shoulders or calloused hands. She purchases a beautiful house for us, just as grand as any Big House and it is ours. Ma speaks up for herself and does not drop her head or eyes as she handles her business. She is a proud woman and I am happy for her. No more cleaning for the Mistress; I clean our own house.

No more working in someone else's fields; we have our own land now. We have nice clothes, and more than one pair of shoes. I see us both in school learning to read and write. I like the feel of books and their smell is divine. And the best part is that we will not be punished for holding a book. No one has papers on me and Ma. We are free and freedom is good to us.

Beyond the window I see Ma's fancy little hat shop. It's called Drusilla's Millinery. She has many styles of hats too; some come from Paris, France. The ladies, black and white, come in to browse and swoon over the great selection Ma has. The sales are great and Ma makes lots of money working for herself. She has the key to her store and when she locks up, we walk arm-in-arm down the sidewalk. People, black and white, greet us with a smile. The men folk even tip their hats. We ride back to our beautiful home in our well-made, but modest carriage.

As I soar beyond the window, I don't look back. I don't think about the ills of slavery, this peculiar institution they call it. It's mighty peculiar all right; one man owning another just like he owns his horses and pigs. I focus my attention on what lies ahead, what opportunities we have. Even the air smells fresher and the sun shines brighter when freedom is on our side. I'm certain life is better beyond this window, it has got to be.

The sharp tone of Silas' voice interrupts my thoughts. "Lucy! You dreaming again, Gal?" I turn to see him standing in the doorway, apron around his waist and a large spoon in his hand.

"Oh, Silas, you frightened me," I say as I stand. "I was dreaming of a betta place," I explain.

"Well, right now, we be's in dis here place, so come on down and help wit' de supper. Massa an' de Missus be home soon an' de absolute last thing you want dem to see is you sittin' here dreaming. You know Massa Pearson reminds us dat idle hands are de devil's workshop. Got dat from de Good Book, he say. Dat could be de cause for a severe punishment." He pauses, then continues with a softer tone, "I used to dream. I could see myself bein' on my own, goin' places where everythin' is fresh, where I be free. I gave up dat dream, don't dream no more. What's de use? All dat talk 'bout de war; Massa and his friends say de war s'pose to set de slaves free. Well, de war's been goin' on for over a year now, an' we ain't free yet. So stop your dreaming an' help me wit' dis meal 'fore de family gits back home."

I hear Silas make his way down the stairs. I turn back and lean out the window just enough to see Ma working much farther in the field than before. A few others are working in the heat of the day all over the grounds and the water boy is busy making his rounds. There's so much sadness here. Tonight, the slaves will gather down in the quarters to do their own work before the end of the day. I love to hear the faint sounds of the harmonica and fiddle when the slaves dare to take time to relax, laugh, and maybe dance after nightfall. I want to share those times with them, rather than be held hostage here in the Big House. They are my people and I belong with them.

I didn't realize how long I sat looking out the window, but it was a beautiful journey to a place called freedom. Silas is right, I don't want to be caught wasting time and bring 'bout a punishment. My eyes search for Little Birdie, who is nowhere to be found, probably far away from this wretched place. Little Birdie is free. I only wish I could be like Little Birdie and enjoy life beyond the window.

THE BEST DISASTER EVER
by L. Andrew Ball, Chesapeake Bay Writers, 3rd Place

Looking back, I guess I really should have told Mom. But Grandpa said we should keep it a secret between just the two of us, and of course I told him I would. Me 'n Grandpa often used to have secrets; I kept them inside me like candies you keep in your pocket: little packets of happiness. But it's difficult, isn't it? When you've made a promise that seemed like a good idea at the time, and then you start to wonder about it.

But this was last year, of course. I'd only just started in first grade and really knew nothing. Back then, I was so naïve! That's a word Grandpa taught me; it's one of my favorites, 'cos it's got these two little eyes peeking at you like over the garden fence. Grandpa told me what they're called — the eyes — but I don't remember. And another reason I like it is because only girls like me can be naïve; boys have to be naïf instead, Grandpa said. Isn't that cool?

Anyway, if Grandpa did something like that *this* year, I'd tell Mom right away. He and Gran had come to live with us a long time ago — back when I was in kindergarten — which was good 'cos it meant there was always someone to talk to when I got home after school, and a lot more laughing than there is now. For my sixth birthday, Gran gave me a teddy bear *her* Gran had given to her. It must have been about a zillion years old, and one of its eyes was coming loose, so it had a sort of squint when it looked at you. But I loved it — I still do! It's nice having someone to sleep with, even if he is a zillion years old.

Gran told me his name was Gladly.

"That's a funny name for a bear," I said, and she told me she'd explain when I was a little older. But then one day she decided to go to Heaven instead — maybe she thought the food would be better there — and that left Mom, Grandpa, 'n me all on our own. She'd clean forgotten to tell me how Gladly got his name, and neither Mom nor Grandpa knew. And this year, Grandpa doesn't even remember who *I* am, except on his good days.

I guess I should explain, in case you're wondering, I never had a dad like other kids. Grandpa said that makes me real special — just like the baby Jesus, he said — and I try to feel that way, I really do; but it gets lonely sometimes, particularly now that Grandpa is getting ready to join Gran in Heaven. I can't say I blame him; it's hard to be truly thankful for Mac 'n Cheese *every* night, even with the Lord's help.

And that's why Thanksgiving was going to be such a big deal: real food for once! We discussed the menu over our Mac 'n Cheese for weeks beforehand, it seemed like. Grandpa said he didn't care, so long as we had roast turkey 'n stuffing ...

"Oh, and mashed potatoes 'n gravy, and braised carrots and corn pudding and cranberry sauce and pumpkin pie and ...." Well, you get the idea.

And Mom said she didn't care so long as we had something green for a change. I tried to think of a green food that wasn't a vegetable, but all I could come up with was green marshmallows, and Mom said that wouldn't do. So, in the end, we decided we'd share a Cornish hen, because they didn't make turkeys small enough; have a sweet potato each, because they were cheaper than the real ones; and some broccoli, because I said I'd barf if we had Brussel sprouts.

When the man on TV said the average cost of Thanksgiving Dinner had fallen for the third year in a row, Grandpa said, "Must be because of what *we'll* be spending; they should give us a medal," which made Mom cry; I didn't really understand why.

Back then, there were lots of things I didn't understand, because I was still trying to sort out where Truth came from. Still am, as a matter of fact, although I think I've narrowed it down a bit. I figured there must be *somebody* who knew what was going on; all I needed to do was to work out who it was. I told you I was naïve.

It wasn't Mom, that's for sure: there were mornings when she needed my help just to get out of bed.

Grandpa? Much as I loved him, I had my doubts even back then, and nowadays he doesn't even know which way is up half the time.

My best friend Corey seemed to know lots of stuff — both her parents were teachers, after all — so I figured I could learn a lot from her. That was until the day I told her I'd never had a dad, and she told me how babies were made. I *knew* she was making it up; my mom would *never* do anything like that, not in a zillion years! So, I stopped believing in Corey.

Then there were my schoolteachers, of course; but they were trying to teach me to read and, frankly, they weren't doing a very good job of it.

And TV was no help, either. It all depended on which channel you were watching, and even back then I felt truth shouldn't depend on the click of a remote.

So that was when I turned to the Church. Grandpa and I always went, every Sunday; Mom usually stayed in bed. We both loved the singing, but I found the other bits boring. My favorite hymn was *To be a Pilgrim*, particularly the bit about Hobgoblins and Foul Fiends, but I liked the one about bears, too — you know, the one that goes:

> *Can a woman's tender care*
> *Cease toward that child she-bear?*

I should think *not!* However, my discovery that there were hymns about bears suddenly made church a lot more interesting for me. Could that be where Gladly got his name?

Grandpa said *his* favorite hymn was *Jerusalem, My Happy Home*, which goes:

> *Our Lady sings Magnificat*
> *With tune surpassing sweet;*

And all the Virgins bare their parts,
Sitting about her feet.

That's what it *sounded* like, anyway. Grandpa never explained why he liked that one so much, and now I guess I'll never know.

After the hymns, of course, there were readings from the Bible. I have my doubts about the Bible, to be perfectly honest. Those three Wise Men, for example? I don't think they were wise at all. What were they *thinking* of with those gifts?

Gold? Where could anyone spend it? Didn't they know it was Christmas? All the stores would be closed.

And Frankenstein? Wouldn't that scare the bejesus out of the baby Jesus? (I wonder if that's possible. What would you have left?)

And Myrrh? What *is* that, anyway? Some sort of herb? What? Are they going to cook a meal right there in the stable? The Virgin Mary wouldn't be up to it, not right after having a baby, that's for sure. And stepdad Joseph? There's a loser if ever I met one. I doubt if he could boil an egg.

No, if those men had really been wise they'd have brought a pacifier, to give Mary and Joseph a bit of peace on earth; some disposable diapers; and maybe a mobile to hang up over the manger. One of those cool ones that plays *Jingle Bells.* The baby Jesus would've loved that.

Anyway, there we were, me 'n Grandpa, in church one Sunday morning, when suddenly, this hymn I'd never heard before came up:

Keep Thou my all, O Lord, hide my life in Thine;
O let Thy sacred light over my pathway shine;
Kept by Thy tender care, Gladly the cross-eyed bear.

Hear Thou and grant my prayer, hide my life in Thine.

It was Gran, talking to me, directly from Heaven! She'd kept her promise and was telling me where Gladly got his name; I should have guessed.

After that, my devotion to the Church was absolute. The Minister had my undivided attention every Sunday. At last, I knew *this* was where I would find the Truth.

My favorite bit of church is when the Minister stops being the Minister and turns back into a normal person — it's like magic! Reminds me of that bit in *The Wizard of Oz,* when Toto pulls back the curtain; and our minister did it *really* well. At the end of the service, he'd look up and smile at us, sitting in rows in front of him, like we were in a school bus, and ask if anyone had any announcements to make.

Grandpa and I usually sat glued to our pew while other people got up and talked about bake sales, and quilting parties, and weed-whacking the graveyard, and so on. But the Sunday before last Thanksgiving, to my astonishment, Grandpa got up and said:

"Ahem, yes ... My family is having a bit of a celebration this Thanksgiving, and we'd be real pleased if y'all would join us."

Well, *that* got everyone's attention! We live in a small community where everybody knows everybody, but we'd always kept ourselves pretty much to ourselves. I wasn't the only one to be amazed by Grandpa's invitation. On our way back home, I asked: "Shall I tell Mom?"

"No, sweetheart; I'll tell her," he said, which came as a relief, because I didn't think she was going to take it too well.

But as Thanksgiving Day approached, I was surprised that Mom seemed to be her usual self: no fits of crying, no panic attacks, no refusing to get out of bed. It wasn't until the great day dawned that it occurred to me that maybe Grandpa had forgotten to tell Mom — or maybe he'd forgotten he ever extended the invitation in the first place! — and by now it was far too late to do anything about it.

As the neighbors began to arrive, it crossed my mind that this might be a suitable moment for me 'n Gladly to run away from home. Mom was upstairs putting on her face, so she didn't know what was happening, and one look at Grandpa confirmed my worst fears. I was the only one who understood why twenty or thirty strangers were coming up our front path, expecting food. By the time Mom came downstairs, the front room was full to bursting, and people were spilling out into the front hall. Grandpa was nowhere to be seen.

"What on *earth* are all these people doing here?" asked Mom, the familiar signs of panic creeping in around her eyes.

"They've all come to wish us a happy Thanksgiving, Mom; isn't that nice!" I said, hoping to avoid a complete meltdown. She tried to rise to the occasion, greeting people and making polite noises and so on, but I could tell she was waiting for them all to leave again so we could start our meager Thanksgiving dinner.

Of course, our guests were all waiting for the same thing. Who would be the first to crack? I was betting on Mom. Her bottom lip was just beginning to tremble— that telltale sign I knew so well — when the kitchen door opened, and Grandpa stepped out. So *that* was where he'd been hiding!

"Food's ready, folks!" he said cheerfully. "It'll have to be buffet style, so just grab yourself a plate and fill it up."

With 3% of a Cornish hen and 10% of a sweet potato? I thought; *I should have run away from home after all.*

Leaving Gladly to fend for himself, I slipped past Grandpa into the kitchen, heading for the back door ... and stopped dead. I'd never in my life seen so much food in one place outside of a grocery store; certainly not in our kitchen. Our wobbly kitchen table was groaning under the weight of turkeys and hams and potatoes and green beans and corn pudding and broccoli and dinner rolls and pumpkin pie and ... it just went on and on. Giving the Brussel sprouts a wide berth, I headed straight for the green marshmallows. It was truly a miracle.

"Just like the feeding of the five thousand," Grandpa said later, after we'd all stuffed ourselves silly, and all our new friends had left.

I overhead Corey's Mom thanking mine for the party. "Thank you, Mrs. Johnson; that was *lovely! Such* a generous idea!"

"Er... It was nothing," said my mother, smiling faintly through her confusion.

"But I hope you weren't offended by all that food, my dear; some of our neighbors never seem to know when enough's enough. For the life of me, though, I can't *think* who could have brought the Cornish hen. For Thanksgiving? *Really!*"

THE TOW TRUCK DRIVER
by Don Waldy, Hampton Roads, 1ˢᵗ Place

Dirk's battery lost its charge in the parking garage. He must be at the Captain's Choice by five o'clock or lose what he judges as a once-in-a-lifetime romantic opportunity. Dirk is meeting Victoria at Happy Hour.

She is tall, sinewy, and stunning. He claims God sculpted her endless legs. Her brunette hair waves at a passerby. If that does not catch their attention, the four freckles under each sapphire eye reach out and seize them. Women covet those two immaculate reflecting pools for the night's stars.

Upon first gaze, Dirk appreciated that her small bosom was ideal for collaborating with Victoria's appeal. The style of hair complemented the dimensions of her face perfectly. Clothes design was in synchronicity with her body form, and the colors were captivating. Loveliness plus wardrobe gave a flawless presentation. She walked with the zephyr of a goddess. Dirk judged her unrivaled by other candidates at work or in the dating scene. No doubt in his mind she was the match for him. He planned to make it so. They first met at the Captain's Choice, and for the past two months he has been calculating if Victoria was a long-term relationship. This week, he reached his conclusion. Dirk desires to elevate their involvement to be exclusive.

Today, he meets Victoria where they first began, and he has to get his car fixed to get there. His watch shows five o'clock. Screams produce gothic echoes yet do nothing to relieve his anger.

The complex traps him in this foul-smelling, dirty concrete building, with rubbish scattered everywhere. Oil droppings from parked cars dot the floor the same as polka dots on a stone canvas. A breeze brings urine-scented air to his nostrils. He takes long, controlled breaths, encouraging himself to think positive thoughts. His best friend, Rob, tells him that is how one answers life's random and unaccommodating moments.

Dirk yells at walls and ceilings. "How inconvenient! I have to be somewhere important, and you imprison me in cinder-block purgatory." He reaches for the cell phone and makes two calls. The first to a tow truck company to come jump his car, and another to friend Rob.

"Hello, Rob, Dirk here. I am stuck in a parking garage with a dead battery. Victoria and I are meeting at Happy Hour, and I am late because of this car malfunction. You and I discussed how I care for her. She is a *3F*. She has *Finances*, she is a *Fit* in my social world, and she has the resources to help develop and support a *Future* of prosperity for both of us. Intimacy's consideration is secondary to these big three. That darn tow truck driver needs to show up soon."

While holding his cell, physical movements betray anxiety. His free hand jingles change in the pant pocket when not being a finger comb through gel hair. The fidgeting repeats throughout the call.

"Okay, Dirk. I appreciate how important for you to catch up with her. For the past several weeks, you mention her at every chance. I never heard you speak of a contender as you do with Victoria. You and I have been together through grade school, high school, college, and work. We played on the same athletic teams. Our business careers are parallel, but they lace yours with promotions because of your aggressiveness. You turn a *no* into a *yes*. I am a family man who barters doing family chores for two hours of Friday Happy Hour once a month. I receive that as my reward for being a good husband and father. I do not have the knowing to offer you advice."

"Rob, I am having a rough day. Karma is amusing itself by toying with me."

"Do not lose your mind, Dirk. Problems, when anointed with liquor, either go away or are not terrible the next morning. I detect the urgent tone in your voice. As for Victoria, you never used your usual cache of witticisms for a social candidate with her. I stand by to help. Want a ride?"

"No. Thanks for offering. The tow truck driver is coming. I hope he saves my day. He better save my day."

Dirk does not stop peeking at his watch. The hands mock him as they move through their chronology. He wants time to slow down, and his late arrival not judged offensive. They refuse to cooperate and speed up to annoy him.

Dirk sees empty parking spaces on both sides of his car. Pools of oil, antifreeze and condensation have used those spots for their selfish purposes. It looks easy for the driver to maneuver in, hook up the cables, charge his battery, and Dirk is on his way in minutes. At the Captain's Choice, Dirk always brags that a certain bar stool with arm rests has his name on it. His favorite social playground is hospitable, not too chic, and unlike a sports bar. Its ambience blesses members of the digital age. He describes the prices as enticing as a body on a magazine cover. This watering hole functions as a home base for every business group. The female patrons are sociable and confident, secure in branding their brains, looks, and financial independence.

"Hello, Rob, Dirk again. While I am waiting for the tow truck, I need to ask you something that puzzles me as regards Victoria. I know you are at the Captain's Choice, holding a drink, surrounded by cohorts. Got a minute?"

"Go ahead. I will tell my associates I need to take this important call and move away from the group. Give me a few seconds."

"Dirk, I am off to the side. Tell me, what is with you? I have not sensed this unease in you since Monique left you for that hosiery salesman."

"Rob, let us get serious. For over two months, I have been an ardent suitor of Victoria. I find it easy to serve her, and she tells no stories of old boyfriends, no family demands, and no embellishments on the subject of job dissatisfaction. She resembles a Hollywood star. Victoria does not interrupt our conversations by texting or answering calls, and she does not talk to me as if holding a microphone. She does not proclaim omniscience concerning every person or circumstance. She does not declare negative issues as regards anyone. Not as to friends, strangers, relatives, or even coworkers. It does not bother me she never says I am handsome, or that I am smart, or even that I wardrobe in the latest fashions. I do not miss that because everybody tells fibs to gain leverage. My ego allows merging with her money, mind and body."

"I am not sure where you are going with this, Dirk. I am your social historian, having watched you in the dating arena for years. I admired your resilience; still, your Victoria attraction has either slowed you in middle age or convinced you that a stable relationship is in your best interests."

"Hold on, Rob, that might be the tow truck driver now. No, my mistake. Let me continue. I seek a fulfilling relationship. What a coincidence that she is eye candy and comes from money. She has no unreasonable dating requests, no unsolvable man-woman tug-of-war issues. I do not recall her mentioning something she desired I could not deliver. This woman is a real catch."

"Rob, how could this woman still be available, being in her late-thirties, boyfriends except never married, and she is gorgeous and wealthy. I answer that question by saying she is waiting for the perfect match. That is when my ego says, 'That a boy, Dirk, she waits for you.'"

"Dirk, she is not a statue to gape. She is human, is she not? Do not overthink. Just speak to her as you talk to me. Nowadays, that approach is refreshing, considering what goes on out there. Many attempted hookups are an extreme indulgence in sensuality. They get those techniques from the movies, television and the Internet."

"You think I tell her how I feel about us? Thanks for listening and advising. Stay in touch."

A thunderous boom in this stone canyon announces the tow truck. Dirk waves at it in the same way an enthusiastic chorus girl does when a high roller comes into the room. The driver pulls alongside the car and gets out.

Dirk wonders if he sees a likeness of mythic beauty, or is it a hallucination? The driver gets out of the truck, only he is she, with legs elongated to the ground as limbs of a willow tree. Amazement sheens on his flushed face, eyes sparking and radiating as night-lights on a Ferris wheel. She captivates him with her simple, greasy work uniform, the color of azure promises.

Her greeting is brief and discourteous, honed from on-the-job dealings with many people, most of the male gender. "Need a jump?"

"Yes, my keys. I got distracted. Thank goodness I did not lock them in the car."

"You must be a prize at home, too."

"I am, I, I, I am not married and I..."

"Save it."

He sees she enjoys minimizing interaction with a customer. She ignores his gawking by discounting him as another pair of unworthy eyes, comparable to a beauty contest judge.

She brushes him aside and leans into the driver's side window to retrieve his keys. He observes that her work pants fit reminiscent of snow on a mountaintop. And her hair disappoints neither. She tries to hide it under a baseball cap whose emblem says *Best Towing*. Her eyes behave as stars auditioning for a full moon. A work jacket veils her middle body, such as closed drapes do a room. Dirk holds his breath while his imagination opens those drapes. She meets his highest expectations. She works on his car with precise motions, wasting no efforts, enhancing her mystique and spellbinding abilities of a mechanical masseuse.

He recognizes the much-traveled path of his tapered mindset. He presses onward. First, he summons his imaginary social coach for helping him date this extraordinary person. "Coach, proposing a thrilling date is more engaging than offering conversational foreplay at a coffee shop, correct?"

"Forward march."

He probes his coach one more time. "An explicit, nonintrusive message is important in capturing her interest. This blue-collar woman may not be unsociable toward a professional. Do you agree?"

Coach does not respond.

Dirk's adrenaline is flowing as Niagara Falls, and he is rising to the challenge. His line of attack manifests as biblical lightning. "Coach, I use this approach. I refer to my style as, *'The guy on a white horse wearing a black leather jacket.'* To be different creates interest. She converses with men every day, many single-minded types."

He prepares to use his opening. Excitement builds. He begins the delivery. "Up to now, I have never…"

"I am not interested."

Her remark disappoints him. He is a fast thinker, though now he is sitting on his rear, not sure how to overcome her disinterest. Dirk knows he has to deliver a worthy comeback.

"Do not appear so dismayed. I am tired of getting hit on by guys, married or single, whose car I fix. Every one of you is so obvious with your eyes straining beyond their sockets when you see me. I am familiar with it being born in your genes. Do not put me on your bull's-eye or trophy case just yet. I may give myself to one or several, and I may wind up disenchanted when their actions do not match their words of promise. I do not demand they be one hundred percent pure. I keep looking for a man who delivers a relationship that satisfies my needs. Yes, that includes the sex part. A few pimples do not bother me."

Her verbiage communicates never being a prisoner of an unfulfilling relationship, whether it is exclusive or open. His eyes fixate on her. He finds it hard to face elsewhere, if not impossible. The spontaneity of how she describes who she is lures him in smoother than a politician's spiel. He cannot stop himself. He goes as a willing pet at feeding time.

"You are in the group of men who do not have the know-how to react to a woman's declaration of independence. My candidness drowns your blueprint for superiority. Why do men not say what is foremost on their mind? Your face looks blush. Let us talk about sexual positions to loosen you up and make you relax."

Dirk's next inhale starts at his feet and flutters up to his lungs before he responds.

"I never had that conversation. I am not against the varying techniques to satisfy."

"Oh, so you assume that what you need, if it feels good, is right for her too?"

"Ah, not exactly, but..."

"I am a woman. I do not trust in the old rules telling me how to act. They take the fun out of a voluntary expression of my individuality. For example, in the vein of afternoon delights when I make loud noises doing the deed. My passion comes out in different fragrances and gets me through the day. I do not speculate about the man. A man has to grasp what to do, so I spend my time enjoying the receiving."

Her eyes produce a flash, and Dirk hopes that is the sign nearing the goal line.

"Even if I raise my legs to heaven for you, it does not bear out. I am easy. My companionship has requirements, and they go from chocolates, flowers and jewelry to include compliments concerning my clothes. Just because of my job, and I enjoy it, it does not mean I wish to live untouched by expensive possessions. Besides, I own this business. I expect any lover to champion my after-work lifestyle if they yearn for my favors. My decision to drop out of college and do this job was because of boredom. The boys who put their hands on me felt timid, bordering on needing a GPS. I prefer experience. Know what you want and want what you do not know."

"What is your name?"

"Angelique. And do not call me Angel because I hate that. I am no angel. If I favor a guy, I am amenable to the relationship. I might save you from yourself, but you need rewiring. I believe at the top of your repertoire, it says, 'Having your way with many accommodating women.' You forgot that the person in front of you has their own aspirations to fulfill. They are not there to serve only you."

It troubles him to question his ever getting to first base. The white horse, black leather jacket pickup line has remained unused. He intends to conjure up stud-luck before again jumpstarting this approach. Dirk longs to engage her emotions with endless promises of romance, fantasizing what one night with her does for his manhood.

"Angelique..." He stops as a police car pulls alongside them.

The officer looks over the scene and then shouts to her, "Need any help, Angelique?"

"No, I have to finish charging his battery. If you get to my house before me, put the chicken in the oven and set the heat for three fifty."

When he hears that, Dirk knows to kiss opportunity goodbye. He got run over by a thresher, and his expression was as downtrodden as a cornfield in late October. His facial color is that of a cloudy day. He ponders whether to act heroic alike a Greek god and continue with the challenge. She interrupts his thoughts.

"Hey, you, whatever your name is. I have been playing with you. You are a good sport."

"Angelique, does this mean we may spend time together? You are a wonderment rivaling a neon sign advertising an oasis. I was never with someone comparable to you."

"Yes, you have. Many times. You did not realize it because you focused on yourself.

As for you and me, you do not appear equipped to spend time with me. I stick with the guy I have for now. Go back and reevaluate why you get into one-sided trysts. Let me finish with your car, and you are free to leave." Minutes pass and he hears the car's engine running.

Angelique takes his credit card and gives him a receipt. She includes departing words of wisdom. "When looking to impress a woman, practice your pickup lines on toll takers, embalmers, librarians and waitstaff. They heard every line. Put recognition and respect into the words. Be sincere because you are incapable of foreseeing how things turn out."

She fixed both his car and him. He heard laughter as she drove off, remarking, "Do not be a callow fellow."

He muses whether she is heading for a chicken dinner or another male neutering. From this time forward, whenever Dirk sees a tow truck, he remembers Angelique. He arrives at the Captain's Choice for the rest of Happy Hour. As he approaches the front door, a cell call comes from Victoria. He inhales and refocuses on her and their rendezvous. Before he speaks, Victoria informs him she is not coming.

"Victoria, I have been thinking about us. During these past weeks, it has been intolerable waiting to be with you."

"Oh, Dirk, I know your wish. It will not happen."

"What is wrong? Is it me, Victoria? Is it something I did or said to you?"

"I need to tell you. I tried to bring it up the other night. It was not the right time. I could not find an opening because you always control our conversations. You are a talker, not a listener, and you have the need of listeners because you are not one, nor do you care to be one. Your life drives you, not what your companion wants. That has not bothered me because of my circumstances."

"Did you not notice how much effort I was putting into building our future? Is there someone else?"

"Dirk, I am fond of you even though you ignore what people say during the few times you give them an opportunity to speak. There is no easy way to say this. I did not become attached to you. I am dying of cancer. After last week's tests, my doctor tells me the cancer is back, and my living longer is doubtful. I am going to the hospital tomorrow for surgery to hope for an extended time."

"Victoria, what do I say?"

"Move on and do not glance back. Always search for good qualities in a person. If they do not surface, there may be a reason. Search for what unlocks that door. My hands will soon inspect the emerging skeleton of a grotesque nobody. The mirror must show unfurling deterioration. Ugly and decomposing are inescapable qualities of my future. I am sorry. I must go. I could see you wanted us to be together. Listen and pay attention to your next companion. I have to go." The click on the dial tone delivers the last goodbye to Dirk.

The call stuns Dirk. He does not realize the emotional state this conversation has deposited on him. Victoria has undermined his social aspirations. That has never happened.

His dispirited entrance into Happy Hour is second only to those when he enters his dental office. His shoes have sticky, emotional glue on their heels and soles, making him slog to the bar. He recollects the times with her, their conversations, their activities, and, in a melancholy retrospect, his activities when she was not around, and he was free to roam. He questions whether during their short time together he had given her at least one memento that was helping her now. Perchance he gave without knowing. Considering today's unexpected happening, Dirk questions his understanding of the relationship game. There are other 3Fs out there. From her comments, he examines his behavior toward Victoria. He accepts no realization of his narcissism. If time were to rewind, he swears he would show caring qualities.

"Hey, Dirk, over here. I saved your favorite seat. Where is Victoria?"

LITTLE RED RIDING HOOD

by Denise Peters, Hanover Writers, 3rd Place

The little red sports car pulled into Spring Woods Assisted Living Complex. All the visitor parking spaces were empty. Unusual. She lifted a crock pot out of its box from the trunk, balancing it on her hip while taking out her phone. No one picked up. *I just spoke to her fifteen minutes ago.*

Silence replaced the ringing. She must have answered. "Hello, Grandma. I brought you dinner like you asked."

Grandma's drowsy voice mumbled a reply.

Pressing the crock pot against the back of the car, she switched the phone to her other hand. "What was that?" No reply. A tractor trailer roared by, stirring her red hair. *Why did I bother coming?* Replacing the phone to her back pocket and picking up the pot, she went to the double wide doors and rang the bell with her elbow several times, an inconvenience she would have avoided if her father's mother had been up.

"May I help you?" the intercom at last commanded in a man's voice. How strange! Madge worked the front desk alone on Sundays.

"Yes. I'm here to see Barbara Hood. She's expecting me."

Bzzz... Although the buzzer freed the door lock, it didn't help her. She elbowed the doorbell again.

"Come in!"

"My hands are full. I can't grab the knob. I...." At the sound of swearing, a chill shivered her shoulders. "I'll be right back." Setting the food down, she returned to the car, taking a handgun out of the glove box and tucking it into her belted pants. *Which window is Grandma's?* Sprinting to the side of the building, she counted. *Twelve, that should be it.* It took a moment for her eyes to adjust to the darkened room. She gasped at what she saw.

Returning to the corner of the brick building, she fumbled for her phone. "Jack? I need you.... I'm at the assisted living home and... Listen. I peeked through a window. Grandma's room has been ransacked. She's lying on the floor. I think she has a gash on her forehead.... No, Madge isn't here. A gruff-sounding man was on the intercom.... Yeah, I'll stay out of his sight."

In less than five minutes, a state trooper's car crested the hill. It pulled into the adjacent lot of the convenience store, the next closest parking to the senior living apartments.

After he grabbed a flashlight and closed the squad door without a sound, she waved him over and hurried back to her grandmother's window.

He shined the light into the bedroom. And swore. "A robber hit a place yesterday. We don't think he's acting alone. I'm going to call for backup. I hope Madge isn't in there."

"Why?"

"They killed the receptionist in Hanover." Then he jogged to his car.

A movement caught her attention. She stared at the dumpster for Spring Woods, her hands covering her mouth to stifle a cry. A mahogany brown arm was slung over the partially opened door. She couldn't wait for Jack. Stealing her way over, she hunched under the windows until she had a direct line. Then she sprinted, trying to keep her church dress from entangling her feet. Heart racing, she arrived at the smelly container. Ugh! Rotting chicken and bananas. The hand moved again, and a moan met her ears. It was Madge! Praise God, she was alive.

Not knowing what else to do, she swung herself into the dumpster and examined the receptionist. A large bump crowned her head, but otherwise no outward signs of injury were obvious. Lowering Madge's hand from where it dangled, she tried to reassure the groggy, gray-haired woman. "Help is on the way."

A siren split the air for a fraction of a second before it was silenced. Then the sound of car after car pulling into the lot. Shouts, and a door being slammed with an axe. *Lord, protect Jack and Grandma.* Shots rang from inside the building and glass shattered. Footsteps ran toward the dumpster.

She eased Madge down, which freed her hand to pull her gun out. Now she had a clear line of fire without being in the intruder's immediate view.

Large hands gripped the dumpster's gaping maw, the left hand awkwardly because of the gun it held. Greasy blond hair that covered a man's eyes emerged next. Blood smudged his t-shirt. He looked over as she emptied the Walther's cartridge—blue, his eyes were blue—and he toppled headlong into the trash, dropping his gun to clutch his chest.

Men had been shouting orders. Jack's voice rang out at the last. "Isn't the building clear?" It was. "Send in the EMTs." Rushing feet crossed the lot, an organized mayhem to bring care to the elderly victims of the robbery.

Jack's voice shook. "Have you seen Miss Hood?"

Pushing through the bags, she reached the dumpster door. "I'm here! Madge needs medical attention!" She glanced over her shoulder. "And so does he."

Jack pulled out his gun and ran to the dumpster. "The one who escaped through the window? Good job, Miss Hood." He pivoted and waved. Within moments, another officer and two EMTs arrived.

After helping her out, Jack gazed at the groaning man.

Miss Hood stepped to his side. "Do you know him?"

He nodded. "Yep."

The second officer peered at the trash before smiling at her. "Looks like you apprehended the elusive Mr. Wolfe."

BEFORE WE LEFT THE LAND

by Dreama Wyant Frisk, Northern Virginia Writers Club, 1ˢᵗ Place

Summer of 1942

Tired of begging to go down the road to play, Emogene sat on the large swing under the silver maple. She'd tried pouting for the longest time when she found out June—as Junior was called—had left her behind. But no one paid her any mind as they were busy eating, and forever drinking coffee and crying. Trucks had gone back over the mountain, after pulling and shoving the casket from the hearse to the porch and through the parlor door. It had taken the longest time. Bonnie shut herself up in her room. Her grandma mostly stayed in bed, and Sistie waited on everyone. Her mom and dad had come during the night and slept in June's room. Now her dad didn't feel good.

Boring. Her good white sandals dug into the dirt while she eased the swing back and forth. She wore a store-bought sundress—flowers and pink stripes—with the wide straps over her shoulders. Her sleepy mother had told her to find it in her suitcase this morning. Then she smiled and winked at her before she fell back to sleep. The dress was a size bigger than her last one.

When they'd chained the old, battered porch swing onto the huge limb of the tree, Carl said it wasn't for swinging, but for sitting—like the glider on the porch. The swing always came into her daydreams back home with her parents. As if they were her paper dolls, she set different people in the swing at different times, her favorite being her grandma shelling peas or stringing beans.

Only now, she was in the swing by herself, and June had disappeared again, this time with Erron. Told her maybe Grandpa would play checkers with her.

The red August sun burned down on brilliant orange marigolds along the stone pathway up to the kitchen porch. Like a cradle, the to-and-fro of the large swing lulled her for a good long while from the agitation of the morning. Except for the squeaking of the porch chains, the yard was quiet, until a burst of nervous laughter from the kitchen startled her. Her mother's laugh rose above the others. She bolted to her feet. All she could think to do—and she wanted to do something, was find out what those two guys from the Air Corps were doing in the parlor. Stomping—just to hear it—she stopped on each step before moving to the next.

A fairyland of flowers spread out in the parlor. In place of furniture, large baskets of flowers and bright-green lacy ferns crowded the walls. A beautiful vase of red roses sat on the mantel. An Air Corpsman stood on either side of the ivory, silk-skirted platform where the coffin rested. The two men reminded her of toy soldiers, except these guys never moved and kept their eyes straight ahead, even as she saw sweat running down their necks and into their uniform collars. Behind the casket, branches of the cherry tree brushed against the screens of two opened windows.

At first, she kept an eye on the corpsmen, but forgot them when their stillness became part of the spell. Inside the room, the coffin looked different from when the men had slid it from the hearse. She had never seen one. An open lid showed a tufted satin lining. She circled the room once to get an idea of all the magic, then started over again and studied the baskets of flowers, especially the frames holding sprays of tall blooms. Amazing. She touched the gilded edges of a dark-blue ribbon and tried to read the card, but the writing was too bunched.

At the foot of the coffin, where the flag was tucked into folds at the corner, she trailed her fingers over the red stripes. When she stepped to the edge of the casket's opening, she pushed up on her toes, gripping the side. Her hand was close to a beautiful silk pillow with an edging of lace. Then the smell hit her—like the ether when she'd had her tonsils out. As she pushed from the casket to get away, her gaze fell on a white, waxen face, and she turned and ran from the parlor—this time leaping over the steps.

She landed hard in the swing, and it lurched sideways, almost hitting the tree before straightening out. When she pushed with her feet, the swing wobbled; she used her weight to create momentum, moving faster and higher. She extended her arms to hold on to the chains at each side, even though it hurt her hands, and began pumping—stretching her legs out straight. The face on the pillow? The swing strained to go higher, until it reached its peak, held still for a lofty moment, then lost its balance and careened from side to side. It hit the silver maple once, but Emogene rode it out, using her body as ballast until it returned to its normal sway. Was that the dead body? But where was Carl?

Again, she pumped, but couldn't stabilize the movement this time. Where was June? When the swing reached its limit, it fell backward and dumped her. Like a cat, she landed on her feet with her knees bent. Nobody had seen her except a mockingbird on the nearby fencepost. He cocked his head toward her, calling in a quarrelsome tone. She stood and angled her head back at him, and they stared at each other for a long moment. Rather than return to the swing, she chewed her nails until she thought of playing checkers with Grandpa and hurried to the dining room to find the checkerboard.

When she got to the long dining-room table, she sucked in her breath. Instead of the usual salt and pepper shakers and a round dish of butter on a tablecloth, it dazzled with cakes, pies, cookies, and breads. People had been bringing food all morning. Cakes with chocolate, caramel, and white icings filled the table. In the heat of the day, some icings appeared to weep as the swirls melt into little damp tears.

The flourishes in the coconut icing looked like ruffles, and before she knew it, she was running her nail-bitten fingertip along the edge of the plate where the icing puddled. She sucked it and the sweetness sent her to gather up another, and another, until she'd moved higher up the side of the cake. All at once, gouges sent crumbling yellow pieces falling. Before anyone could wander from the kitchen and see the mess, she stuffed some in her mouth and turned the plate around to the back. She licked at the leftover smudges on her fingers, then rushed to pull the checkers and board from the cupboard.

She was surprised to find Grandpa in the parlor—he hadn't been there earlier—slumped on the settee. His glasses slipped forward on his nose. His vest was buttoned tight over a long sleeve white shirt. At breakfast, when Sistie had told him not to wear it, he said he'd lived through too many cold winters to mind the dog days of August. His coffee sat cooling on the table, nestled beside a tall spray of white flowers.

"Grandpa?" Clutching the checkerboard to her chest, she stood in front of him. "Grandpa? Don't you want to play checkers? Let's go out on the porch and play checkers." She kept her back turned to the casket to keep away the hospital smell.

Raising his head slowly as could be, Grandpa adjusted his glasses and widened his eyes. "Child, be quiet." He frowned and his eyes narrowed. "What's that all over your mouth?" With some effort, he pulled his handkerchief from his back pocket and pressed hard against her lips. Then he folded it and wiped the corners of her mouth. "What in tarnation is that?"

"Coconut. Pieces of coconut. It's from the cake. There's all kinds of cakes in the dining room."

His watch ticked in his vest pocket as he inspected her face.

"Let's you and me go out on the porch and play checkers." She chewed on the edges of the checkerboard.

"Stop chewing on that board."

Knowing he seldom stayed mad at her, she kept her eyes on him and lowered the board.

"Don't you know Carl is lying dead right there behind you? He's come home to be buried and live with our Lord forever."

"No, it's not Carl." She heard her voice, and it scared her, giving lip to Grandpa.

"You stop that back-talking." He didn't look too mad. "It is so Carl. He's dead and been fixed up by an undertaker for his funeral tomorrow. A lot of people will be coming here today to view his body."

"I already looked. It's not Carl." She wrinkled her nose. "And it smells awful."

"Look at you." He frowned. "Go get Sistie to comb your hair. It's all tangled up. And wash your face too."

"Don't you want to go out on the porch and play checkers? Please, Grandpa."

He paid no mind. There wasn't any use in begging him—he never, ever changed his mind. When she looked through his dirty, round-rimmed glasses, she wondered how he could see. She dropped onto the settee, wishing he put sugar in his coffee so she could sneak a drink. She looked from him to the coffin, and back again. It always turned out he was right. Maybe she should try another look. Letting out a big sigh, she walked the few steps to look at the body again.

The afternoon sun streamed through the windows behind the coffin. Holding tight to the checkerboard, she stretched up on her tiptoes and swiveled her eyes so she could only see the white silk pillow. Then she straightened and took a fuller look, seeing the hair, dull and dark against it. It looked like Carl's, so she continued until she took in the strange face, shaded by the coffin lid, but as the smell of ether hit her, she backed off until her heels struck the legs of the chair.

If Carl could just be real, they could go into the dining room and get a big slice of cake, with thick coconut icing, just for her and for him. He would wink, and they'd tiptoe to the front porch and eat the cake, and he would blow on his sweet coffee and hold the cup out to her for a sip—that's what he always did. Then they would play checkers, and she might win, because sometimes she did.

Grandpa knew all about being dead. Maybe he could die, wear his suit and tie in a casket and put his bald head on a pillow with lace instead of sitting there and slurping his coffee. She tucked the checkers and board under the chair.

More people came. *Doesn't he look natural? Hard to believe he's gone and him so young. In the prime of his life. What will Helen do without him? We are so sorry. How's Bonnie? Heard she's taking it hard. Nobody should have to go through this. Was it just last summer, Carl and Emogene drove up and down the road?*

They looked down at her. One said he was Grandma's brother. She tried to remember him but couldn't. The seats in the parlor filled, and the porch hummed with voices and the clinking of glasses and scraping of forks on plates.

The sun had moved away from the windows when June and Sistie entered the parlor, leading her grandma to the coffin. Sistie's skirt brushed against her leg. Grandma, her hair perfectly combed and braided, leaned upon them; her feet, in dark, felt slippers, dragged, and she swayed once almost toppling forward. Emogene wanted to run away but couldn't think where.

The three moved toward the casket while the room of friends and family turned silent and watched Grandma's first viewing of the body. When they stopped at the coffin, she looked down at the strange face for only a second before she twisted her arm loose from June and leaned over, reaching toward Carl's face. The Air Corpsman at the head of the casket rushed forward, as if to grab her hands, but Sistie stood tight against her mother, and June was in the way of both. The other corpsman looked on. Her grandma pressed against the silken pillow, pushing it away from Carl's head.

A god-awful groan, seeming to last forever, came from her grandma. "That...that's not his head. What is it? What is that?"

Emogene had never heard that voice. Was it her grandma's? Something inside said, "See, it's not Carl."

"What have they done?" Grandma crumpled to the floor and her dress pushed above her knees, showing her white cotton slip.

Out on the porch, someone laughed. "Have you ever tasted a pie crust this good? It must be Mrs. Davis's. Do try it."

The hot August day continued to burn outside while in the parlor the air grew thick. Emogene watched tears run down Grandpa's cheeks and drip from his chin. Part of her went far away.

The shade of the silver maple had deepened as the day grew cooler. June watched Erron sip his iced tea while the swing moved them back and forth. If only he could bide his time like Erron. His stomach hurt—no iced tea for him. "Uncle Marsh drove straight home to use his own phone. He called MacDill Air Station. Said they all blamed the war and they're doing all they could. He phoned a bunch of people. Hell, we don't know anybody important."

Erron barely raised his voice. "At least when my dad got hurt in the mines, we knew immediately the coal company was to blame. Somebody's got to know something about Carl."

"Well, they don't. Or they're not telling." Erron's eyes betrayed very little.

June knew he was giving something hard consideration. Maybe what needed to be done. Whatever it was, he didn't want to talk about it. "Say, you think we could go up Jane Lew and get a beer? Maybe two? Play the pinball machine?"

Erron wiped the damp glass on his trousers. "You're not going to go off and do some half-baked thing, are you?"

"Carl would say, 'Let's go.'"

"Goddamn cocksucker. That's why he's lying in a casket with half his head missing."

June crossed his legs and took Erron's glass for a gulp of tea.

"So, you got a good look?" Erron asked.

"Hell, yes. Same time as Mom. Nothing's there. The back of his goddamned head is missing—'bout as big as the palm of your hand—and they built it up with something like plaster. Then they tried to cover it up by pasting on some of his hair."

The kitchen's screen door slammed hard, and they both looked up the hill. Bonnie ran across the back porch as fast as her long legs could carry her and headed off in the orchard's direction.

June shifted on the swing and moaned. "Oh, God, somebody's finally told Bonnie. I was dreading it. She probably had to go see for herself, and those Air Corps guys couldn't stop her. I know that."

Erron's eyes were slits as he followed her movement up the hill.

June shook his head. "I keep thinking it can't get any worse."

The door slammed again, as Sistie took off after Bonnie.

"If he'd waited, we could've signed up together," Erron answered.

June closed his eyes and took a deep breath. He couldn't take any more of what might have been.

When Erron looked down for a long time at Queenie lying in the grass, it was plain to see that he was more unsettled than he showed.

"Will—you know him, barely says anything—said he's seen enough accidents down at his factory, and cover-ups. Things we never heard of around here."

"Things we never heard of around here—" Erron broke off and looked toward the parlor windows. "Ever think about how much danger we're all in? All the time? For Will, it's about those furnaces smelting all the metals for the war. For my dad, it was about getting coal out of the ground. It's what we get for living in West Virginia."

"Our state is rich and we're poor." June gave a short laugh.

"That's what we're used to." Erron handed him the empty glass.

It dawned on June that Erron was getting ready to leave. His stomach twisted at the thought of being left alone.

Erron looked up at the sun. "Getting late."

"You want something to eat? The place is full of food. The ladies of the church are carrying in other stuff for supper."

"I gotta go. Wanted to tell you, I got me another job the other day, at least until I get my orders to leave."

June swallowed hard. "Quitting the glass factory?"

"Need to. This way I can leave money for Dad until my army pay comes in regular. They're hiring for strip-mining near Lost Creek. Pay's good."

"Everybody's talking about strip-mining."

"They dynamite their way down to the coal. No more digging it out. Faster. But the thing is, I can't come to the funeral. Either show up and work or lose your job. No benefits. Get hurt? Too bad."

———— ✣ ————

When Erron stood up, June remembered Grandpa calling him a long drink of water. He walked with him to the gate.

"Be back to see your mother when everything settles down," Erron told him.

A wave of unbearable loneliness came over him as Queenie joined Erron at the gate. Erron stooped on one knee and held her face right under her jaws, so they were looking eye to eye. Anyone might have thought he was talking only to Queenie, but June knew better.

"You know, my mom's grave's not far from y'all's plot. Gonna have mine close to Carl's."

June found himself with a hand on Erron's shoulder. Then, all in one movement, Erron was out the gate. "See you, June."

MEG

by Lee Bullock Schwentker, Northern Virginia Writers Club, 2nd Place

"If they have pumpkin, get pumpkin. If they don't have pumpkin, but they have apple cider, get apple cider. Whatever you do, don't get blueberry," said Lark.

"I've never even *heard* of a blueberry donut," said Meg.

"Me neither, but it sounds like the worst," said Lark.

"Got it. Any instructions from you, Thomas?" asked Meg.

"Whatever. I like them all," said Thomas.

"Thank you, Thomas. I can always count on you to go with the flow," said Meg.

While the kids finished their cereal, Meg put on her shoes, so she could dash out the door to the Dunkin' Donuts' drive-through before coming back home to watch them gobble their donuts and walk them to school. The whole outing seemed unnecessary. What mom adds a superfluous errand to the morning of the first day of school? But, given that everything else was different on this first day of school, Meg figured she could keep the donut run tradition the same. Usually, Brent would have been home with the kids while Meg took care of this annual errand, so leaving them home alone felt odd, though Lark was a trustworthy ten-year-old and Meg would be back in 15 minutes.

There was no line at the drive-through. The previous September, the line of cars had stretched around the block and the kids were almost late to school. Meg placed her order, noting that they did indeed have blueberry donuts. She ordered one for herself—it didn't seem so different from a blueberry muffin, and she had always had a weakness for blueberry muffins. Her high school boyfriend had hated blueberries so much he would pick them out of a muffin, leaving a trail of destruction on his plate at their local coffee shop. One afternoon, looking down at his plate of rejected blueberries, Meg decided they had nothing in common other than both having last names that started with Z that put them in the back row of their AP U.S. History class.

Meg wished other decisions had come so easily for her. When she switched careers, she didn't just open an Excel spreadsheet one day, see a deep abyss, and decide she wanted to be a family therapist. No, after genuinely liking her job as a data analyst at Potomac Group for several years, over time, the repetitive nature of the work bored her. And while Potomac Group served real human clients, Meg didn't. She crunched numbers all day, which other people explained to clients.

Soon after Lark was born, Meg decided she wanted to *help* people, so she went back to school to take the prerequisites to become a nurse, but chemistry wasn't much better than it had been during her experiences with it in high school and college. Around this time, Lark fell off her tricycle in their driveway. Meg passed out at the sight of Lark's slightly bloody knee. While Lark barely shed a tear, Meg collapsed in their front yard. Fortunately for any of Meg's would-be patients, she realized soon after the tricycle incident and *before* starting a BN program that nursing probably wasn't a good fit.

A multi-year process of elimination landed Meg in a Master's degree program in family counseling. The full name of the program was marriage and family therapy, but a woman who has just finalized her divorce has the right to drop the "marriage" and refer to herself as just a "family therapist" if she chooses. How Meg identified her job had led to some minor confusions over the past few months. Another mom at day camp pickup had asked, "So you are a child therapist? My youngest is a terrible sleeper."

"Actually," Meg had explained. "I don't work with children. More with their parents."

"Oh. So, you're a *parent* therapist?"

"Sort of. I focus on relationships."

"Ah, like a marriage therapist."

Meg nodded, an imposter in her second career. She felt like she needed new suffixes added to her name—Meg Zimmer, MFT, *Divorcee*. She coached couples through rough patches, affairs, financial ruin, and grief all the time and, if they chose divorce, she worked to help them see divorce as a path, not as a failure. Of course, when Meg and Brent chose it, it felt like failure—old-fashioned failure with a big red "F" on their report card, not the new-fangled and, somehow softer, "E" used these days.

As Meg pulled out of the Dunkin' Donuts parking lot with a fake smell of blueberries emanating from the passenger seat, she felt a sense of relief. After she walked the kids to school, she would drink her coffee in a quiet house. There would be no stewing, no snide remarks, no unkind silences as she put her laptop in her briefcase and threw a frozen burrito into her bag.

Brent had gone on a health kick a few years ago. He would try to persuade Meg to join him by setting a good example. He would mention the grilled salmon salad or the gazpacho he ate for lunch and Meg would remind him that part of his job was schmoozing and being schmoozed, so lunch was sometimes with a client at a good restaurant, where he had both time and a full menu in front of him.

Meg ate her lunch between her session that ended at 11:50 and the one that began at noon, leaving barely enough time for a frozen burrito to get hot, cool down enough to handle, and be eaten. Brent had encouraged Meg to skip the noon sessions to give herself sufficient time for lunch. But, of course, that would mean seeing five fewer clients each week. And while Meg didn't hold any grand delusions that she was saving her clients, she felt she was helping them, even if only incrementally Besides, it didn't seem Brent was going to pick up the kids from aftercare just so Meg could move her noon sessions to 5 pm and enjoy a leisurely lunch. Is that when things went downhill? When they started fighting about how Meg was or was not lunching?

Meg was just like her clients—they were always trying to find the fault line, the breaking point. She tried to get her clients to focus on the future instead of the past—how they would heal, how they would cope with their new normal. She hated that phrase *new normal*. As though normal were a thing that most people experienced. It wasn't just Meg and her clients investigating the moment their relationships fell apart. The Point of No Return seemed to be what everyone else wanted to talk about, too. Meg's mom had inquired gently at first, but then with greater specificity and urgency. "Do you think your changing careers put extra pressure on the marriage? Do you think Brent should've taken that job in Charlotte? Then, you all would've moved here with family and you two wouldn't have to do everything on your own."

"I don't know, Mom. Just like any relationship, it wasn't just one thing."

"Should I have gotten to know his parents better? We just had Mary and Ron over a few times. I know they live in Davidson, but 20 minutes can be just a *world* away, you know? We should've invited them to the symphony with us. Sometimes two of our tickets sat empty when Charles and Linda couldn't join us."

At this point in the conversation, Meg was usually on speakerphone, doing what she called home admin—ordering groceries, scheduling a haircut, texting the kid who mowed their lawn—while her mom shared her theories about why Meg's marriage ended.

Her mom continued, "And there was that time his parents invited us to the Raptor Center, but you know how I feel about birds."

"I do, Mom."

When Meg told her two best friends from college that she and Brent were separating— over a group FaceTime because Jill lived in Tulsa and Ana was living in London—her friends wanted to know where the marriage had broken. Jill asked if things went south after Thomas was born. (She and Mark were thinking about having another kid.) Ana asked if Brent's long work hours had been the problem. (Ana and John had moved to London for John to open a London office of his company and Ana and the kids had barely seen him since the move.)

Everyone worried about themselves, fixated on their own potential fractures. Meg was accustomed to this; she dealt with other people's preoccupations with their lives all day. But this was *her* marriage that had ended. It was *her* kids whose parents were living in different houses. All she wanted was for her close friends and family to focus on her situation for a moment. Would it have been like this if Brent had died? Would people have brought over casseroles and worried about themselves and the test results *they* were waiting for? Maybe. In some ways, it seemed like a death. In other ways, it didn't. Meg was certainly grieving, but there was this whole promise of a new life at the same time. Like the promise of that quiet house after she walked the kids to school.

By the time Meg pulled into her driveway, the blueberry scent was so pungent she wondered if it had penetrated the leather seats of the car. When she walked in the front door, Lark and Thomas were standing in the foyer.

"You were gone a thousand years," said Thomas.

"I mean, it seemed like longer than 15 minutes," said Lark.

"I think time slows down when a kid is waiting for a donut," said Meg. "I bet I was gone for 12 minutes."

"What d'ya get?" asked Thomas.

"One pumpkin and one apple cider," said Meg.

"Why does the bag smell like blueberries?" asked Lark as she took the bag to the kitchen and dumped the donuts onto a plate. The blueberry donut tumbled out. "Oh," she said. "I guess blueberry donuts exist." Lark looked up at her mom. "You got one for yourself?"

"I did."

Lark grimaced, unsure why anyone would pick blueberry over pumpkin or apple cider, especially in early September. The three of them huddled over the kitchen counter, devouring the donuts. Meg was grateful she had convinced Lark that fifth grade was the proper time for a child to make her lunch and help pack her brother's. One task Meg could cross off her list.

Thomas pressed his fingers into the crumbs on the plate. Meg looked at her watch. "Get those last crumbs and then grab your lunches and backpacks. It's time to go."

They had only a three-block walk to school, but it followed a route that many of their neighbors took, so Meg knew she would see at least half a dozen parents she knew on the way. When they arrived at the first intersection, Meg saw a large group of kids with their parents trailing. The families lived all over the neighborhood, so they must have met at one of their houses, probably Amy's, to walk together.

All the kids' parents had joined the caravan. Liz and Matt, Amy and John, Lauren and Joe, Danielle and Dan (if you could believe it), and Tara and Jen walked behind their dozen kids. The parents were smiling and laughing like this was the beginning of a vacation day. How could they *all* be available to walk their kids to school at 8:30 am? Even in years when Brent didn't have an early meeting, he didn't walk the kids to school, even on the first day. He would stay back to watch the morning news and have a second cup of coffee before he left for the office.

"Mom, did you know Wikipedia is sexist?" asked Lark.

"Not really. How do you mean?" asked Meg.

"Only 20 percent of biographies on Wikipedia are about women," said Lark.

"Wow," said Meg.

"Maybe more men do important things," said Thomas.

"Can you even *believe* him? What are we supposed to do with that?" said Lark, glaring at Thomas.

Meg had a block and a half to impart some parental wisdom. "Men have had more opportunities to do important things. Your grandma couldn't even go to the college she wanted to go to because they didn't accept women. We don't even know about some of the incredible things some women did hundreds of years ago. So, women are probably underrepresented on Wikipedia."

"Underrepresented?" asked Thomas.

"Yeah. If 100 women did amazing things, there are only Wikipedia articles about 10 of them."

"There are only 10 Wikipedia articles about women?" asked Thomas.

"That's just an example. There are a lot more than 10 articles about women."

"But not enough," said Lark.

"I'm sure not enough," said Meg.

The procession of kids and parents caught up to them as they waited to cross the street. Amy scooted past the kids and walked over to Meg, offering her forearms. "How *are* you?"

"Hanging in," said Meg. "How are you all?"

"I was just so sorry to hear. You and Brent were so...well, I always thought you were anyway," said Amy. She thought they were what? A cute couple? Perfect for each other? A mess!

"Yeah, well. We're doing ok," said Meg, looking down at the kids. Thomas was watching the crossing guard who was doing a little first-day-of-school dance. Lark was looking straight ahead.

"Well, just let me know if we can do anything. We're happy to take the kids anytime. Or I could pick up something from the store for you. Anytime. Really."

While awkward, at least the exchange with Amy didn't include any of the usual navel gazing or prying questions.

"Thanks, Amy. That means a lot," said Meg.

The crossing guard started her "right this way" motions, and the group crossed the street.

Amy leaned over to Meg and whispered, "He always worked such *long* hours. I don't know how you stood it as long as you did."

Amy looked at Meg as though she were expecting a response. As though Meg would say, "Yep. You hit the nail on the head. Brent was working 80-hour weeks last year. If he could've cut back to 70 or 75, we would've made it."

Meg just nodded. "Who's Michael's teacher?"

"Ms. Winston. I've heard good things. What about Thomas?"

"Ms. Laura Moretti!" said Thomas. "I've heard good things."

Meg smiled and picked up her pace to get ahead of the prying parents. As she did, her shoe caught a seam in the pavement and she fell forward, landing hard on knees and then her chest and chin. The parents and kids behind her stopped quickly to avoid trampling her. There was silence and then lots of clucking and murmuring and are-you-okays and what-a-tumbles.

Meg rolled over and looked up at Lark. "Am I bleeding?" she asked.

"Yes, but not much. Really, Mommy, not much at all." Lark held out her hand. "Let's go to the nurse's office."

Meg stood up, grateful that nothing seemed to be broken. She turned and gave the parents and kids a little wave like an injured athlete walking off the field. Amy called out, "Truly, Meg. Just let us know what you need. We're here!"

Meg and the kids walked past the flagpole and to the principal, who was wearing a bright yellow "Welcome, I'm Principal Patterson" nametag, waiting at the door to greet families. She opened the door and said, "Mrs. Abrams..."

"Zimmer," Meg corrected.

"Sorry. Ms. Zimmer, I'm so sorry you fell. Ms. Robinson is in the clinic, if you want to see her and get some bandages."

"Thank you. I'll at least try to rinse my chin off," said Meg. She could tell it was bleeding but hoped Lark had been honest and it wasn't bleeding much.

"Some start to the school year," said the principal. "Maybe it's like in Spain, where it's good luck to step in dog poo on your wedding day. Maybe a parent tumble is an unlikely sign for a great school year!"

Or maybe, thought Meg, it's a sign that trying to do the same things when nothing is the same is really hard, dangerous even.

Meg stooped down to look in the bathroom mirror and saw three minor scrapes on her chin. She looked at her knees and saw the beginnings of a bruise on her right knee. She smiled in the mirror. Her teeth and mouth looked fine. Not bad at all. She was just a little scraped up. Her heart was no longer racing. She cleaned up her chin, dried off with a couple of scratchy paper towels, and headed out of the bathroom.

Lark and Thomas were waiting for her, just as Meg had waited for them outside these same bathrooms at pickup when one or the other of them just couldn't make it home to pee. She gave them a quick squeeze, one under each arm.

"I'm fine. Good as new. Run on to your classrooms," Meg said.

"OK, Mom," said Lark. "Glad you are OK."

"Have a good first day!" Thomas called to Meg as he turned to the third-grade hallway.

A first day indeed, Meg thought, as she waved to the staff in the front office and walked out of the school and back up the hill. She glanced at the spot where she'd fallen, making sure she hadn't dropped anything. No keys. No wallet. No chapstick. Nothing of consequence. The seam in the concrete where she had caught her shoe was barely noticeable, innocent.

The house was as serene as she had imagined. The coffee pot had shut off. Meg poured herself another cup and sat at the end of the kitchen table, which seemed longer than usual. She pulled up Wikipedia on her phone and searched for "famous women," expecting to come up with a long list of famous women—Joan of Arc, Madeleine Albright, Rosa Parks, Harriet Tubman—the usual suspects. Instead, the search took her to an entry for *De Mulieribus Claris*, a book written in the 14th century, Latin for "concerning women." It was the first book devoted to biographies of women, containing 106 biographies of women who were renowned, either for good or wicked reasons. Meg scanned to the list of women. Of the 106, most were listed as "wife of," "widow of," or "daughter of," except Minerva, the Roman goddess of wisdom and justice. Only the goddesses weren't tied to men.

Meg put her phone on the table and closed her eyes. Her chin throbbed, but only a little. She straightened her back. Her dress felt cool on her shoulders. Of all of her dresses, this one was the most like a toga, with its loose fabric draped at the neck and sleeves that weren't quite sleeves.

THE MONEY CAN

by A. J. George, Northern Virginia Writers Club, 3rd Place

 After graduating with the Harvard class of '48, I paid a visit to my Great Uncle Wilfred. I was now an educated man of the world with the knowledge that would propel me into a successful career; and I had him to thank. He had paid the tuition, even providing me with a modest allowance.

 Comfortably seated in his parlor, we drank brandy while he weaved a yarn of rich tales and folklore associated with the surrounding region, some handed down for generations. With each glass, the stories took upon themselves a more colorful charm, and one sparked my imagination.

"Well, young man, let me tell you the tragic and sinister story of Lucius Stone, whose empty estate stands on a hill some distance from here," he began. "I was a younger man in those days, but I remember it like it was yesterday when the very powers of hell visited our quiet community, for only the devil could have orchestrated the events that led to his untimely fall.

"He often traveled abroad, sometimes months at a time, leaving his butler carte blanche in the estate's management. During his last trip, he toured Eastern Europe for a lengthy span. He returned in possession of arcane knowledge—a kind of knowledge that called for the highest qualities of will and intellect—knowledge of the black arts. It was said among the servants that he had a secret room in which he practiced this abominable craft, summoning dark forces and consorting with demons. Some servants, frightened by the goings-on, packed, and departed in haste. In time, he developed an eccentric character and became increasingly reclusive. An element of dread and misery became associated with his name, chiefly owing to the gossip. He discharged all but two of the remaining servants, retaining Ancilla the housemaid, with whom he was rumored to be having an affair, and the groundskeeper."

He leaned forward in his wing chair, a lustrous gleam in his eyes, and continued.

"It seems Lucius acquired a preference for keeping his money close, for he converted much of his wealth into precious gems and gold coins, which he stashed away in a large coffee can that he supposedly hid somewhere in the house. After that he lived a life of near total reclusion and was rarely seen, and Ancilla alone ventured into town to purchase necessities for the household. Eventually, she could no longer conceal what had become obvious. She was with child; and gossip, spawned by the grocer's wife, spread swiftly through the town and beyond.

"Then there came a time late in Ancilla's pregnancy that she failed to make her customary trip to town; and her prolonged absence ignited concern, such that the sheriff went to the Stone House to investigate. What he discovered was nothing less than a gruesome scene out of a nightmare. Ancilla lay on the kitchen floor amidst a pool of congealed blood, her throat slit; and Lucius Stone dangled from a noose in the foyer, the other end of the rope tied to the balustrade at the top of the winding stairs. His obsessions drove him beyond mere eccentricities to the point of madness and destruction. As for the child in Ancilla's womb, it was determined that she had given birth prior to her demise, but the infant was never found.

"A distant heir inherited the property and put it up for rent with an agent in town. No renter stayed more than a week, and some deserted the house with such abandon that they never returned for their belongings. The house gained a reputation of being haunted, and they say that Lucius and Ancilla still walk the halls of Stone House. It still stands to this day and has remained unoccupied all these many years with no prospective renter or buyer, and the locals avoid the property entirely."

His snifter empty, my uncle left his chair to replenish the measure he had consumed. Standing by the fireplace, he swirled the brandy in his glass, a far-away look in his eyes.

"Shouldn't there be more to the story?" I inquired, regaining his attention. "Whatever happened to the can filled with riches? Did anyone ever find it?"

"Oh, some tried," he answered. "But those who dared to discover the whereabouts of the money can, as it came to be called, returned empty-handed, reciting incredible tales of terrifying forces at work within those walls."

He then informed me he would be away most of the next day on a business errand that could not be postponed, and that I should enjoy the hospitality of his home until his return. The hour being late, he finished the remainder in his glass and retired for the night. Alone, I sat by the dying fire for a time, my curiosity stirred by the thought of hidden treasure just waiting to be uncovered.

Late next morning, I left a note for my uncle stating my intentions. A bicycle with a basket in the shed provided me with transportation, and after gathering a few items, I started for town. The country lane wound its way past green pastures spotted with grazing livestock and crept along lonely patches where bordering pines swayed in a gentle breeze that played whispering music among the branches, while the dreamy scent of spring flowers floated on the fresh sparkling air. A covered bridge spanned a rolling creek and soon the provincial town jutted out from the rustic landscape.

I called upon the realtor's office, and presenting myself as a prospective renter, I requested the keys to the old Stone House that I might inspect the house and grounds before deciding. And probably because of the assumption that I was unfamiliar with the house's reputation, the agent gladly handed me a single key; and making an excuse that would relieve me of his company, he pointed out the location of the property on a plat map of the region and supplied me with directions.

After enjoying a leisurely lunch at the local inn, I mounted the bicycle and was again off on the adventure. I once lost my way. Rambling hills retarded my progress, and a passing rainstorm forced me to take shelter in a dilapidated barn. By the time I reached my intended destination, the sun had dipped below the crest of the trees, its last defiant rays shooting prisms of light between the trunks and speckling the foliage with flecks of gold.

Two stone pillars flanked an unlocked iron gate and letters on the arch above the gate spelled the name "Stone House." A rugged pathway gently sloped upward beyond the gate. It was overgrown with rough grasses and small shrubs. I laid the bicycle by the gate; and taking with me a flashlight, a candle and box of matches, and my trusty Swiss pocketknife, I opened the squeaking gate enough to slip through the gap and began the trek. A genuine interest impelled me in my enterprise, but I also had to confess to a certain sinking in my heart as I trudged along the strenuous path, for I approached what might prove to be the place of a real country legend, and a house already lifted by the imaginative thoughts of a considerable number of people who deemed it haunted and ill-omened.

At first sight of the house, I must admit that I nearly succumbed to the sharp trepidations creeping up in me, for its very appearance impressed upon me the picture of some mournful creature that concealed within its confines a dark and dangerous power better left undisturbed; and then I reminded myself that I was an erudite, educated man, versed in conventional reason and bold in the notion that I had nothing to fear from brick and mortar.

The Victorian manor, marked by the river of time, stood lugubrious against the twilight. Lonely, darkened casements glowered at me with an unwelcoming countenance. Like watchful guardians, they appeared to discern my every movement as if I was some uninvited interloper. At one corner stood a tower adorned with tall, slender stained-glass windows and crowned with a conical roof that sported a weathercock, and an iron railing traced the outline of an angled roof.

Stalwart double doors marked the entrance, and even with utilization of the key, opening the reluctant door required a bit of forceful persuasion. Immediately upon crossing the threshold, I was greeted by a wall of silence and a stillness that was both palpable and foreboding. Before me a winding staircase draped in shadows rose in a sweep to the upper story, and a survey with the flashlight revealed a hall that stretched, ever narrowing, into a long dark passage that led to the back of the house. To my right, a pair of pocket doors opened to a spacious dining room. Beyond the open doorway to my left awaited what appeared to be a parlor.

Reason dictated the basement to be the first location searched by previous seekers, and cleverly devising a reverse strategy, I decided to start at the top and work my way down in a thorough search. Night settled over the house. Gathering darkness shrouded the interior in a sea of shadows, and the flashlight now became a necessary and comforting source of illumination.

I was maneuvering my way up the stairs, when halfway in the ascent a sense of opposition confronted me, warning me, almost compelling me not to advance further. A chill swept over me, and I felt keenly aware of something lurking in the dark recesses, something of dreadful malignancy, watching—waiting. Hesitation seized me, and I half-expected some hidden menace to pounce out of the shadows. For a few moments, I questioned the rashness of my impetuous undertaking; then boldly gathering my wits and dismissing what my rational mind considered being the product of imagination, I mounted the remaining distance.

Atop the stairs, a balustrade overlooked the staircase and provided a partial view of the foyer below, and a lengthy hallway stretched in both directions. I was deliberating on which course to take when a definite sound broke the stillness. Footsteps on the floorboards, accompanied by what seemed to be the rustling of a skirt, arose from the far reaches at one end of the hall, becoming more audible as they approached at a steady pace. Thinking a squatter had taken up residence in the old house, I projected the flashlight toward what might be a threat; but to my utter astonishment, the beam of light exposed no visible impression—no person—no presence at all. A rush of air like a cold breeze brushed past me, and every nerve soared to the pinnacle of alertness as I became conscious of a creeping sensation that crawled up my spine and rippled over my skin in prickly waves.

"Why are you here?" A female voice whispered in my ear, so close that her icy breath touched me and made me shudder.

Startled, I turned about to watch in shock and dismay as the cobwebs billowed from a passing movement of air that glided along the hallway toward the other end. Then a door slammed shut with a bang that resounded throughout the house! So unreal was the episode that it left me lost in a fog of bewilderment. Were my senses playing tricks on me? Had the oppressive atmosphere of the house affected me?

Furtively, I crept down the corridor like a burglar in the night while the dream of worldly riches and a lifetime of comfort without want or need impelled me onward. Hollow murmurs, emerging out of nowhere, it seemed, acted upon my imagination. Shadow called to shadow as they grew and gathered power. Discarnate voices now spoke in ghostly whispers that swirled in constant motion around me, haunting me, threatening me, and conveying to my mind something that was quite terrible and overwhelming. They hovered at my side; brushed past my shoulder; and circled round me, always pressing closer and closer in horrible proximity. An open door nearby invited retreat, and gathering my scattered senses, I flung myself headlong through the doorway. In one swift motion, I grasped the doorknob and shoved the door closed in a desperate measure to shut out the virulent whisperings.

Pressing my back hard against the door, I fell into a violent trembling and the perspiration poured from my face. A rapping at the door developed into a persistent knocking. Finally, the knocking ceased, followed by an outburst of maniacal laughter from the other side that lingered menacingly then gradually faded away down the hall, and all was draped in a quiet but uneasy calm in which I remained rigid, afraid to even draw a breath.

Hardly had I relaxed when a furious pounding erupted upon the door with such force that the wood shook in its frame. Wholly disconcerted, I swung around and reeled backwards, every nerve battered by an onslaught of fear that repeated with each blow upon the door. Tripping over a sheet-covered ottoman, I tumbled to the floor. Immediately, my feet and elbows were in desperate motion, applying every effort to scoot away from the assault until I bumped into a wall, where I curled up and cringed in a crouching position. My whole body shivered uncontrollably, my limbs were locked in a horror-stricken state of immobility, and my mouth was incapable of uttering even the slightest sound. The pounding abruptly stopped, and after a moment of silence, the doorknob rotated. An unbearable tension gripped me as my eyes beheld the knob, turning back and forth by the power of some unknown force. Fortunately, I was spared the agony of whatever was on the other side of that door, for it abandoned its attempt at ingress, leaving me to tremble for a time.

My composure returned, and in my effort to stand, I grabbed hold of a gaslight sconce to pull myself up. It gave way, ratcheting downward, and to my amazement and wonder, a panel opened to reveal a concealed portal. A narrow staircase rose from a small landing, and thinking that my inauspicious adventure might yet reach a successful conclusion, I climbed the steps to find myself in the attic room of the tower. Curious-looking designs and enigmatic symbols were arranged in a circle on the floor below a thin layer of undisturbed dust; and within the circle, the skeletal remains of an infant lay upon a blood-stained slab.

The room was empty, yet I was not alone, and an unearthly cold clutched my soul with a shuddering sense of dread. Something or someone was in the room, moving cautiously back and forth, watching me, almost touching me. I was sure of it as I was of myself, and I am bound to admit that a certain weakness came over me and that I felt that strange inclination for action, which is probably the beginning of the horrible paralysis of genuine terror. I should have been glad to hide myself, if that had been possible, to cower into a corner, or behind a door, or anywhere so that I could not be watched or observed. Then I experienced what I can only describe as a vivid tactile hallucination. I was touched! My arm was clasped by fingers.

First, I heard them—the thump, thump of two hooves on the planks, and then I saw them—a pair of goat-like hoof-prints in the dust coming toward me. Some compelling force sent me headlong down the narrow stairs, as if the haunting forces of the whole world were at my heels. Upon reaching the door to the hall, I tried to fling it open, but someone or something on the other side held it shut. The hoof-beats pursued, descending the stairs behind me, looming closer, and I pulled hard on the knob, turning it and straining in a frantic frenzy to open the door. Suddenly, it popped open as if something had released its grip, and I ran wildly down the hall to the winding staircase and bounded down the steps. At the bottom of the staircase, I caught my breath; and though the hoof-beats were no longer audible, I clearly detected a pair of eyes that pierced my back like icicles, and a rancid odor, like the stench of death, assailed my nostrils. I wheeled about and gasped. For all my learning, all my worldly education could not have prepared me for what I now saw on those stairs. The phantom vision personified all my nightmares stored in a bottle, which had been uncorked, unleashing every dark dream, every nightmare upon me in a single moment.

I recoiled in terror before the fiendish abomination, and in a sudden jolt of alarm, I dropped the flashlight, which hit the floor and extinguished, plunging me into impenetrable darkness. In a panic, I reached out for something, anything I could use as a point of reference; and finding the wall, I felt my way along it until I came to the entrance of the dining room and slipped inside.

One by one I closed the pocket doors, and then engaged the vertical bolts, locking myself in. I retrieved the candle and box of matches from my jacket pocket. With a shaking hand, I lit the candle, and the darkness fled on shadowy wings into the corners and recesses of the room. Two empty candlesticks rested on an elongated table. I made use of one.

In anticipation of the inconceivable, I sat on pins and needles, helplessly it seemed, powerless against the terrifying and maddening forces that had taken up residence in the old house.

The door to the kitchen stood ajar, and from beyond it I received the audible impression of a woman sobbing, her grief-stricken wails overwhelming me with an unwelcome sense of sadness and gloom. I cautiously approached, and as I pushed the door open to its full extent, I placed a hand over my mouth to stifle any cry. For a second, I stood stock-still, my heart stopped beating and my blood turned into ice.

Facing me, directly in my way between the doorposts, stood the figure of a woman. She had disheveled hair and mournful staring eyes, and her face was white as death. Her throat had a gash that stretched from ear to ear, and blood issuing from the wound soiled her nightgown with crimson stains.

She stood there motionless for the space of a single second. Then the candle flickered, and she vanished—utterly gone—and the door framed nothing but emptiness.

Primitive emotion now seized full control, overruling any remaining vestige of reason, and I took flight. Not caring what awaited me, I unbolted one of the pocket doors, slid it open, and raced into the foyer where I encountered an apparition that surpassed all the horrors I had endured. The corpse of a man dangled from a noose, the head cocked to one side, and the rope straining from the weight of the body that swayed back and forth. It slowly turned and his pale face came into view. The eyes flashed open and glared at me with extreme malice, and his lips curled in a sardonic, menacing grin. A surge of terror swept over me with uncanny swiftness and all the strength ran out of my body with a rush. Overcome by an overpowering weakness, I fainted and dropped on the spot.

In a half-dream, I heard my uncle's voice calling me, and I opened my eyes to the comforting sight of his face. He was bent over me, gently caressing my brow, and speaking soft words. I gratefully grasped his hand as he assisted me to my feet. Beams of early morning sunlight streamed through the dingy gray film on the windows, illuminating the interior. The apparition was gone, and the candlestick still lay where it had fallen, but curiously, the candle had been snuffed out as if someone had pressed the wick into the wax with their thumb.

Once outside, I related in a faltering voice all the horrifying events I had experienced and swore that I would never again enter that house. He listened attentively, and then as we tread the overgrown path to the gate, he imparted these words to me. "I'm going to be honest with you, trusting you will keep a secret. I told you that Lucius had discharged all the servants except Ancilla and the groundskeeper. I was the groundskeeper. How do you think I acquired my wealth?"

The Virginia Writers Club
The Golden Nib, 2021, page 169

The Lady in the Bar

by Norma E. Redfern, Riverside Writers, 1st Place[2]

I noticed her as soon as she walked in. Her black stiletto heels clicked against the bar floor. It was just after one in the morning. We closed at three. She was tall and had shoulder-length dark hair with silver strands peeking through. She was wearing a long black dress covered in hundreds of shimmering sparkles; it had slits that went up on both sides of her legs, revealing slinky black stockings. She had on a long black and silver scarf wrapped over her shoulders and held a matching bag in one hand.

I knew she did not belong in a place like this. Not at this hour in the morning, dressed the way she was. Unless she was a high-dollar hooker, although she did not carry herself as one. She looked like a woman who was a member of the Marsh Manor Country Club. A place where she went with her husband or her girlfriends for lunch. Somewhere she could play tennis and go to the pool. Not that my bar was a dangerous place, but we never got customers that came in dressed or looked like she did.

She looked around and headed for a small table in the far back corner. She looked nervous; her hands were shaking as she sat down. My only waitress, Wanda, walked over to take the woman's order. I overheard Wanda start her standard greeting, "Hi, I'm Wanda. Do you want a menu or just a drink? I'm your waitress for the evening." Wanda paused, "Wait, sorry, it's not night; it's after midnight."

I then heard the mysterious woman speak for the first time. "Thank you, could I have an ashtray and a pack of matches?" she said; her hands trembled as she took a pack of smokes out of her bag.

"Would I be able to have a Long Island Iced Tea?" She looked up at Wanda and smiled nervously, her hands fingering her smokes. "If it's not too much trouble." "I'll check this out with Bart to see if he has the stuff to make one. Normally, we only serve beer and bourbon shots, nothing classy here. I'll be right back with your matches and ashtray." "Thanks," she said as she looked down at her hands.

---

[2] Norma passed away October 23, 2021. She was a talented writer. She will be missed by all those she touched with her writing, those who knew her, and those who loved her.

Wanda whispered, "Bart, you won't believe what she wants to drink. One of them fancy drinks. She called it a Long Island Iced Tea. I told her I would have to check with you. Something's funny about her; she's shaking like a leaf."

"Tell her there's no problem. I'll fix her drink. You just take care of the crew at the end of the bar."

Turning, I watched Wanda take matches and an ashtray to her new customer.

"Just wanted you to know Bart will bring your drink in a minute. You want anything else? Maybe some food. We serve a great sandwich," Wanda said with a smile as she was hoping for a nice tip.

"No, thanks."

I watched her again. She picked up her smokes, took one out, and lit it. She took a deep drag, blowing out the smoke, then reached up and touched the side of her face, wiping a tear away. I fixed her drink. Since I did not get many Long Island Iced Tea requests, it was nice to make something special rather than bourbon shots or a beer.

I own the bar for nearly ten years, bringing in more money every year. Most everyone liked to have a drink after work before going home to a nagging wife. I have been here a long time, seen a lot of things. I've never had a woman come in here dressed like that, looking the way she did.

I walked over to the table; I sat the glass down on a napkin. She looked up and softly said, "Thank you." Her hands were still shaking as I bent down close to her body. I could smell a luscious scent, like jasmine blooming in summer, coming from her hair and body. Long sensuous lashes framed her green eyes speckled with brown flecks. Her lips were a dark pink against her fair skin, and her throat was exposed; it was long and lean. A thick gold necklace hung from her neck, and it looked expensive.

"Is there anything else I can help you with, anything, Miss?" She looked at me; a tear rolled down her cheek as she looked away. "I'm sorry, no one can help me." Her hands clenched around her drink. I wanted to reach out and touch her, hold her, and let her cry her heart out. It was strange; I did not understand why I felt an attachment to her. Maybe it was the way she looked. Did she remind me of someone from my past? I knew I had to help this woman.

"Can I call someone for you?" She looked up at me, her face pale and her eyes puffy from crying.

"There's no one to call."

I offered, "Stay here after we close. We can talk then if that's okay?"

A thin smile. She said, "Yes, that might be all right. Thanks for being so kind."

I watched as tears began rolling down her porcelain face. I wanted to reach out and wipe them away, but I knew that would probably startle her. I decided right then, and there, I would close the bar for the night. Not many customers. "Last call, everyone! We're closing early."

"Wanda, why don't you get out of here early. I'll finish the cleanup. You need a break." I turned and gathered all the empty glasses. A shocked look came over her face. "Don't worry, I will pay you for the rest of your shift. Get your bag and get home to your kids while I'm in a good mood."

Wanda sputtered, "What's come over you? You never let me leave early." Sher hestitated. "You do not have to tell me twice. I'm leaving."

Out the door she went; when the last customer left, I locked the door.

I walked over to the dark-haired beauty. "Do you want another drink?"

She looked at me. It appeared like she had been crying this whole time. "Yes, I would."

"I'll be right back, and we can talk, okay." She nodded yes and smiled.

I had one of those tissue boxes under the bar counter. I went over and put it on the table in front of her, and she smiled. I went back behind the bar to fix her another drink. I could not take my mind off her. I thought about what it would be like to touch her soft, silky skin, smelling her scent that flowed like water over her body, running my fingers through her hair. I pictured holding her in my arms, pulling her in close. I had not been with a woman for a long time.

Most women who come in here are only looking to trade sexual favors for a meal ticket or a free drink. I would give up everything to have a woman who looked the way she did, someone to love me, just me, someone in my bed at night. I wanted a change, maybe marry a special woman, have some children, and start a new life.

This time I fixed both of us a drink. I thought I might need one. She looked up with half a smile. Sitting down, I sat the fresh drink in front of her. I put her empty glass on the next table. I looked at this lovely creature. I wondered what had happened that made her come in here and start drinking. I knew she needed to talk. I had lots of experience listening to customers; sometimes, they just needed someone to listen to their woes.

"Are you okay? Are you sure I can't call someone for you?"

"No, there's nothing you can do," she said as another tear rolled down her cheek. She pulled a few tissues from the box and blew her nose.

"Now, you can call me Bart. Is that okay with you? Let start from the beginning. I never got your name." She took a deep breath. I did not know if she was going to say anything at all. Her skin was ghostly pale. She looked past me, deep in thought.

This was a woman, the kind I would have liked to have. I'd love to take a woman like her to my bed. I would drive her crazy. Most women who I had said my package was extra-large. They could not get enough of me. They were not what I wanted. These women were all rode hard and put away wet. Something fresh was to my liking. This woman looked delicate and sweet. I reached for her hand, lightly touching her with the tips of my fingers. "If you talk about it, maybe it won't be so bad." I squeezed her hand.

"My name's Alison Anderson. I have been married for fifteen years." She paused as she bit her lower lip. "My husband, Stewart, planned for us to meet for dinner and a play. He called and said something came up. He had an unscheduled meeting and could not meet me in the city. Stewart said he would stay at our condominium since his meeting would not be over until later.

"We talked, and he suggested I come into the city tomorrow night for dinner. He said he loved me, and we hung up the phone. I did not know what to think when he said he loved me. It had been a long time since he told me that. It was not like him. I sat there holding the phone in my hand.

"He had been acting strange the last few months. I wondered why I felt something was going on. I went upstairs to change my clothes and sat on the side of the bed, thinking, *Why should I stay home?* I had the tickets to the play. I could go into the city by myself, have dinner and see the play. Then I would head over to the condo and surprise him."

She stopped at this point and stared off into space; a few tears fell as she wiped them away. I asked, "Are you okay?" She looked at me with those big green eyes; another tear fell down her cheek. I grabbed a tissue from the box and gently wiped her tears away. Her lips quivered, and she nervously clutched her hands and looked away.

Her voice aroused me. She was in such pain; I knew I wanted to take away that pain. I wanted to take her in my arms and kiss her hard on that delicious mouth, driving my tongue deep within, making her mine. I wanted to take her to bed, love her, and give her the ride she would never forget. I reached across the table, taking her hand in mine, squeezing it. I looked into her tearful eyes and felt like I could see into the depths of her soul.

After moments passed, I said, "It's going to be okay. Tell me why you're hurting so much."

"You don't understand; it's what happened. I can't change the past."

"I'm here to listen and help you." My heart went out to her; her pain was my pain. I wanted to hold her close and take her fears away.

"I'll try." She had a strange look on her face, as though she did not know what to say. "Last evening after Stewart called, I went to the city and had dinner, then saw the play. Thinking about what he said when he told me he loved me. I wanted to have a special night, just the two of us. Perhaps it might mean he had feelings for me again. I knew his meeting would be over late. The play had lasted longer than I thought. It was around eleven-thirty when I arrived at the condo.

"I opened the door. The light was on in the kitchen. His jacket was on the chair. I walked towards the bedroom. I could hear two voices, so I cracked the door open just enough to see in. I stood frozen; he was not in bed alone; someone was with him. My heart pounded. I couldn't turn away! The light was on in the bathroom, enough for me to see the silhouette of two naked bodies intertwined. They were whispering. They didn't know I was there. *Why had this happened? I thought we were happy.* I felt like I would die; they made love again. The words they spoke to each other cut me like a knife. Stewart never talked to me when we made love. He was saying tender, loving words to this woman. I could not help myself. I stayed there, watching and listening.

"I didn't know how much time had passed. It was like watching a movie on TV. How could Stewart do this to me? I could not turn away. At last, they fell asleep in each other's arms. Stewart always kept a gun in the drawer in the bedroom. I took my shoes off and went in. I grabbed the gun out of the drawer, not making a sound. The safety was on. It was loaded.

"Walking to the side of the bed, I looked down at them both. I stared at the woman, a rather young-looking girl. She must have been half his age. Her long blonde hair curled against her face. Their bodies entwined the way we used to when we were first married. His hand was cupped around her breast, and his head was nestled against her neck. Stewart had not held me like that in years. I had longed to be held like that again. How would I be able to face my friends and family? Standing there, I do not remember pulling the trigger." She hesitated. "Until I saw the blood dripping down the side of the bed."

Allison stopped talking, her hands held the side of the table. "I don't even remember leaving, just walking down the street until I saw the neon sign. Barts Bar and Grill." I reached over and touched her hands. She looked down, and suddenly, she cried, not holding back but sobbing hysterically. I moved to her side of the table, took her in my arms, and held her. If only I could keep her forever. Her scent was driving me crazy. I could take her on the table. It would be easy.

"I'm here for you."

Allison pulled away from me. "How can it be okay? They're dead! I killed them both!" She fainted in my arms. I had splashed a small amount of her drink on her face. She opened her eyes and looked at me. She was confused, not knowing where she was. "Allison, do you know where you are? My name is Bart, you are in my bar. Bart's Bar and Grill, you came in around one a.m. Are you okay?"

She started crying. I held her close. I felt I would never let her go.

Allison screamed, "Let me go! I need to get out of here. I have to go home!"

I backed off. "You told me what happened. I have a friend who might help. He's a lawyer. I think we should call him for advice."

She sobbed hysterically, "I can't. I killed two people!"

"How do you know they are both dead? You might have missed it. Did you check for a pulse?" I attempted to hold her steady, but she pulled away. I reasoned with her, "I'm trying to get you some help. I am calling my friend for legal advice! Just stay calm. We'll figure this out together!" I pulled my cell from my pocket. I dialed the number. It rang.

"John, I know it's, yes, it's important. Can you come to the bar ASAP? Thanks, buddy, see you in a few." I looked over at Allison, and even though she was frantic, she was the most beautiful creature I had ever seen. I wanted her badly.

Clutching her purse, Allison screamed, "Why did you do that? Why would you call anyone? I thought you would help me!?"

Before I could even answer... *Bang! Bang!* I fell to the floor.

The door slammed as she left.

THE OLD NEAPOLITAN HUSTLE

by James F. Gaines, Riverside Writers, 2nd Place

It was ten thirty in the morning and the fellow in the pork-pie hat was all alone except for the bartender. It was meant to be that way because this was not the type of place where a mommy would stop in for her daily latte on the way home from yoga lessons. The owner was an old bookie who didn't want his principal business to be disturbed, so he didn't clean up much. He was especially rude to strangers and paid off the local cops to stay away. Johnny was counting on its shabby appearance to have an immediate effect on Mooney, who liked his booze from a fancy bottle with red sealing wax and served in a clean glass. So when this Mooney walked in and scowled, Johnny knew things were working his way. Mooney sat distastefully at the streaky table and didn't mind at all that the bartender never offered to serve him.

"So what's up, Scapino? I don't see you or that crummy Billy of mine for six months while you're screwing around together and suddenly it's old home week. Lemme guess; he wants an advance on his trust? He ain't gonna get it. I don't bust my ass every day so he can piss through the family money, and he knows it."

"It isn't that, Mr. Mooney. Billy doesn't need any money himself. It's something a little more delicate."

"Oh, sure, delicacy was always his specialty."

"He's had this girlfriend, Angelina Campos, since last year and now it looks like, well, like he's knocked her up. You know those Latin types don't like the feel of rubber, huh? Well, she herself really doesn't care because she's been there before, if you know what I mean, but the trouble is her brother. This Campos guy is in with the gangs somehow and it seems he found out that even if Billy's got nothing but debts, you own plenty of businesses, so he wants money to set things right, mostly with him. Angelina says he'll make her sue for paternity and child support and all kinds of emotional hardship crap. Of course, she's lying, you know, *mentir para vivir*, like they say, and Campos will take all the money or beat it out of her and tell her to go get an abortion and the Pope be damned. But right now she's hanging it over your head."

"And why the hell are you here saying this? Since when is Billy too ashamed to drag his own disgrace out in the open and smear it all over the Mooney family?"

"He's afraid to leave their apartment. This Campos guy is really mean. Angelina says he was down in Mexico with the Zetas and he's former military police and killed all kinds of guys south of the border on both sides of the law. She says a guy up here owed him money for some drugs and he stuck him in an oil drum with pieces of tires and baked him alive, what they call a *pozole*, like a stew. Billy's afraid Campos will come after him just to give a sample of what he can do if he doesn't get the money quick."

"Screw them all. Let them try to sue that worthless Billy and me, too. Our money's all safe in trusts. See what they can do to a white man in court."

Johnny took a sip from his bottle of Coors and tipped it towards the bar to offer one to Mooney, but the older man simply scowled. Not his style. Mooney straightened the yacht club necktie he wore over his immaculate blue shirt, scanned the room impatiently, and looked at his watch. Today it was the gold Vacheron-Constantin. Johnny didn't need an ad from the Times to recognize it. He had lifted a few of them not too long ago.

"Are you sure, Mr. Mooney? After all, just to defend yourself, you're talking lawyers, you're talking hourly charges, an hour for a five-minute phone call, a couple hundred dollars for a letter. It mounts up. I wouldn't want to go through it just for the frustration."

"To hell with it, Scapino. I'm protected and I'm in my right." Mooney's right eye twitched a bit, right next to where he had taken a grazing bullet once, but you couldn't tell now.

"Yeah, but what will it cost you to prove it? You know, there's doctors and medical tests and labs. And then lawyers can get into all these expert witnesses who'll charge a hundred dollars a mile and stay in four-star hotels for a week just to give ten minutes of testimony. Sure, you can get better lawyers than a Campos, but what if they string things out? I heard of a guy with an insurance scam who kept missing hearings every time he had a runny nose and dragged a little case out for three years and believe me, every day the lawyers were tacking on another charge and insisting they get paid. Finally, the big insurance company coughed up over a hundred fifty thousand just to stop the lawyers' bills from getting any higher."

Johnny's wolfish face was all lit up now. He was in his rhythm.

"I can last longer than they can," barked Mooney. "They can't tie up the courts forever."

"How can you know that? Campos was telling the two of them he's got some pull with one of these civil rights law outfits that can bring in big wigs from New York and Washington. Poor Latina victimized by money-hungry WASPS. Even if you ain't strictly speaking a WASP, Mr. Mooney, they don't make any exception these days for the Irish, you know. You got a face that isn't brown, so you're the enemy. Look at the DA, the Attorney General, the judges—women, blacks, browns, not many faces like us. Who knows what they're going to do? They can throw writs at you right and left, mess with your operating licenses, make you audit your books and pay extra for it. If you can't do business, how are you going to pay your ordinary bills? I'm seeing six figure liabilities even if you win."

"Don't scare me, Scapino. I've been in scrapes before. I know when I'm safe." Mooney looked at his Geneva special again. His face was as smooth as a baby's butt and his hair impeccable, but he was late for his bi-weekly visit to the barber.

"But listen, Mr. Mooney, it ain't just you. It's Billy, it's Billy's sperm, and it's a little Billy maybe growing right now. In just a few months, that's a live kid. And as for Billy, he's my best pal and all, but we both gotta admit, he's no asset. What if he dredges up his past? Just a little over a year ago, there was that other thing, and that girl's still in town.

She's quiet now, but if she hears there's more money at stake, she'll start squealing fast. And you don't have to go too far back to find more. What about your daughter? She wants to marry that doctor she's been seeing, but do you think a plastic surgeon wants to have a story like that when he's trying to build up a tony practice? You might have to lay out more just to keep her happy than this trial might cost…"

"Okay, I get your drift. But I gotta think about this and sit down with my people. What does this Campos want anyway?"

Johnny leaned back in his chair and opened his leather jacket a bit to pose in thoughtful recollection. "At first he was talking eighty large with Billy. Do you believe that? But I talked with him and he came down to fifty."

"Fifty grand? What the hell! What does he think he wants fifty grand for?"

"He wants a new Cadillac."

"Is he fooling? I can get him a fine Caddy for a lot less than that."

"But he wants a new one. An Escalade. With fancy tires and sound. And those flashy rims. The whole show. To these street guys, their wheels are everything."

"He can be happy with a lot less."

"It's not just him. It's his posse, too. They want to show off around the barrio."

"Let them take the fucking bus, and Campos, too. I'm not giving them an Escalade, or fifty large, or fifty frigging cents. I'll break them if I have to. To hell with this guy Campos and his damned…"

Scapino raised his hand and hushed Mooney in mid-sentence. "Sssh. Quiet. Oh my god, here he comes. It's Campos."

Mooney instinctively took a step back and half concealed himself behind his son's buddy. He looked furtively over Scapino's shoulder to see a stocky bear-like man approaching. Tall for a Latino, well over six feet. His bare forearms revealed an illustrated novel in blue and red ink, and it wasn't *Snow White*. As Campos came closer, several scars became evident on his face—from fighting with the Zetas, from fighting against the Zetas? Mooney couldn't stand to look directly at him, but only squinted out of the corners of his eyes.

"Where is that *maricón*, Mooney?" Campos sneered. "I heard you might meet him sometime soon. I want to know where he lives. Where his family lives. What kind of car he drives. That shit Billy told me something, but of course I don't believe him without some proof. What you call corroboration, no?"

"I swear, Campos, I couldn't tell you. What I know is that he won't pay you the fifty grand."

"*Plata o plombo!* Then I will kill him. I will gut him myself." Campos drew a wicked-looking knife from inside his jacket. The bartender went on wiping off his glasses like any normal morning. Mooney shrunk back a little more.

"Hey, Scapino, who's that behind you? Do I know him?" asked Campos, craning his neck to get a better angle.

"He's nobody, Campos."

"Maybe that's one of Mooney's friends," he snickered.

"No way, in fact, that guy doesn't like Mooney at all. He has a score to settle with him, too, he was just telling me."

"Well, I'm happy to learn that, yes, I am. So you, amigo, are also an enemy of this Mooney?"

Mooney himself was too choked up to answer, so Scapino jumped in, "Absolutely, Campos, I can guarantee it myself."

"Well," Campos beamed, sidling around to the stranger, "Put it there, my friend." He stretched out his paw and grabbed Mooney's quivering hand. "Any enemy of a Mooney is a friend of mine. You should be happy. Because if I don't get no money, I'm gonna take that Billy and cut his nuts right off!" He jabbed the dagger right up against Mooney's crotch and the older man gave a little "eek" sound. "I'm gonna cut those Mooneys off before the end of the week. You can take that to the bank," he added, as he jabbed again with the same result.

Scapino tried to reassure him. "Listen, Campos, you won't need to do that. This is a quiet town and you don't need to get rough."

"I got nothing to lose," Campos snarled, pushing Mooney back another step, still holding Mooney's hand in his right and brandishing the knife with the left.

"Besides," added Scapino, "He will have some security. He wouldn't walk right into your hands unarmed." Mooney's face showed signs of panic as his brain realized this was exactly what was happening.

"I ask for nothing better," boasted the Latino. "He can have bodyguards, one, two, three, four even. I don't give a fuck. I'll cut them down. The first one, I'll cut him right in the liver. The second one, I'll take him from the front and get him right between the ribs so I can see the blood come out of his mouth like he was puking. Now the others will run, but I will get number three right in the back straight into the heart." He said all this, staring Mooney in the face. "The fourth one, I will grab from behind and slice his throat. And then that Mooney, him I will do like this." He raised the knife right up against the lens of Mooney's glasses and pressed so the glasses squashed back against his face and then the tip of the knife scratched the lens. Mooney was too transfixed to even close his eyes, and one big tear traveled down each cheek.

"Hey, Campos," Johnny said, with a weak laugh, "You don't have to take it out on your friends, too."

Campos suddenly backed off with a satisfied snort and said, "That is what I will do, I promise you," as he started for the door.

"That's a lot of guys to kill for fifty thousand bucks. I hope you won't have to do it."

Mooney said, after a stupefied pause, "I'll be right back," and headed for the men's room.

Johnny looked at the bartender after he'd left and said, "I sure hope he brought another Depends with him in his pocket, because I could smell piss when Campos went for the eyes." The bartender nodded with a faint smile.

Mooney came back, looking a little more composed. "Look, Scapino, I can see what you mean. I think I better pay him."

"For me, I'm glad you're going to do that."

"Let's run after him and give it to him part of it right now. I've got about four thousand on me for a deal I was gonna do this afternoon."

"No, wait, I don't think that's a good idea. If he decides you were trying to trick him just now, he's not gonna be pleased. You better give me the money you got now, and send somebody you trust with the rest by, say, two PM. I'll make sure he gets it. Besides, in person, he just might ask for more."

"Look, Scapino, it's just that I'd feel better seeing my money change hands myself."

"Mr. Mooney, I feel you're disrespecting me just a little. I mean, either I'm honest or I'm not, right? Would I want to trick you after exposing myself to that guy and vouching for you just now? When have I ever given you reason to believe I didn't have your son's interests and yours, too, in mind? Look, I give up. If you don't trust me, I'll just pull out of this whole thing. I don't need this hassle. You can take care of your own affairs from here on. So long!"

"No, hold on!" exclaimed Mooney. "Wait. Take this," he added as he shoved his billfold to Scapino.

"No." said Scapino, holding up his hands. "I want nothing to do with your cash. I don't want to touch it. From now on, I'm thinking only of my safety."

"Please, take it, I give up. I trust you completely. Take the cash and wait here for the rest. I know you'll take good care of it and take good care of yourself, too."

"All right, sorry," sighed Scapino. "I'll take care of everything. I'm your man."

Around four that afternoon, Scapino met Billy at the gym, where they had adjacent lockers. Nice and cozy. Billy was just buttoning his shirt after a workout and a shower. He asked Scapino, "Everything copacetic?"

"You bet," answered Johnny, handing him a briefcase he carried along with his gym bag. "Here it is. Thirty grand. Stakes for your little jaunt to Miami."

"Is that all? I thought you said you might get me forty."

"Well, I couldn't shake out as much as I thought. Besides, there was a little finder's fee, and I had to pay off Campos for his Oscar winning performance. You should have seen it. Academy award quality at least. Then again, it's better you weren't there. You would have laughed so loud it would have spoiled everything."

"Thirty will have to do. Best I make myself scarce for a while now. Anyway, thanks for setting it all up."

"Your servant, sir," replied Scapino with a mock flourish, "All in a day's work."

A SURGICAL NIGHTMARE

by Madalin Jackson Bickel, Riverside Writers, 3rd Place

"Good morning Mr. Kelly. Welcome back. How do you feel?"

John Kelly gazed at the nurse with bleary eyes and retorted, "A bit sleepy to be truthful."

She smiled. "As you should be. The doctor will be in to see you in a few minutes. He has several things to tell you."

With a sideways grin, John replied, "I hope it's that I have a great heart pumping again."

"I'm sure it will be good news." With that, nurse Baily left the room.

John took a minute to look around the room. He assumed he was in a room for recovery. It wasn't where he began early in the morning when the anesthetic was administered. He wished there were a clock somewhere. *How long had he been under?*

He craned his neck around but still could not find a clock. There was a TV but no remote. That was good news. They were probably going to release him soon. He hoped his daughter was on her way.

As he waited, he vaguely remembered his dream, if that's what it's called when under anesthetic for an operation. It was a strange dream and disturbing in its content.

John took a moment to permit his mind to focus on what he had dreamed. It had been a nightmare in reality. He closed his eyes and let his mind wander back to eight thirty this morning. He had counted backwards from one hundred and apparently fallen into a deep sleep.

In the dream, he was in a much larger room. Bright lights glared in his face, making it difficult to focus. Someone was speaking with an accent. "Mr. Kelly, welcome to our new facility for special patients. We will open your head to view your brain. Fortunately, you have been cleared for all necessary procedures."

"Uh, what brain procedure? I'm here to get my heart repaired. It's nothing to do with my brain."

"I'm afraid you were misinformed. With all the new guidelines in place, we are now permitted to do more in depth and exploratory surgeries. You are one of our first patients and were chosen because you are in fit shape. That is healthy and mentally active."

"I think you must be mistaken. Are you sure you don't have me mixed up with another patient?"

"Oh, no, we do not mix up patients or make mistakes."

The white scrub clad man with the strange voice turned and nodded to a group of men and women dressed in green. They quickly surrounded his bed. He was tied to the gurney, and a mask was placed over his face. The last thing he remembered was the whirr of a drill. He tried to scream, but nothing happened.

Eventually he wakened. He was groggy, and his thinking was not clear. A voice spoke, but he could not turn his head to see who was speaking. "Mr. Kelly. You have come through this procedure remarkably well. I need to check a few things. Please try to move your right hand."

Both of John's arms were securely attached to the side of the bed. He tried to move his head to look at his right hand, but it wouldn't budge. There was some type of brace, a frame of sorts, attached to his head. He concentrated on moving his hand. He felt nothing.

"Good John. You did just what we expected. Now, let me explain. You have had a probe inserted into your cerebral cortex. It is rather like a robotic device." The speaker mischievously laughed. "It permits us to control parts of your brain."

John's only expression to this catastrophic announcement was to blink his eyes. *What the hell was going on?*

"The first time I asked you to move your hand, nothing happened. I am going to have you try again, only this time I am going to assist you." John could see an arm in his peripheral vision. It held what looked like a two inch by three-inch flat box. "Now, John, try to move your hand again. This time I will push a button to assist you."

John did not know if he moved his hand. As far as he could tell, all that moved were his eyes. The figure moved around to the front of the bed. Dressed in a dark military uniform, stood a tall, thin man. He smiled, but his eyes stared back hard and black. "As you can see, John, you cannot control your body and probably not much of your mind. That is what we wanted to occur."

He held up what looked like a remote and gently rocked it back and forth. "You see, thanks to this little box, I now control you, your body, your mind, and..." the man pierced his lips and snickered, "your finances."

John could not react. He thought of his work, his home, his family. He did not understand what was happening.

"You see, John, this is occurring all over your wonderful country. My people are now in control of your government and thus in control of all aspects of American life. Following this experimental operation today, thousands of citizens will undergo the same procedure. Once we are in control of your citizens' bodies, we will take over large buildings and turn them into sanitoriums for you and your fellow Americans. By the time our work is completed, we will own almost everything in your failing country. Well, at least everything worth owning. That is your banks, your media, your so-called businesses, everything.

"I can tell by the fear in your eyes that you do not understand. The great people of your country put us in charge and now we are. Some thought our movement was about religion. They were small-minded individuals thinking in terms of a middle east take over."

He laughed like he was making a joke. "I can assure you this has nothing to do with the middle east or countries like China and Russia. We are taking them over too. It is a new World Order. Common man, his needs, his accomplishments, his dreams no longer interest us."

At that moment the strange man in the black uniform moved toward John. He could feel something being placed over his face. The world became dark.

— ❖ —

"Mr. Kelly, I am Doctor Morgan. Are you awake enough for us to talk?"

John realized he was back to reality, but the dream had left him dazed and depressed. He nodded and was able to say yes, but he did not feel normal.

"Good. I'll have the nurse raise your head slightly. I don't want to move you too much until I'm certain the anesthetic has worn off." He motioned for a nurse to adjust John's bed.

She used the bed's automatic system to raise one end of the bed so John's head would be slightly raised. She then took a glass from a side table and, using a straw, let him sip some water. He realized his throat and mouth were dry. After the sip of water, he moved his tongue around and felt like he could speak.

"Better?" the doctor inquired.

"Yes." John replied hoarsely.

"Good. Now, John, you came in this morning for us to check your heart for malfunction and the need for a stint in the case of blocked arteries. I'm pleased to tell you that little damage has been done to your heart. You may have had a mild attack. That being said, we found it necessary to place one stint in an artery feeding blood to your heart. I have spoken to your daughter and son. They understand what we did and that your prognosis is good. You should be able to leave in a few hours. You are not to drive for at least one day and you are not to lift anything over five pounds for several days. You have a plug in your artery, and we want the opening to heal."

John had several questions to ask about the procedure and any possible side effects. The doctor amiably answered his questions, then left to check on another patient. John could feel his body relax. Between the dream and the knowledge that he now had something stuck in his heart, he felt disconnected. He leaned back and let his eyes close.

"Dad, dad, it's Susan. Are you awake?"

John opened his eyes. His lovely twenty-year-old daughter was smiling. "They said you can go home now. I'm going to get the car while you get dressed. All the paperwork has been finished. You need to try sitting up and then see if you can put on your street clothes." She helped her father get to a sitting position and waited while he tried to clear his head.

"Is that better?"

He squeaked out a yes and she responded by smiling and offering to get an orderly to help him dress. She then leaned over and gave him a hug. He could see she seemed relieved. Maybe it had been a rocky road he had traveled this morning, but everything seemed to be okay now.

As his daughter was leaving, a burly orderly came into the room. He assisted John with dressing. It was embarrassing, but John wiggled into his pants and T-shirt. He was handed his socks. While putting on his socks, he noticed the orderly handling his trainers. *What in the world was he doing?*

He was handed his shoes and slipped them on his feet. He double knotted the laces. The orderly left and quickly returned with a wheelchair. "Your daughter is waiting. Let's get your jacket, then you can slip into this limousine. I'll whisk you down to the front of the building and get you settled into your daughter's car. It'll be easy."

John was rolled to the elevator, down to the first floor, and then to the front door. He could see his daughter's car. She was standing beside the open passenger door. The orderly rolled the wheelchair out to the car and helped John move from the chair to the car. When John was all settled, the orderly leaned in and whispered. "I left you a message in your shoe."

He closed the car door, turned, and wheeled the chair back into the hospital.

Susan buckled her seatbelt, then inserted the key into the ignition. "What was that all about?" asked his daughter.

John turned and looked at her. "I have no idea. He just whispered that I had a message in my shoe."

"Where in your shoe?"

"I don't know. My right shoe seems tight. I'll check it when we get home." John tightened his seat belt then added, "Can we stop somewhere for coffee and a Danish? I haven't eaten since dinner last night." He looked at the clock as he said this and was startled to see it was after two in the afternoon.

"Sure dad. I could use something to drink, too."

"I didn't realize it was so late. There probably won't be any breakfast items. Get me a chicken sandwich and a cola."

It took less than a half hour to visit a drive through and get John back to his house. His daughter pulled into the driveway and turned off the engine. "Come on, I'll help you into the house. Mark is here and plans to stay over until tomorrow morning to make sure you are okay."

John smiled at his daughter. She thought of everything.

A few minutes later, the three of them were sitting in John's TV room. Susan stopped and looked at her dad. "Did you check to see what was in your shoe?"

"No, I forgot about it." John slipped off his right trainer. Inside was a small, folded paper. John pulled it out. It had been folded over several times. He unfolded the paper and pressed it flat. There was writing on one side. It was a small, neat manuscript.

After reading this, please destroy it or I could get fired. The hospital has been ordered to do additional procedures. You should know there is now a GPS unit in your heart. Be careful.

John read the note aloud to his children. His son, Mark, took the note and quickly burned it in the fireplace. Mark then put a finger to his lips. None of them spoke.

Mark grabbed a notepad and wrote: *The house may be bugged too.*

John leaned back in his chair. Should he tell his children of his dream?

The next day, he walked outside with his son. When he felt it was safe to talk, he shared his nightmare. Mark shook his head. "Dad, if anything like you have dreamed is true, heaven help us all."

"Mark, it's not the dream I'm worried about. It's the GPS. Why would someone need to know where I am at any given time?"

Mark gave a nervous laugh. "Well, I suppose there are some wives who would like to keep track of their husbands. Seriously, are you involved in any projects at work that some outsider might want knowledge of?"

"I don't think so. Even if I were, I couldn't tell you."

"Okay. Let's go back to the house and have some lunch. I suggest we occupy ourselves with innocent sounding banter. In the meantime, I'm going to get all three of us burner phones for private communication. I'll tell Susan." Mark looked around the porch and garden. "Let's hope the weather stays good until you can get back to work."

Mark helped his father through the door. He closed the door and initiated the dead bolt. He wondered if it was time to look at better security for the house.

Mark headed for the kitchen to make sandwiches while his dad walked into the den and switched on the television. Across the street, well-hidden behind shrubs, a small man dismantled an extreme sound-amplifier bionic listening device and slipped away.

THE RETURN OF THE BLANCHED COVIDIANS

by Betsy Ashton, Valley Writers, 1ˢᵗ Place

The Seer proclaimed the role of the Scribe on the last day of the Before-Times that After-Times history should be remembered in writing. Oral history-tradition of Before-Times fell out of fashion with the loss of electricity across Dry Earth.

The Seer ordered all followers to seek shelter underground until a divine signal appeared in the sky. The Scribe for the Blanched COVIDians of the Sunrise Mountain region wondered how anyone would see a divine signal in the sky if they were underground. He kept his thoughts silent, because oral history was replete with reports of Scribes being slain for treason for questioning any words of the Seer.

The Scribe for the Sunrise Mountain Blanched COVIDians kept a secret journal on a tablet left over from Before-Times with his thoughts, fears, and happenings that didn't correspond with the imagination of the Seer. History demanded it. If, that is, the Blanched COVIDians were ever to leave their shelter. And even if they never left someone in After-Times might find the haven, just as his Clan had.

After months of seeking, a scout stumbled upon what appeared to be a refuge and led the remaining members of the Sunrise Mountain Clan to a sealed entrance. The Clan Liege used the butt of his unloaded firearm to rap on what looked like a door. The Clan had run out of ammunition when their last hunt resulted in two does and nothing else.

Echoes responded.

"There is a room of some sort behind this. Men, open the door." The Liege commanded.

He stepped aside to watch his loyal followers, clear dirt, and rocks from before the wall. What appeared to be stone at first slowly revealed a fitted metal door.

"If this is large enough, we can shelter within while we await the sign."

When the workers finished clearing the entry, the Liege laid his hand on the metal door and commanded it to open. It did not. He searched for a hidden latch. He found none. The Shaman chanted. Nothing happened. He looked for a crack where he might use a tool to pry the door open. There was none. The door refused to surrender its secrets.

The Liege commanded the Scribe to cease recording what could later be construed as personal failure. He stepped back and stared at the door. The Scribe, too, searched for an anomaly that might lead to a switch.

"There, my Liege. Just to the left. There's a tiny indentation." The Scribe pointed.

The Liege glared down at him. "I saw that." The Liege didn't tolerate anyone seeing something he'd missed.

He walked to the door again, ran his hands around the lower portion, and placed his hand on the indentation. Nothing happened. The door remained closed. The Scribe approached.

"If I may..."

"And you, oh master of words, think you can work magic to open this door. For all of your vast knowledge, this could be a tomb filled with corpses of the Before-Times Spotted Death."

"That may be, but the old records spoke often of secret, well-stocked hideouts for the elite. This may be one of them." The Scribe remained stalwart in his belief that this was the haven for which they'd searched for years.

"And how did it open?" The Liege sneered.

"If I may..." The Scribe stepped forward and placed his smaller fingers into the indentation. He felt around until he found a lever of some sort. He pulled it. Nothing happened. He pushed it. Nothing happened.

"Ha!" said the Liege. "You lack the strength of character to open this haven." With that, he tried to push the Scribe aside.

The Scribe's smallest finger felt a button. He pressed it even as the Liege shoved him. The door moved.

"All hail our Liege for opening the door." Dutiful followers chanted an expected response. The Scribe kept his silence.

The door slid into a secret compartment to the left. It stopped with a loud clang of metal. The Liege and his followers surged forward into an antechamber. Stone walls as smooth and unmarked as glass, ended in another door. The Liege searched and found another secret lever. This door creaked and groaned as it swung inward. The Liege led his followers into a huge room filled with tables and chairs, long-abandoned machines of unknown use, and reflective mirrors lining the walls at one end.

"What was this place?"

"Is it magic?"

"Can we stay here?"

"Is there food?"

Questions came from followers as they peered into every corner. Doors led to corridors lined with more doors. Behind some doors lay rooms for sleeping; others contained large communal cooking areas. An old-fashioned lock on a metal loop secured the very last door. The leader of the Clan's protective force found a metal rod and pried the lock free. He stood aside to allow the Liege to enter.

The Scribe wondered why the Liege would want to go first. The locked room could be the last resting place of those who built this facility. It could be contaminated with remnants of the Spotted Death. Before the Scribe could speak in warning, the Liege opened the door to reveal a warehouse stacked with boxes of dried substances. The Liege picked one up and held it to the ceiling, which had glowed with the opening of the outer door. Writing on the packet was faded. The Liege could not read it. The Liege could not read.

The Scribe took the packet and copied the words onto his tablet. "I think this is food."

"Do you think it's safe to eat?" The Liege asked.

"It would appear so. I see nothing alien growing on it. We should open one packet and test it."

The Scribe carried several to the communal kitchen where women had laid out the last stores from their packs and were busy slicing plants for a stew. They looked at the packets with distrust. The Scribe opened one and laid its contents on a metal counter top. He asked for some hot water.

The Liege's wife, the senior woman of the Clan, poured steaming water into a bowl and carried it to the Scribe. He soaked one sealed packet in the water until it softened. Then he peeled off the outer covering. Mouth-watering aromas filled the room. The Scribe requested a spoon. He tasted the hot food and pronounced it safe to eat. Women crowded around, each reaching out with her own spoon.

"I don't know what it is," said the Liege's wife, "but it's delicious."

The women opened more packs to find different food.

The Liege entered and ordered the Scribe to make a count of the packets in the warehouse. The Scribe spent the rest of the day counting boxes, listing each type of package, and adding his count behind the strange words. By his calculations, if each member of the Blanched COVIDians ate two packets a day, there was enough food to last for three cycles of the sun.

The Scribe kept his private journal. In it, he noted the irony of sheltering in this odd haven from the military his Clan so thoroughly loathed. They had previously fought skirmishes, winning a few, losing more. Men and women fell in defense of what the Clan felt was their right, the right not to recognize a government. They believed the Spotted Death came from that government, an attempt to destroy all the Clans across the land. The Liege told the same stories about the rise of the Clan, its sacred mission, its near disappearing by the government it so hated.

The Scribe knew these stories were lies told to keep the Clan intact. He had read the Before-Times histories of his Sunrise Mountain region. He found no references to government conspiracies like those the Liege repeated until they assumed the false mantle of truth. The Spotted Death came to Dry Earth on hot winds that scoured the land and drove water from its soil. Had the Liege told stories of ancient plagues, floods, wars, and famines fostered by man and nature, his teachings might have held some semblance of truth. As it was, his words reflected the ravings of a mad man, the Seer, who spouted vitriol at unseen enemies.

The Scribe held his tongue, wishing to keep it in his mouth. He reviewed his lists of foodstuffs, medical supplies, and other necessities. He recorded writings on the packets, each with the same identifying marker. The Scribe felt the Clan would grow soft in these safe environs, that the Liege might not be able to hold them by fear and false theories. The Scribe pondered what would happen should some sign appear. Would they leave the underground haven? Would they wander again through the wilderness? What would become of the Clan should the Liege have one of his revelations and lead the group out of safety and into danger?

One day, a young lad entered the warehouse and grabbed a packet of dried crunchies. The senior woman found him, crumbs on his mouth, orange dust on his lips and fingers. She marched him in front of the new tribunal, which the Liege had established to punish anyone who didn't follow his rantings.

"My Liege," his wife began, "I have caught this wicked lad eating something in the warehouse."

The Liege stared at the boy, the youngest son of his third-in-command. "What do you have to say for yourself?"

"I, I was hungry, my Liege." The boy threw himself at the Liege's feet, his orange fingertips staining the floor. "I'm sorry, but I could not help myself."

"And where did that orange stuff come from?"

"From the crunchy things." The boy harbored hope that he would escape punishment. He held up the packet.

"Be that as it may, you have stolen the crunchies. I order you to receive ten lashes as your punishment." The Liege snatched the packet from the lad. He nodded to the head watchman to take the boy away and flog him. As soon as the boy was out of sight, the Liege dipped a hand into the packet. "He was right. These are tasty, but no one can steal them without getting caught."

The Liege handed the nearly empty packet to the senior woman. "Get rid of these."

The Scribe dutifully noted the crime, its punishment, and the name on the packet of crunchies that led to a child being flogged.

Life settled into a new routine, a new normal, underground. The Scribe kept his daily log of quotidian details: foodstuffs consumed, water culverts cleaned, meetings of the tribunal, all the while laughing inside at what he knew.

Two and a half cycles of the sun into their disappearing, a strange sound penetrated their haven. The ground throbbed like a beating heart. Fear spread through the Clan, followed by hope that this was the long-awaited sign from the Seer. Watchmen crept to the main door and tried to listen through the thick metal. They heard nothing, but the throbbing continued. Something large, something alive, was outside.

The Liege sought out his Shaman to determine what was on the other side of the door. The Shaman burned mystic messages on scraps of paper. He ingested magic smoke. He sat with eyes closed, waiting for a word from the Seer. After many hours in a trance-like state, the magic smoke wore off. He rose and proclaimed that the Seer had spoken. What was outside had come for them. They should open the outer doors and emerge into the sunlight of a new world.

"Gone is the Spotted Death. Gone is the Dryness. Gone is the old world of government oppression. Gone is the military, which sought to destroy us. Found is the glory of the Seer in green leaves and plentiful water."

The Liege gathered his small band of Blanched COVIDians, now pale as flour. He ordered them to prepare to exit the underground into a new world where they would live in peace and harmony. "The Seer has spoken through the Shaman. We are to leave this place."

The Clan bowed. The members made ready to leave, packing all sorts of remaining foodstuffs into carry-bags. They left their useless weapons behind, believing they would never need them again. They gathered behind the outer door and awaited the Liege to appear and open it. At long last, it slid aside to let in a great burst of brilliant light. Large machines parked in a circle bellowed and belched, shaking the ground and deafening the ear. The Scribe recognized them. Until he was asked, though, he would offer no advice.

Men wearing brown-patterned clothing emerged from the belching machines and advanced toward the opening in the rock. They carried weapons at the ready. Despite the weapons, the Liege, believing the men were emissaries of the Seer, moved forward to welcome them.

"Who are you?" shouted a man with odd metal ornaments on his shoulders. "Why are you here?"

The Liege tried to explain that they, too, followed the Seer and were ready to welcome the newcomers into the Clan.

"How the hell long have you been here?"

The Liege beckoned the Scribe forward.

"We roamed the wilderness for two and a half years after the Spotted Death came. We found this facility and moved in over two and a half years ago. We've been waiting ever since for a sign from the Seer. My Liege believes you are that sign."

"What the hell are you talking about?"

The Scribe handed the man in the brown-patterned uniform a packet of food. "Join us in celebration."

The man looked at the packet. "Do you know what this is?"

The Scribe nodded. "It is food stored in case of a disaster like the Spotted Death. No one was here when we arrived, so we thought it was meant for us."

The man handed the packet to another one, standing slightly behind him. "Are you part of that crazy anti-military militia that tried to overthrow the lawful government in years past?"

The Liege claimed the government was unlawful because it denied the Clan's right to live as it pleased. "Old documents said we should have the right not to recognize any government over our freedoms."

"Who are you?" asked the first man again. "What do you call yourselves?"

"We're the Blanched COVIDians from the Sunrise Mountain region. We follow the COVIDian Seer of All the Mountains."

"Well, I got news for you. Your 'Seer' was a guest of our fine military establishment until the coward killed himself rather than face his punishment."

"That cannot be. You're the sign we've been waiting for. You came to save us."

"We are not from your Seer. We're from the government you hate."

"This cannot be. You are our sign."

“The central government you denied kept you alive in your haven. You might be the dumbest group of survivors we've found. “

“Well, ain't that just funny as hell. You all hid out in a government facility, fed with food from the very entity you claimed had no rights.” The second man laughed. He held up a packet of foodstuffs. “Shit, they survived on MREs, Meals Ready to Eat.”

SCRAP

by G. W. Wayne, Valley Writers, 2nd Place

"You gotta I.D.?" Cal asked the jittery tweaker, knowing he wouldn't.

"Uh, why ya need that?" The skinny derelict sneered, his arms stretched over the welter of twisted copper pipe he had strained onto Cal's counter moments ago.

"State law," answered Cal. "Keeps refuse like you from cashin' in on stuff you've ripped outta walls."

The junkie stared defiantly at Cal. "This here's legal. Found it in a dumpster next to the Dunkin' on Prescott Boulevard."

Cal glared back. *Addict logic. So, this piece of shit's gonna get in my face? Must be way overdue for a hit. Might have a knife. Gun?* "Get out of here," Cal said. "Get out before I call the cops." His right hand pulled up his sweatshirt and rested on the grip of his 9mm.

The stick man rolled up the sleeves on his dirty plaid shirt.

Was he going to fight?

"Don't try me, man," Cal responded. He saw the tattoo on the right forearm.

"Fuck you. Fuck you," the meth head wailed at Cal, sweeping his clattering swag back into the lopsided shopping cart in which he had wheeled it into Cal's office.

"Try City Scrap over on Richmond Road," Cal called out to his departing visitor. "They don't give a shit where you get it." *Semper Fi on his arm. Another homeless vet trashed to the curb. No room at the VA? Denied disability? Discharged unfit?*

Cal let go of the gun, reached into his rear pocket, pulled out his wallet and removed two twenties. Leaving the billfold on the counter, he hurried outside and caught up with the man rattling his burden toward the scrapyard's front gate.

"Use it for food," Cal said as he pushed the money into the stunned addict's shirt pocket. "Use it for food, soldier."

Up close, the metal vendor caught the odor of unwashed body. Festering teeth. Clothes stained by urine.

"There's a shelter on East Jefferson Street," he offered. "Try it."

"Yes, sir," said the unfortunate. He tried to stand at attention. Wobbled.

"But don't come back here," Cal ordered.

"Yes, sir."

"At least until you're clean."

"Yes, sir."

Why did I say that?

Cal waited until the man and his cart had rattled out onto the sidewalk. Then he returned to his office, pocketed his wallet, and hit the switch to close the gate leading into his business. Scotty had left it open after Rick's Removal Service had honked its way in with a metal load from the Kmart demolition cross town.

How many times have I reminded Scotty to close it?

Too many. And too many lost souls wandering dazed among the underpasses and mud flats near the Rivanna River.

"Hey, who was that?" called out Scotty as he walked back toward Cal's office hut from deep in the yard.

"Just some freelancer," answered Cal.

Scotty laughed. "Yeah, more an' more of 'em, huh?"

"Yeah," echoed Cal. "More an' more of 'em."

"Your son's hauler brought in quite a load. Must have bought another bunch of flips."

"Good stuff?" asked Cal.

"Not really. Toilets, bathtubs, some eighties-style light fixtures. A few old mirrors in frames. A nice fridge. Some new-fangled thing I don't recognize. Should I add it up at the goin' rate?"

Cal stared out the gate. *Semper fi. Semper fi.*

"Hey, Cal, should I ..."

"Yeah, of course," Cal answered. "Gonna leave early today, Scotty. Mind the store. Close at the usual. No tweakers."

"I know the rules, boss."

"Except the gate. You never remember to close the gate."

"I will. I will," Scotty promised, watching Cal get into his Cherokee. "Hey, ain't you forgot something?" Scotty pointed to Cal's hip.

"Oh, yeah," said Cal. He took sidearm and holster off his belt and handed them to Scotty. "Be sure this gets locked in the safe before you leave."

"No problem, boss."

Cal waved at Scotty as he reached the SUV.

Scotty saluted back. Looked down at the gun. "Wouldn't want anybody to steal us blind of all this precious merchandise," he muttered as the Jeep backed up and growled out onto Route 29.

Why do some of us make it? Why can some of us get up afterward and walk over guts and smashed faces back to the line? Why? I made it through twenty years. Some don't last a single hitch. Why? Cal parked opposite Brother's Open Door on East Jefferson. He passed several bunches of homeless smoking on the old benches he had donated from his yard. The skinny junkie that had visited him was not among them.

"Excuse me," Cal said to the day manager at the front desk. "I'm looking for a, well, younger man, obvious addict, meth most likely."

"We gotta lot of those," said the supervisor flatly.

"This one's a vet."

"Yeah. Some of those too."

"Semper fi tat on his right forearm."

"Nobody like that," said the man.

"If he does show, call me," said Cal. He opened up his wallet and handed over a business card. "Gotta pen?"

"Yeah, sure. Here."

On the back of the card, in some white space, Cal carefully printed his cell number. "If it's off-hours, call this number."

"Relative of yours?" wondered the attendant.

Cal hesitated. "Yeah, yeah." He inhaled slowly. Thought a second. "A brother."

"Will do," the shelter employee said. "And I'll pass the word."

"Thanks," said Cal. He turned and walked slowly back to his car, glancing at the huddled homeless knotted about the sidewalk between the shelter and East Jefferson. *A different kind of scrapyard.*

Traffic was heavy along Richmond Road heading out to Monticello Shores. Cal turned on the radio. News channel. Iraqi protesters demanding the withdrawal of all U. S. forces. *Thankless bastards.*

On impulse, Cal turned off at Morglen Way and drove the looping, wooded lane up to his son's house. Up the twisting driveway. Over a small brook. Overarching crepe myrtle in fulsome bloom. Deep, intoxicating barbecue aroma carried on savory hickory smoke drifted to him as he parked close to Sam's Lexus. Flipping homes was paying off handsomely for his son.

The ghosts from Nasiriyah dissolved when Sam came out to greet Cal.

"We got some brisket tonight," said Sam. "The way you like it. Slow-roasted and tender."

At least Sam had gone a separate path. His mother's influence, thank God. I spent too much time away. I should call Elaine. See how she was holding up under the stage three diagnosis.

"Your brother showed up," said the caller when Cal answered the telephone in his scrapyard office. "Came in last night."

Cal had been inputting new inventory on his laptop. "My brother? ... Oh, yes. I'm sorry. Yes." He looked down at the date in the right-hand corner of his screen. It was the sixteenth. Thursday. Three days after he had left word at the shelter. "I'll be down there later. Say, four o'clock."

"Okay, but if he wants to leave, I can't hold him."

"Oh, right." Cal paused. "Give me a few minutes."

Leaving Scotty in charge was dicey. End of day close-up was one thing, but it was only nine. The prematurely ancient Viet vet was vulnerable. Had lost much of his memory in drinking games with the Walker brothers. Couldn't lift much. Would probably lose any confrontation with a junkie waste picker's rage.

I must go.

"I've got something to attend to," Cal said to Scotty, gazing at piles of newly deposited copper piping behind the office. "Hold the fort."

"Sure," said Scotty. "I'll keep the gate closed."

"This stuff Rick brought in early's pretty rich."

"Yup, pretty rich," echoed Scotty.

"Did he say where he found it?"

"Some demo work down toward Lynchburg. Your son's stuff."

"My son's using Rick? Pretty far afield for him. For both of them."

"Yup, pretty far afield," repeated Scotty. "See ya!"

Why am I leaving, anyway? What am I going to do when I get to the shelter?

"Where is he?" asked Cal of the lanky male attendant, at least it seemed to be a male, at the desk at Brother's. *Top knot bun. Was that the latest? How to tell anymore? Should I use they to refer to ... them? Gender neutral but not genderqueer. Wasn't that an insult? Not anymore? The more I read, the less sure I am.*

"Where's who?" shot back the desk operator.

Cal sighed at the abruptness of his words. *He probably gets a lot of odd questions. Soft voice. Could be a ... What? Who? Oh, hell, it didn't matter!*

"Oh, sorry, lost in space," apologized Cal.

The person wrinkled their brows.

"You, I think, called me earlier. I'm Cal. I was looking for my brother, and you think you found him here?"

"Oh, yes, Marty. He's in the back. Cleaning the kitchen."

"Cleaning the kitchen?"

"Yes," said the attendant. "He's very industrious. Rather sweet."

Sweet. Was this a joke? "I'm going in there, okay?" asserted Cal. *Damn. What if "they" here had their sights set on Marty? What if ... Stop it. You're being bigoted. Can it. Remember your objective.*

"Sure," said the person. "Do you need back-up? In case your, uh, brother, becomes unsettled?"

Back-up. Need back-up. Cal had a momentary vision. The LAVs in evening light leading the team through Ambush Alley north of the Saddam Canal. He crushed it back into his subconscious. At least for now.

"Sure," said Cal. "Might be a good idea."

The two worked their way through some old hallway narrowed by boxes of donated clothes and other flotsam. At its end, a dark staircase. Cal hesitated at first. His companion passed him, turned on an overhead light, and beckoned for Cal to follow. Kitchen smells greeted them in the alcove below. Remaindered drifts of hot cooking oil and cheap beef, cut by a brief sting of disinfectant at a small sink at the end of the galley kitchen they entered. A thin figure bent over the fry surface of a large oven, scrubbing it vigorously.

"Marty," called out the shelter employee.

"Sammy," answered Marty.

"Your brother's here."

"My who?"

"I got this," interjected Cal. *Sammy or Sammi? Damn, my son's name if it's Samuel. Same name, worlds apart otherwise. I'll assume with a "y." Oh, frickin' drop it, you old dog.*

"My who?" repeated Marty.

Cal turned crisply on his heel and smiled at the desk operator. "Brother-in-arms," he said crisply. "We both served."

"Oh, I see," answered Sammy.

Cal approached Marty. "Do you remember me, soldier?" he asked.

Marty stared warily at Cal for several seconds, clenching a steel wool pad dripping with grease in his left hand. His head cocked to one side. Cal stopped a defensible distance away, noting a pile of knives on a nearby table. He waited for Marty's next move.

Marty snapped to attention. "Reporting to duty, sir! As you ordered, sir!"

Cal smiled. "Excellent work, soldier. Carry on."

Marty turned back to the stove and continued his scouring.

Cal hesitated, then added, "This is your post now. Guard it."

Marty nodded. Kept at his work.

Sammy shook his head but worked up a weak smile. Cal motioned they should leave Marty. On the way upstairs, Sammy sighed. "Some people, uh, circumstances, I guess I'll never understand."

Cal laughed. "Ditto, but you're doing right by my buddy." *I can deal with this person.*

"We try to help everybody we can, regardless ..."

"Understood," said Cal. "Understood."

He patted Sammy on the shoulder as they returned to the front desk. "I noticed he's got new, well, different clothes on, and he seemed clean."

"First things first," said the clerk. "He had to be clean ..."

"You mean drugs clean, don't you?"

"Yes, and weapons and paraphernalia. Maybe we find an I.D.."

"Did you?" asked Cal.

"Can't tell you that."

"What's his last name?"

"Don't know," said the attendant. He smiled.

"Thanks for telling me what you can't tell me," responded Cal.

"You've said a lot in a strange way yourself ..., sir."

"Does he board here?"

"He can, but we can't fit everyone forever. Usually, they move on though. Typical stay's about a week."

"Sammy, please let me know if Marty shows any intent to leave. Let me know immediately. Let the staff know that." Cal pulled out another business card. Grabbed a pen from several lying around on the desk and carefully printed his cell number on it, as he had the first time. He handed it to Sammy. Then he pulled ten twenties out of his wallet. "For the shelter," he said. For one ludicrous moment, he wanted to add, "You're a good man, sister." from the Maltese Falcon. Smiled broadly. Chuckled at his own joke.

"Glad we were able to help," said Sammy. "And thanks."

"I'll be back soon," said Cal.

Sunday after lunch, Cal sat deep in his recliner, feet up, laptop on his thighs, watching The Washington Football Team announce the signing of two over-the-hill wide receivers on ESPN streaming. *They'll never go anywhere with those lumbering has-beens.*

It occurred to Cal Elaine had not returned his voicemail message from yesterday. That uneased him. He surfed through his on-demand platform looking for an old movie to absorb him. One where right and wrong were clear. Mostly. He found The Big Sleep. The original. It was four when it ended.

He was invited over to Sam's for dinner. *Should get up and shower soon, dress, maybe bring Terri a bouquet. She's due in three months. Finally, after seven years.*

Cal clicked over to Central Virginia News. Improvements on Route 29 coming. UVA having signed a promising forward for Tony Bennett.

A report on vandalism hitting empty houses. Usually for sale in remote locations or on the market for too much time. A bunch down toward Lynchburg also hit. Campbell County, City of Lynchburg, and Albemarle County police coordinating an investigation. Putting the blame on addicts desperate for fix money.

No way anything would happen there. Cops were stretched too thin on violent crimes as it was. Defund the police. Jackass Antifa. Wait until one of them got assaulted, and watch him/her, oh, them, squawk for help.

"So, key lime pie for dessert. Love it," said Cal to Sam and Terri. "Great meal. Business must be good. That's a new Lexus outside."

"It's great," said Sam. "Booming."

"How's that?" Cal asked.

"Lots of folks exiting the Northeast, or just looking for a less hectic lifestyle," answered Terri. "Charlottesville has UVA, wineries, a foodie culture, and the Blue Ridge and Wintergreen nearby. Prices are lower ..."

"Especially in the out counties," continued Sam. "Activity in Louisa, Greene, Buckingham's picking up. Why even ..."

"Down south to Lynchburg," finished Terri.

"Aren't they pretty much ramshackle has-beens?" asked Cal.

"Gotta be picky," said Sam. "Look for where an owner's too greedy. Home's been on the market long, neglected ..."

"Sometimes vandalized?" questioned Cal.

"That too, but not always. Terri's my detective," said Sam.

"I look for those types of situations. I swoop in and make a cash offer," Terri affirmed. "We did pick up a few down by Lynchburg. Ones that had been ripped up. The owners feel hopeless. Even a low-ball offer looks good. I also picked up some property with old single-wides on them. We demo'd them down, slabs and all."

"Can I swoop in on another piece of pie?" asked Cal.

"Sure," said Terri.

"Dad," said Sam. "Why not join me? Part-time, if you want. That junkyard can't be getting you much profit."

"It pays my bills. Let's me invest my pension."

"And gives Scotty a job," said Sam. "That old derelict's useless."

"He has a Purple Heart," asserted Cal. "People like him are the reason we're free."

"Here's your pie, Dad," said Terri.

At the front door while departing, as Terri picked up the dishes in the dining room, Cal felt Sam's hand on his shoulder. "Mom's not doing well," he whispered. "You should call. Maybe try to see her."

"I have called," said Cal.

"Drop in on her?" suggested Sam.

"Some things may not be salvageable, son," sighed Cal.

On his way home, with the pie unsettled in his stomach, Cal pulled into his scrapyard, parked near the office, entered it, and hit the lights. *Some new-fangled thing I don't recognize.* Scotty's words kept coming back to him. *What was it Scotty saw?* He walked reluctantly back to Sam's load from the prior week.

Cal remembered the interview that had accompanied the vandalism article he had read. A high-end, on-demand hot water system had been ripped out of one of the stripped homes.

There it was. Under the floodlights' harsh glare. *Irreparable, twisted junk.*

Cal shivered. *Irreparable.*

No. Had to be a mistake. Not Sam. But the pie sat leaden in him. *Should he report it? And what if the hauler was involved–as a side hustle, but not Sam. And his call got Sam wrongly involved?*

What if the cops came by? Why hadn't they already?

Cal checked his cell. No, Elaine had not responded.

It wasn't until just before dawn on Monday that Cal clicked off the TV after numbly watching a string of more old Bogart movies while surfing through Zillow offerings on his laptop. He drove bleary-eyed to work, gave Scotty a week's pay, and closed the yard for the week. Texted Sam he needed a break.

I'm ready. I've flipped my schedule. And, I have a candidate. Long shot. Will probably fail. But gives me time to think. And maybe delay any police inquiry.

Just before closing the blinds and tossing and turning into interrupted, fitful sleep, he left another message for Elaine.

Cal slumped down in his Cherokee hidden off a wide trail, watching an old van pull up to an isolated, near-by fixer-upper off Route 29 south of Charlottesville he had been observing weeklong. The van cut its lights and parked at the foot of the empty home's long, gravel driveway. It sat without any activity for a good half hour.

About one, a bent, slender figure emerged from the driver's side. It closed the door softly and disappeared in the direction of the house. Cal left his car and cut his way silently on an oblique path after it.

What if it was a sting, somehow? What if cops were waiting? Could I avoid getting pinched? And if not, what to say? A scrap dealer! No way out, reasonably, just so the case could be declared closed.

Would it be worth it if it scared Sam away from this stuff? If Sam was involved.

Close to the home, Cal heard the clang and crack of pipes and fixtures being torn out of walls and off bases. To his right, he heard footsteps. A second figure vague in the moonlight walked up to the back of the home. The voice, however, that called in to the demo artist was unmistakable.

Cal left, crying softly. He gunned his Jeep and flew out toward Route 29, passing the van and the Lexus just behind it. He hoped he had been heard.

Late Saturday morning, Cal called Sam. He asked about Elaine. Sam's voice was calm, if sad about his mother's latest operation.

"There's not much chance," he said to his father. "Doctors give Mom about three to six months, tops."

"I've tried to get in touch, son. I really have. I guess I've failed."

"Don't blame yourself," Sam said. "We each take the path we think is best."

"And how's business looking this coming week?"

"Great. Got offers on a few flips, and a lead south of here. Remote place off 29."

"Well, all my best," concluded Cal. "Got some business of my own to attend to."

I wasn't heard. Maybe I should have walked in on him? Without a weapon? That would have been stupid. Maybe just taken as another illicit moonlighter?

"How would you like to work for me, soldier?" Cal asked Marty in Brother's Kitchen. "I can put you up in a small trailer in my scrapyard."

"Yes, sir," grinned Marty, saluting. "When do I start, sir?"

"Grab your gear. Let's go," said Cal. *I hope Scotty returns on Monday. One week off, you never know. Well, either Scotty will have a subordinate to keep busy, or, I have a new yard boss.*

Cal called Charlottesville police while Marty fumbled together his bags.

At his scrapyard, after the police had taken Cal's info, and Marty had settled in, Cal left another message for Elaine. As he ended the call, he thought about Casper Gutman's remark in The Maltese Falcon. "But, well, if you lose a son, it's possible to get another. There's only one Maltese Falcon."

Cal drifted back to where the cops had set up a mobile CSI and were photographing and picking at the suspect salvage.

The words swirled inside him and dizzied him: *And what* rara avis *am I pursuing?*

TWO TYPES OF MEN

by Albrecht Inhoff, Valley Writers, 3rd Place

The song of a mockingbird, the default setting on Allen's alarm clock, interrupted his emotion-charged dream. Still dazed, he turned his head toward the clock, squinted to decipher the digits, and rested longer. He rolled onto his left side, closed his eyes, and to ward off sleep, he sought to revisit his dream. But the dream was like a coin that had rolled off a table and could no longer be found.

With his mind's eye, he kept searching, but it was like staring into a void. It was his mind's ear that heard the beginning of 'America the Beautiful', and using this cue to jog his memory, Allen found the images in his dream: There he stood with a raised arm conducting a Baptist women's choir whose members wore festive red robes with white collars. The key for the music was changed, however, from major to minor, so that the singing sounded mournful, and toward the end the somber voices were overshadowed by the song of a mockingbird.

Over breakfast, he and Claire had often analyzed their dreams. This could reveal a totally different side of a person. Standing on a pedestal and directing attractive women with a little stick should be the symbolic fulfillment of repressed sexual wishes, according to Freud. Claire would have laughed if he had told her that. The music sounded sorrowful, perhaps because he missed Claire. But there was more. If dream content descended on thin threads from a higher reality, as taught by Taoist priests and Tibetan lamas, then it could mean something much more ominous.

He pulled up his knees into a fetal position. With the fingertips of his right hand, he explored a small bump below his navel. Maybe here was the beginning of his end. When he arched out of his curled-up position, he felt a soreness in his lower back. Maybe here was the beginning of an infirmity. Why did the mockingbird sing? Was it just the intruding alarm clock? He yearned to go back to sleep and wished that a higher reality would unite him with Claire. A look at the clock told him, however, that he had already stayed in bed too long. He pushed aside the cover, *brrr*, pulled an XXL flannel shirt with a red, white, and blue checkerboard pattern over his torso to stay warm, *so soft*, and looked for his slippers, *over there*.

The shower consoled him. Jets of warm water hit his head and upper torso, and he watched small rivulets of water wiggle down his legs. He adjusted the shower head and turned around to let the water hit his lower back, hoping it would ease his discomfort. He could not remember having ever had a dream in which he took a shower. He used a corner of his towel to wipe condensation off the mirror and then turned his head from right to left to examine his face. He wondered what Claire had seen in him. He had asked her, and she had replied that she liked his square chin and his big eyebrows. "They give you presence". But those two features did not even look attractive to him. Without being asked, he had told Claire over and over that he loved everything about her. When she asked him for details, he added he loved how well her body fit into his when they were spooning in bed. So, here was the difference: he liked everything about her, and she liked two things about him. It showed he loved her more than she had loved him. He checked his watch. Time was slipping away.

He used his foot to push the bathroom door ajar and then aimed for the kitchen. There he said "good morning" to a hand-size rubber ducky that sat in the bay window over the sink. Ducky was a present from Claire. They would sit in the oversized tub, squeeze a long high-pitched 'wheeee' out of ducky, and then push it from one to the other. For half an hour, Ducky was their naked, joyful child. His eyes fell on Claire's note that was affixed to the fridge: "Allen, you are so incredibly different. You opened my eyes."

Still looking at the note, he reached for the handle of the fridge. He assumed she wrote the note to make him happy, and it did. The magic of these words used to increase his energy, make him think faster, work harder, soar higher, and smile more often. With Claire, he could be the man he wanted to be. Now he felt flat, as if three dimensions had been reduced to two. He could not understand why she was gone, as if she had been swallowed up by a great void. He had done nothing wrong. All his intentions had been good.

She had accompanied him to the department's graduate student picnic. It was her presence, the blue afternoon sky, and the consumption of red wine that made his spirits surge, and this surge made him feel secure and witty. This wittiness made him flirt with female graduate students and two younger faculty members. When Claire asked why so much of his charm was directed at others and so little at her, he did not think she was upset or that he had done something wrong. It was innocent, and he thought that his demonstrative popularity would impress her; it would show her what a desirable man he was. He knew he loved her with every fiber of his body. If she saw his charming personality, she might love three rather than just two of his features. Their what-do-I-love-about-you equation would be more balanced, and that would be a good thing. Love has its own logic. It is not a strictly linear affair, and sometimes you have to pull away in order to get close. Couldn't she tell he was an insecure man who would use the attention and affection of other women to make him a more confident person—a stronger person who could love her more? He told her she should enjoy the moment. They had all the time in the world after the picnic. She did not look upset when she walked away. He even decided he would banter longer and would look for her afterwards. Then he would give Claire—with bolstered confidence—all his loving attention.

Allen could not find her when he left the group of women, and it confused him. He concluded she waited for him in the car. He had given her the keys, and she was to drive home because she drank relatively little alcohol at parties. The car was not in its spot, however, perhaps because Claire felt hurt and had driven back without waiting for him. Allen felt misunderstood and annoyed; Claire should not have left him in the lurch. Perhaps she did not realize that here, away from town, he could not simply hail a ride. No, he had to go back to the party and ask someone for a ride. That would be awkward because everyone would think that there was something wrong with him and Claire. The women would side with Claire, and the men would feel superior.

He had no choice. He had to go back and beg. He asked one of the female faculty members who had been amenable to his charms, Dr. Margaret Golden. He felt awkward asking Marge, and it also felt awkward when she suggested leaving right away, although it would have been equally awkward if she had suggested to leave a little later. Either way, Allen suspected everyone would conclude that he and Marge had hit it off and that Claire was out of the picture. Yet, nothing could have been farther from the truth.

He loved Claire with all his heart. Marge was a fine colleague, but his interest in her was -more or less- marginal. Yes, she was attractive, but she was not his type: too tutorial, too detail oriented, too much need for control. He could not fathom getting involved with her, and flirting with her was easy and enjoyable because there was so little at stake. Allen felt awkward while Marge went around saying 'good bye' to too many people, and he felt even more awkward sitting next to her in her car, as she kept looking over at him. She laughed freely at what he said, and, as far as he could tell, she was an unattached modern woman with an open heart and an open mind. Her doors seemed open.

Marge told him that Claire had abruptly left with a third-year graduate student, Peter French, who did not seem to be well. Everyone assumed that Peter French was the student's real name, that he was from Paris, and a connoisseur of sensory pleasures. But this was all wrong. Truth be told, his real name was Guillaume Vidal, he was from Clermont-Ferrand, and he liked soft cheese that smelled like dirty socks. Because Guillaume sounded strange and because he was French, everyone called him Peter French, and because most people had some dazzling ideas about Paris and no inkling about provincial Clermont-Ferrand, polite Guillaume had not bothered to correct them. So Claire was off with "Peter French".

Marge did not know any details because Claire and Peter had rushed out. Allen did not like it because Peter was a dangerous man. Allen thought of Pao Yu's dream in the Chinese classic, 'The Dream of the Red chamber'. There the Goddess of Fearful Awakening from the higher Realm of the Great Void visits Pao Yu and tells him that there are two kinds of amorous men: the carnal and the intellectual. Allan was the intellectual type. He loved the company of women, but he did not need to dance to Pan's flute. Peter was young and athletic. He had been on a French cycling team. He had the calves to prove it. Peter was satyric.

Allen tried to steer the conversation with Marge into neutral territory, and the best he could think of was her latest research project, the influence of rat mothers on the sexual behavior of their female offspring. Allen soon realized that this was a slippery-slope topic, and he grappled for safer ground. He shifted the conversation to research designs and to statistical models for the analysis of data, which were difficult topics for Allen's agitated mind; he was constantly distracted by Marge's dramatic body movements and her gesticulating right hand, which should have held on to the steering wheel, in his opinion. In short, his conversation with Marge was disjointed. It seemed to last forever, and he was afraid it would–one way or another–end in disaster. She might crash the car, which would further complicate his situation (assuming he survived the accident), and if Marge reached his house safely, she might expect serious signs of affection.

How odd! The evening had started out so well. Claire looked so happy next to him in the car, and his spirits had soared into the azure sky when they arrived at the picnic. It looked as if he was going to have one of the best days in his life. What irony. Now the day was bound to end badly. In his mind, he saw Peter wearing a colorful, tight cycling outfit that revealed the sculptured muscles of his youthful body. Allen's phone buzzed, and Marge turned to glance at him. With some hip wiggling, he extracted the vibrating device from his pocket, checked the number, did not recognize it, and blocked it. "Scammers", he said, and Marge pushed her lips forward and nodded vehemently. When the first houses of the college town came into view, he felt uncomfortably warm, and his clothes seemed too tight. When the car stopped at a traffic light, he asked whether he could roll down the window. He breathed deeply, looked around, and read traffic signs. The words "Center for Teaching" had some mysterious appeal, and he repeated them in his mind. It was like turning a key that opened a door for a way out.

He would ask Marge to drop him off at the department so that he could make some last-minute changes to his lectures. She was a passionate instructor, and she would accept the urgency of this work. Dr. Marge Golden tilted her head to the right and left several times in response to his scholarly wish. He thanked her affectionately before he climbed out of the car, "I would have been lost without your help", and he felt compelled to pull out his lecture notes when he was in his office. After a few cursory glances, he put them down, fetched a duffel bag with his workout outfit, and headed for the gym. There he pushed more weights than usual, as if triceps must beat calves, and when he took a shower, he felt a twinge in his lower back.

He hailed a ride home, and when the hired car pulled into his driveway, he looked for -but did not see- his car. Despite everything, he longed for Claire. He wanted to smell her, look in her eyes, and feel her hair. He wanted to take her in his arms and press her against his body until he could feel her soft contour. He paid the driver, walked toward the front door, and pushed it open.

When he flipped the light switch, he could tell right away that Claire she was not there. Since she was still with the dangerous Frenchman, he stayed up and waited. It was past 3 AM when he gave up. Hope dies last, but it will die eventually. He had a hard time falling asleep. Over and over, he saw Claire approaching him at the picnic, and after he had drifted into sleep, the Goddess of Fearful Awakening sent him touching dreams with off-key music.

He knew he was still holding the handle of the refrigerator door. What was the matter with him? He checked his watch and was stunned. He had barely enough time for a cappuccino. He fetched a carton of milk and put it next to the espresso machine, then removed the machine's water container and put in the sink. With practiced movements, he turned the lever of the faucet toward cold with one hand and tested the freshness of the water with the other. As usual, he looked through the window and followed the cars that appeared on the stretch of road he could see. He followed their trajectory absentmindedly, while he kept sensing the temperature of the water. A bent-over female cyclist in a racing outfit caught his attention, and because it was obvious by now that Claire had been enticed by Mr. Carnal, he wondered whether he should move on. Perhaps he should join a dating site. He needed a catchy username—how about "All4Love"? Out of the corner of his eyes, he noted a familiar-looking car that did not continue its journey down the road. Instead, it pulled into his driveway.

Allan pulled his hand from the stream of water and turned off the faucet. All dating related thoughts vanished, as if they had fallen through a trapdoor. The car parked outside his range of view, but he heard the slamming of a door, and he assumed the driver would now use the walkway. Allen's heart pounded. He rested the palms of both hands on the rim of the sink to support his weight and leaned forward into the bay window. To see more, he raised his heels high and twisted his upper body toward the front door. He saw a woman, and she must have noticed the movement in the window, because she turned her head toward him, and their eyes met. Allen was startled, and his head jerked back. "This was very awkward", it shot through his mind. He wanted to withdraw from the window, but his body refused to obey.

A deep, painful stab that contorted his face had penetrated his lower back. Clenching his teeth, he slid his hands back until he could hold on to the rim of the counter and then nuzzled his body a step backward. By degrees, he lowered his upper body until it was almost parallel to the floor. Only then did his back pain become bearable, and he could let go of his hold. With guarded little steps, he shuffled toward the front door, feeling like an old man. He counted, and at 25 the doorknob was within reach. With his bent over posture, his head was on par with the knob, and he had to reach up to grip it. The bell had not rung, and Allen wondered whether she had left. It would be good, because he did not want to be seen in this pathetic condition. To be on the safe side, he counted some more and then cautiously pulled the door open to see whether his car was left in the driveway.

Instead, Allen saw the bottom of a pair of jeans and white sneakers. He did not want to keep staring at the ground -with her looking down at him-, but it was impossible to stand up straight. He slowly raised his head to look up.

"I am Kathryn Romero, a friend of Claire."

"Kathryn sounds familiar."

"Claire asked me to drop off your car, and to give you this manila envelope with the keys and a note from her."

Kathryn held out an envelope, and Allen raised a hand to take it.

He lowered his hand and stared at it.

"Why didn't she come herself?" Allen wanted to ask whether Claire was still with the French satyr but suppressed this humiliating inquisition.

"It's all in the note. Sorry, I'm in a rush, I've a ride waiting. I hope you feel better soon."

Allen watched the pair of sneakers walk away. Life was full of unexpected endings. He felt like crumpling the envelope with Clair's mocking song: "I can do what you can do". Why bother reading it? Back in the kitchen, he put the envelope on the counter and returned to his routine. Bent over and with an excruciating awareness of his back, he ground coffee beans, stamped the grind into the porta-filter, locked the filter into the machine, and pressed the 'brew' button. He inhaled the aroma of the espresso. The steaming of the milk was difficult with his crooked posture. Finally, Allen's cup had a white crown; he took a sip and felt reassured by the familiar pleasure.

He called the secretary to cancel his meetings for the day and made an appointment with his physician. He took several deep breaths before he reached for the envelope. He pulled out the car key and the note. It was long. Claire must have felt a need to explain why it was over.

Dear Allen,

You were probably surprised that I left the picnic so suddenly and that your car was gone. Here is what happened. I talked to Peter while I waited for you. He was sipping a Martini when I told him a publish-or-perish joke (your joke, I merely retold it). Peter laughed so hard that the pit of an olive in his mouth was sucked into his windpipe when he inhaled. He coughed, but the pit was not dislodged. Instead, it went further down when he gasped for air. When he wheezed, I became worried and told someone that Peter was in trouble. I rushed him to the emergency room using your car. Because the battery of my phone was low, I used Peter's phone to let you know. I called many times, but you never answered!

Peter has no family around here, so I stayed with him. The pulmonologist was off duty, and it took a while before he arrived. Assuming I was Peter's significant other, he showed me an X-ray with a "bright spot" below Peter's seventh rib in the right lung. It was the pit! They operated. It dragged on. I fell asleep in a waiting room.

Kathryn, who answered Peter's phone, agreed to pick me up and to drive me home. She also agreed to drop off your car because you will probably need it.

See you tonight.

Miss you.

Claire

HILLTOP HOUSE

by K. P. Robbins, Write by the Rails, 1st Place

My spirit moans when I see what has become of my once beautiful Hilltop House. Like me, it has decayed. A horrid chain-link fence surrounds the entrance where I welcomed distinguished guests. Birds now fly through busted windows to foul the rooms I decorated with such care. Yet despite the hotel's boarded up doors, its view, the most glorious in the county, remains, as it always will, to defy the indifference of the town.

From this bluff overlooking the Potomac River, my husband Thomas Lovett built his hotel in 1889. He was the third generation in his family to own property. That may not seem like much to you nowadays, but for a Negro family after the Civil War, it was something.

Oh, the times we had at Hilltop House. We held fancy dress balls for the students at nearby Storer College, a school devoted to the education of African Americans, as you now call us. Many of the students also worked at the hotel, and every night, one of them would play the piano to entertain our guests in the fine dining room. Thomas spared no expense in adding all the modern luxuries. We had electric lights, hot and cold running water for the bathtubs, and even a steam-heating plant to keep our rooms warm in the winter.

The hotel's reputation attracted both white and black visitors, arriving by railroad and later by automobile. City folks from Washington, D.C. and Baltimore traveled on the B&O train, emerging through a tunnel on the Maryland side of the Potomac to a bridge over the river. From the railroad station at Harpers Ferry, they could look up to the west and see our hotel looming over the town. Thomas drove a horse and buggy, and later a Model-T, to carry them up the hill to the circular overlook outside our front door, where they always stopped to marvel at the view before coming inside to register. Mark Twain, Alexander Graham Bell, and even the president of the United States, Mr. Woodrow Wilson, stayed with us, but of all our guests, the most memorable to me was Mr. W. E. B. Du Bois.

When he first came to Hilltop House in the summer of 1906, all Mr. Du Bois could talk about was his Niagara movement, dedicated to gaining full civil rights and greater political clout for Negroes. He had chosen Harpers Ferry for an organizing conference because he considered it sacred ground, the site of John Brown's misbegotten raid that eventually led to the Civil War and our emancipation. He also expected to find new converts to his cause among the faculty and students at Storer College.

Mr. Du Bois took a liking to my Thomas. Both men believed education and hard work would uplift our people. Like my husband, he came from a family of freedmen who owned property. Although his light skin revealed the white blood that also flowed through his veins, Mr. Du Bois dedicated himself to securing equal rights for people of color. Shorter than my husband, with a high forehead made to seem even higher by his balding head, his all-knowing eyes tolerated no disrespect. He sported a goatee and mustache and always dressed formally, in a stiff collared shirt and bowtie under his jacket, and rarely smiled. I could never bring myself to call him Will, like Thomas did. He was always Mr. Du Bois to me.

I was surprised when Thomas told me that Mr. Du Bois' conference would be a man-only affair.

"How can that be?" I asked my husband. "How can Mr. Du Bois exclude women when he says he's for equal rights for all?" I was so angry spit erupted from my mouth as I continued. "Aren't I included in all?"

"Calm down, Lavinia." Thomas reached to stroke my arm, but I twisted away from him.

"Forget about me, Thomas. What about your sisters, Mary, Marcia, Sarah, Julia Virginia, Henrietta, Margaretta and Florence? Or our daughters? What about little Florence's and Charlotte's future?"

"I promise I'll talk to Will. I'll see what I can do."

Two days before the meeting was to begin, Mr. Du Bois fell ill with fever and headache. As I was a trained nurse, Thomas asked me to go to his room to care for him.

"Did you ask him about allowing women to attend the conference?"

"Yes. We talked."

"What did he say?"

"He said he'd consider it."

"Humph. Not good enough."

I was never a meek woman. Before I came to Harpers Ferry, I had graduated from the nursing school at the New England Hospital for Women and Children. I set my sights on Thomas Lovett the first day I was introduced to him. He was taller than me and lean but looked strong. "Very pleased to make your acquaintance, Miss Lavinia Holloway," he said, all proper and shy. I gave him a big smile and boldly replied, "I'm sure we'll be seeing more of each other in the future." He looked surprised but pleased. He had already graduated from Storer by then and was teaching at a nearby school and working at his parents' boarding house.

Everyone in town knew the Lovetts because there were so many of them. Thomas had two brothers and seven sisters, all of whom attended or worked at the college. His family didn't approve of our courtship at first. They thought I wasn't good enough for Thomas. His maternal grandmother was a freed slave who had been given property in Virginia, and they looked down on me because only President Lincoln's Emancipation Proclamation freed me. But I knew I was a handsome woman. I parted my short, curly hair in the middle, brushed back off my face, and I favored starched white blouses and long skirts cinched with a belt to show off my small waist. Besides, I was smart and hard-working like them, and they eventually conceded to the inevitable when Thomas' infatuation with me became obvious to everyone.

On our wedding night, I told Thomas I wanted him to build me a house. He said we needed to save our money, but I soon discovered his pay as a schoolteacher didn't go far. So I began doctoring, and quickly developed a reputation for my cures, most of which I had learned at nursing school but some in the slave quarters and from a Cherokee medicine man who lived nearby. By the time our daughter Florence was born, my cajoling of Thomas to build had turned to nagging, I'm ashamed to admit, but still he hesitated. He said we could afford a house only if we rented out some of its rooms. I didn't want to run a boarding house like his parents, and neither did Thomas. His plans were bigger; he wanted a hotel.

We went looking for land and settled on Magazine Hill, just above the Potomac River, close to where it merged with the Shenandoah. Thomas thought it was the most glorious property in the county and the perfect spot for a grand hotel. Finally, when we had been married for six years and I was hugely pregnant with my second daughter Charlotte, Thomas built my Hilltop House. He, his brothers James and John, and his students erected a magnificent structure, made of local stone and lumber, four stories tall with a rounded tower on the entrance side, a covered porch and second floor balconies. I had to admit, Hilltop House was worth the wait. I wanted it to look just as splendid inside, so I purchased rugs, settees, dishes, and silverware, some from the estates of white families. I sewed pillows and draperies and dried flowers to grace the dining room. Thomas's sisters stitched quilts and contributed their needlework, which I framed and hung in the bedrooms.

So you see, the women had as much to do with the success of Hilltop House as the men. That's why I couldn't let Mr. Du Bois exclude us from his movement.

I went to the kitchen to brew my fever tea—a favorite blend I made from willow and viburnum barks. Then I picked parsley and feverfew leaves, my headache cures, from my garden. I mashed these herbs with butter and spread the mixture on slices of bread. I put everything on a tray and carried it upstairs to Mr. Du Bois' room.

"Come in," he said when I knocked. I entered and found sunlight streaming in and the great man sprawled on his bed, fully clothed, not even his bow tie untied. I lay the tray down on a side table and went to the windows to close the draperies. "You need darkness now," I ordered. "Drink this tea and eat this bread, and you'll feel better tomorrow."

"Thank you, Mrs. Lovett. Your reputation as a healer is well known around here, I understand." I nodded and left the room.

The next morning, Mr. Du Bois appeared in the dining room for breakfast. When I came to his table with more of my special tea, he told me he felt much better and thanked me for my kindness.

"You're most welcome," I said. "Now I have a favor to ask of you."

"Of course. What can I do for you?"

"You can let me and the other colored women in town attend your Niagara conference.

My boldness startled him so much that he stuttered a little. "I, I'm not sure. As I discussed with your husband, I don't think that's appropriate."

"Why not? Since you've been here, women have cooked your meals, laundered your clothes, and cured your headache. I assume you thought that was appropriate?"

He eyed me cautiously. "I see you are an intelligent debater, Mrs. Lovett. I sincerely doubt if any other race of women could have accomplished as much."

But I would not let his flattery distract me from my mission.

"If you are fighting for equal rights for all people of color, doesn't that include women?"

He tilted his head and wrinkled his brow as he regarded me. I held my tongue, and it seemed like a long minute before he spoke. "You are right, of course, Mrs. Lovett," he conceded. "Every argument for Negro rights is an argument for women's rights. I will be honored to have you and the sisters join our Niagara movement."

I'm still proud of myself for speaking up that day. You may know the Niagara movement now as the NAACP. Except for my marriage and my children, that's what I value most about my life.

When we turned seventy, Thomas and I knew we had neither the strength nor the energy to run our fine hotel. We sold it and moved to New York City, where our daughters had both relocated years before. Thomas came back to visit Harpers Ferry many times, but I could never bring myself to return.

After my body died, my spirit broke free and I once again found myself drawn to Harpers Ferry. Sometimes people said they saw a ghost roaming the hallways of Hilltop House, but that wasn't me. I would never do such a thing to upset my guests. It could be W. E. B. Du Bois, still inspiring a movement for civil rights. Although Storer College closed in 1955, tourists kept coming after the government declared Harpers Ferry a National Historical Park. My spirit glowed with pride when America elected its first black president, but by then Hilltop House had already gone to wrack and ruin.

The town declared my hotel unsafe and unfit to occupy because of structural issues caused by an old fire. A new owner wants to redevelop the property, but it won't be the same. The Hilltop House I knew and loved is gone forever. I won't be coming back here again.

No one cares about our history now, about preserving a renowned attraction created by an entrepreneurial, educated black man over a century ago. I wonder what Mr. W. E. B. Du Bois would have to say about that.

The Good Ole Days

by John Dutton, Write by the Rails, 2nd Place

Sometimes, it is better to fix things rather than throw them out. You know, they just don't make things like they used to.

July 10th, 2335

Anthony Viggiani's great-great-great grandfather immigrated to the shores of the land of the free over two hundred years ago, but Anthony never forgot his family's history as he stood in his great great-great-grandfather's repair shop. Tools scattered on the workbench or hung from pegs on the back wall. His father's well-loved toolbox sat at his feet. He worked over the chipped and grooved oak table, and he wished he could hear the stories this workbench carried. It was at this work bench that the name Viggiani became world famous for quality repairs and outstanding customer service.

Viggiani's Repair Shop thrived because, since the days of Amazon Prime, products continue to be mass produced cheaply and quickly. The *Amazon Effect* led to two groups of thinking: One was the throw it out and buy another, or two was the fix it and make it last as long as possible. It was the second set of thinkers that kept Viggiani's Repair Shop in business. The PS 55 was the latest product on the fritz. The virtual reality headset PlayStation offered still could not conquer the eye strain or limit the nausea. Anthony knew Sony's PlayStation [PS] never would. It was his father, Vincenzo, who stumbled upon the secret fifty-odd years ago: Tensor Holography. Vincenzo's technological discovery enabled holograms to deliver a beautiful 3D representation of the world around us. Holograms offer a shifting perspective based on the viewer's position, allowing the eye to adjust its focus of depth while focusing on foreground and background. Not only does tensor holography work well in virtual reality, but it also improves the quality of 3D printing and medical imaging. This year, Vincenzo has been trying to make the entire process work off a smartphone.

Anthony Viggiana pressed the button that powered off the hologram of his great, great, great grandfather's workshop. What remained was a six-foot plastic table where the workbench stood. On it, a small, flat object, no bigger than a credit card, lay in the center of the table. Anthony took the small, flat object and placed it in his shirt pocket. He pressed a button on the table, and it twisted and turned until finally it was in a one-by-one-inch cube resting between his feet. Tony bent and picked it up, flipped open his father's toolbox, deposited the table cube inside of it, and snapped it shut. Besides the cube, the tools inside this toolbox were antiques passed down through generations of the Viggianis. He admired every nick, scratch, and chip in the family toolbox. The tools inside, though old and well worn, were priceless to him.

"Hey, Tony. I love that workshop."

The words pulled Anthony out of his reverence.

"Oh, hi, Sam. I love that workshop too. Your PS55 is now working, and it is better than ever. I'll send your mom my bill."

"I know it is. You are the best at what you do. Hey, how come you never sold out to Sony or Microsoft? Your holograms are the best. It beats this crappy PS technology. You know, this is the fourth time you have been out to fix this hunk of junk."

"Thanks, but if I sold out the family secret, I wouldn't be needed anymore. Would I?"

"No, but you would be filthy rich! You could buy whatever you want."

"No, I would grow bored and restless."

"Bored and restless? With all that money? No way!"

"Listen, Sam. Do you remember what happened to the cure for cancer? The electric car? Or even the diamonds mined throughout the world? No, you don't, because you don't know about them. They all exist alright, but no one ever knows about them because they are all locked away, so that money can be made. When the throwaway society overtakes the fix-it society, I'll sell my family's secrets to the highest bidder, but for now, I will keep the family business afloat. I like to work. I like being needed. I like to make a difference in people's lives, and I like offering quality service at a fair price. Just like my family has done for centuries, and, someday, I hope you will too, no matter what career path you choose. I hope my family's values rub off on my customers."

"I can see all that, but why do you do it, Tony? I mean, does work really matter *that* much to you?"

Anthony patted his pocket close to his heart before pulling out another hologram card from his pocket. He placed the card on the floor and pressed a button. The hologram burst to life. It was a crib and standing in the crib was Anthony's son.

"I keep this one around to remind me why I do what I do. My son is just a bit older than you, and he will finish high school next year. After he finishes college, I want him to take over the family business. I want his children to keep this business going for as long as the fix-it society will have us. They just don't make things like they used to in the good ole days, and I want to keep our old-fashioned service and quality care going for as long as possible. It is these little things in life that matters."

An alarm buzzed and a voice spoke, "Your next appointment is ready for you, Anthony."

"Thank you, Alexa. Please ready the teleport and inform our next client, I am on my way."

"With pleasure, Anthony."

"I have to go, Sam, but it has been nice reminiscing with you. Call me when you need me. You know I will be here for you. Maybe next time I will let you use some of my dad's tools and we can work on your PS55 together."

"That would be awesome!"

The two shook hands and Anthony stepped into the teleport that Alexa had opened. He vanished.

ENDNOTES

- Page 43 Turn of the century postcards are no longer copyrighted unless a reseller has secured a new copyright after satisfying outstanding claims. The US Copyright Office has an index of all copyrights. Academy of Our Lady private school was repurposed and now belongs to the City of Chicago.
- Page 46 Derivative art by Nicolay. All elements public domain.
- Page 47 Postcard, Big Stone Gap, VA Coal Mine. See note, page 43.
- Page 58. "John Grisham doing 1st extensive book tour in 25 years." Jerry Mitchell. The Clarion-Ledger. April 18, 2007. Fair use allows the use of images in transformative work to create a new interpretation of an image. The Clarion-Ledger was notified of this intent and sent a copy of the story. Further, elements of previously copyrighted material can be used in substantive (not major) interpretations. See US Copyright guidelines.
- Page 64 Derivative art by Nicolay. All elements public domain.
- Page 65 Public domain. No attribution required.
- Page 71 Image provided by author, Chuck Tabb.
- Page 76 Public domain. No attribution required.
- Page 83 Derivative art by Nicolay. All elements public domain.
- Page 90. Image provided by author, Peggy Crowley Clutz.
- Page 99 Derivative art by Nicolay. All elements public domain.
- Page 102 Derivative art by Nicolay. All elements public domain.
- Page 108 Postcard. See note, page 43.
- Page 132 Derivative art by Nicolay. All elements public domain.
- Page 136 Wikimedia Commons. Sarah Rector.
- Page 141 Derivative art by Nicolay. All elements public domain.
- Page 148 Derivative art by Nicolay. All elements public domain.
- Page 156 Derivative art by Nicolay. All elements public domain.
- Page 158 Derivative art by Nicolay. All elements public domain.
- Page 163 Derivative art by Nicolay. All elements public domain.
- Page 170 Derivative art by Nicolay. All elements public domain.
- Page 184 Derivative art by Nicolay. All elements public domain.
- Page 199 Public domain. XnSketch.
- Page 205 Derivative art by Nicolay. All elements public domain.
- Last Page Photo provided by John Nicolay from his collection. Humpback Bridge, Covington, VA. Derivative elements.

Humpback Bridge, Covington, VA

Made in United States
North Haven, CT
23 December 2021

13563292R00122